D0875421

Walt Whitman & Opera

By Robert D. Faner

Southern Illinois University Press
Carbondale and Edwardsville

FEFFER & SIMONS, INC.
London and Amsterdam

ARCT
URUS
BOOKS ®

Copyright © 1951 by Southern Illinois University Press
Arcturus Books edition April 1972
This edition printed by offset lithography
in the United States of America

Preface

"WALT WHITMAN'S method in the construction of his songs is strictly the method of the Italian Opera."[1] So wrote Walt Whitman himself in the *Saturday Press* of January 7, 1860, answering attacks upon the poem now known as "Out of the Cradle Endlessly Rocking." Many years later he confided to his friend, John Townsend Trowbridge, "But for the opera I could never have written *Leaves of Grass*."[2] On another occasion the poet spoke similarly to Horace L. Traubel, his most intimate friend in his last years. "My younger life was so saturated with the emotions, raptures, uplifts, of such musical experiences that it would be surprising indeed if all my future work had not been colored by them. A real musician running through *Leaves of Grass*—a philosopher-musician—could put his finger on this and that anywhere in the text no doubt as indicating the activity of the influences I have spoken of."[3]

In spite of such pointed testimony, however, remarkably few of Whitman's critics have attempted to "put a finger on this and that" in his poetry or to treat the subject of his passion for opera in any detail at all. To be sure, all the biographers have mentioned his attendance at opera, but only De Selincourt,[4] in 1914, and Canby,[5] in 1943, have offered critical comment on the importance of the subject to an understanding of the origin and nature of Whitman's poems.

Other brief and somewhat generalized discussions have been presented from time to time. In 1925, Louise Pound called attention to some of the more obvious relationships between Whitman's poetry and his love for opera.[6] Three years later the French critic, Jean Catel, referred briefly to opera as a formative influence on Whitman's poetic work.[7] In 1937, Clifton J. Furness lectured before the Boston Chapter of the Special Libraries Association on the topic "Whitman and Music."[8] The printed account of the talk, however, does little more than indicate the need for study of the subject and announce the fact that Furness was himself engaged in such a project. Unfortunately, the work of this authoritative Whitman scholar was not completed before his death in May, 1946. An important contribution to the discussion of the topic is to be found as a section of *American Renaissance* by F. O. Matthiessen, a work which appeared in 1941.[9] Matthiessen's treatment is in terms of conclusions rather than analyses of the poet's work, however, and is of course brief. Other recent comments on phases of the topic of Whitman and music have been prepared by Julia Spregelman[10] and Alice L. Cooke.[11]

It is obvious that of the mass of scholarly publication devoted to Whitman these studies form only a very small part—surprisingly small in the light of the importance which Whitman himself attached to the topic. It would seem, then, that a study is needed which might examine in detail the nature and scope of the poet's interest in opera and show by specific reference to his poems what the probable effect of that interest was. Such is the purpose of the present work.

The presentation is divided into two parts. The first, which is devoted principally to background material, brings together from a variety of sources information as to what specific musical works Whitman heard or knew and a suggestion of the musical climate in which he lived during the years when he was evolving the technique to be employed in *Leaves of Grass*. Furthermore, it attempts to reveal the extent of his technical knowledge of music and the quality of his appreciation of it. Finally, Part I suggests, in general terms, ways in which the poet's deepening understanding of the art of opera, and his response to it, inspired him to be a poet and colored his conception of what poetry could and ought to be. Throughout Part I Whitman is quoted liberally, for most of his remarks on the subject of opera are neither widely known nor easily accessible.

Part II of the study is devoted to an examination of representative poems in an attempt to show how various aspects of operatic art influenced both their form and their content. In these matters of analysis Whitman himself has given small help, for his comment on his poetic technique was always of the most general sort. Recent scholarship on his unusual and highly problematic prosody, however, has gone far to clarify its nature. What the present study attempts is to contribute further to an appreciation of its precise quality by examining it in the light of one of its probable sources.

The writer has tried not to ride a good horse to death. He is thoroughly convinced that grand opera was a major influence on the formation of Whitman's poetry, and he has treated that influence almost exclusively. He neither insists nor wishes to imply, however, that there were not other influences, often overlapping in their effects. The importance of these other forces is understood. But here Whitman's devotion to opera is the topic, and it is hoped that the following pages may throw light on the nature and the result of that devotion.

It is a pleasure to acknowledge genuine gratitude to Dr. Robert E. Spiller, who has given indispensable critical advice in the preparation of the study. Dr. Sculley Bradley has also been most generous with helpful suggestions. Furthermore, sincere thanks are due to the officers and attendants of the various libraries from which material has been obtained: The Library of the Curtis Institute of Music, The Free Library of Philadelphia, The New Orleans Public Library, The New York Public Library, The Library of Duke University, and, principally, The Library of the University of Pennsylvania.

ROBERT D. FANER

Southern Illinois University

NOTES—PREFACE

1. "All about the Mocking Bird," *Saturday Press*, January 7, 1860. Quoted in *A Child's Reminiscence*, edd. T. O. Mabbott, R. G. Silver (Seattle: University of Washington Book Store, 1930), p. 20. The article is not signed but is convincingly identified as by Whitman.

2. John Townsend Trowbridge, "Reminiscences of Walt Whitman," *Atlantic Monthly*, LXXXIX, 166 (February, 1902).

3. Horace L. Traubel, *With Walt Whitman in Camden*, 3 vols. (New York, 1908), II, 173.

4. Basil De Selincourt, *Walt Whitman: A Study* (New York, 1914).

5. Henry Seidel Canby, *Walt Whitman, An American* (Boston: Houghton Mifflin and Co., 1943).

6. Louise Pound, "Walt Whitman and Italian Music," *American Mercury*, VI, 58-63 (September, 1925).

7. Jean Catel, *Walt Whitman: La Naissance du Poète* (Paris: Les Editions Rieder, 1929).

8. Clifton J. Furness, "Walt Whitman and Music," *News Bulletin*, Boston Chapter, Special Libraries Association, IV, No. 2, 2 (November, 1937).

9. F. O. Matthiessen, "Whitman," *American Renaissance* (New York: Oxford University Press, 1941), pp. 517-626.

10. Julia Spregelman, "Walt Whitman and Music," *South Atlantic Quarterly*, XLI, 167-76 (April, 1942).

11. Alice L. Cooke, "Notes on Whitman's Musical Background," *New England Quarterly*, XIX, 224-35 (June, 1946).

Acknowledgments to Publishers

For permission to reprint portions of the works mentioned, grateful acknowledgment is hereby extended to the following publishers and individuals:

Columbia University Press for *Annals of the New York Stage* by George C. D. Odell and *I Sit and Look Out*, edited by Emory Holloway and Vernolian Schwartz.

Doubleday and Company, Inc., for *The Uncollected Poetry and Prose of Walt Whitman*, edited by Emory Holloway and *The Letters of Walt Whitman and Anne Gilchrist*, edited by Thomas B. Harned.

Farrar, Straus and Company for *Walt Whitman Handbook* by Gay W. Allen.

Clarence Gohdes for *Faint Clews & Indirections: Manuscripts of Walt Whitman and His Family*, edited by Clarence Gohdes and Rollo G. Silver.

Mrs. A. F. Goldsmith for *Letters Written by Walt Whitman to His Mother 1866-1872*, edited by Rollo G. Silver.

Harvard University Press for *Walt Whitman's Workshop*, edited by Clifton J. Furness.

Emory Holloway for *New York Dissected*, edited by Emory Holloway.

Houghton Mifflin Company for *Walt Whitman an American* by Henry Seidel Canby.

The Macmillan Company for *Roadside Meetings* by Hamlin Garland.

Charles Scribner's Sons for *Essays* by J. G. Huneker.

Simon and Schuster, Inc., for *The Opera* by Wallace Brockway and Herbert Weinstock.

Contents

Part 1

BACKGROUND

CHAPTER I

Musical Experience

1

ONLY A YEAR before his death, looking back over his long career as a poet, Walt Whitman recorded his great indebtedness to those individuals who had performed so inspiringly on the New York stage when he was a young man, and to the great masterworks they had interpreted.

Seems to me I ought to acknowledge my debt to actors, singers, public speakers, conventions, and the stage in New York, my youthful days, from 1835—say to '60 or '61—and to plays and operas generally. . . . Seems to me now when I look back, the Italian contralto Alboni[1] (she is living yet, in Paris, 1891, in good condition, good voice yet, considering) with the then prominent histrions Booth, Edwin Forrest, and Fanny Kemble and the Italian singer Bettini,[2] have had the deepest and most lasting effect upon me. I should like well if Madame Alboni and the old composer Verdi (and Bettini the tenor, if he is living), could know how much noble pleasure and happiness they gave me then, and how deeply I always remember them and thank them to this day.[3]

It is significant that from the recollections thronging back to him as an old man, Whitman should identify three persons as deserving an expression of his deepest gratitude, and that these three should be representatives of Italian opera as he had known it. It must of course be granted that Whitman's interest was keen both in the stage generally and in the art of oratory, as it was practiced in his day. It is true that in certain sharply defined periods of his life his absorption in matters of oratory was almost complete.[4] But after his interest in music was thoroughly awakened, it continued throughout his life to be a primary inspiration.

As the quoted testimony suggests, opera was the climax of his musical experiences. Any attempt to explain and evaluate the influence of this operatic music on Whitman's artistic development must establish the extent and nature of his familiarity with operatic

3

literature and the dates of his greatest enthusiasm and most frequent attendance. For if opera is to be claimed as a formative influence on the poet's work, it must be shown that he was closely
familiar with it in the days when he was evolving his unique literary
theory. Incidentally, his interest in other forms of music should be
noted in passing, though they are by no means so important to his
development and came to be completely overshadowed by his devotion to the lyric stage.

Unfortunately, Whitman left no account even moderately systematic of his activity as a young man. He was almost secretive about
his comings and goings in the years just preceding the appearance
of *Leaves of Grass*. There is, however, his statement, already quoted,
that during the years 1835 to 1861 he was familiar with things
musical in New York. (*Leaves of Grass* was first issued in 1855, and
by 1861 a third edition had been prepared and published.)[5] An
early biography of the poet by Richard Maurice Bucke, a friend
who was to become one of his literary executors, places the years of
greatest musical activity from 1840 to 1860.[6] Whitman attended
opera after these years, though the twenty-year period suggested was
undoubtedly the time of the poet's greatest participation in musical
affairs, if for no other reason than that his opportunities were far
greater in those days than in any others.

What this participation amounted to in terms of actual musical
experience may be determined by piecing together all of Whitman's
references to music. These are of two kinds: first, his comments on
music written at the time of his attendance and contributed to
various newspapers and journals; second, his later prose works and
poems in which he attempted to recall the activity of his young
manhood. Such a record will by no means be complete, of course,
for it is wholly unlikely that the poet mentioned in his writings
every performance he witnessed. It will at least provide a structure
of fact upon which may be based a discussion of the effect of his
favorite type of music upon his work.

2

Whitman's contemporary accounts of his musical experience
during his formative years do not begin until 1845, though he had
been associated in one way or another with various papers in the

New York area for five or six years before that.[7] The first comment on the subject concerns not opera, which he was to become interested in later, but the popular music of one of the family troupes of the day. In an article in the *Broadway Journal* for November 29, 1845, called "Art-Singing and Heart-Singing," he comments at length on a performance of the Cheney Family which he had recently heard.[8] This was apparently the first time he had heard the Cheneys, a quartette of three boys and one girl, all children of Simeon Pease Cheney, the distinguished New Hampshire preacher. And he confesses that he had not heard the Hutchinsons, another family group actually more widely known at the time than the Cheneys. This deficiency was corrected, however, by the time he came to publish a reworked version of the article, called this time "Music That Is Music," in the Brooklyn *Daily Eagle* on December 4, 1846, a little more than a year later.[9] Whitman does not list the compositions performed by these remarkably popular troupes, but the records of their programs provide the titles of some of their more often sung pieces: "The Soldier's Farewell," "Our Childhood Home," "My Mother's Bible," "Get Off the Track," "Lament of the Irish Emigrant," "The Mariner Loves O'er the Water to Roam," and "The Old Granite State." The songs were by no means genuine ballads, though they were usually referred to by that term. Instead, they were sentimental concoctions on all sorts of topics, notably those which would be likely to bring tears to the eyes of the uncultivated audiences which heard them. Sometimes the songs were open abolitionist propaganda, like "The Bereaved Slave Mother," which the Hutchinsons introduced with great success in 1843.[10]

By 1846, when he published the article on the Hutchinsons, Whitman had certainly begun to attend regular concerts of serious music by the internationally renowned musicians of the day, for in the article he mentions, somewhat scornfully, "the New York concerts with the florid Italian and French music."[11] He also refers to Ernesto Sivori, the Italian violinist and composer who had been a pupil of Paganini; Leopold De Meyer, the pianist who was somewhat extravagantly billed at the time as "Imperial and Royal pianist to the Emperors of Austria and Russia,"[12] and the Italian operatic contralto, Rosina Pico.[13]

The habit of concert-going, which Whitman himself declared to have begun as early as 1835, became real grist for his journalistic mill while he served as editor of the Brooklyn *Daily Eagle* in 1846 and 1847. Now, as for many seasons while he was a working journalist in the New York area, he was on what he called "the free list,"[14] and it may be assumed that he made the most of his opportunities. In any case, no fewer than thirteen articles of varying length but specifically on musical subjects came from his pen in these months.[15] One of the reviews, published on October 9, 1846,[16] discussed the playing of Joseph Burke, the American violinist who had been a one-time boy prodigy. Burke's playing of "The Carnival of Venice" is declared to be the equal of that of Ole Bull, the reigning master of the violin. Thus we may be reasonably sure that Whitman, like so many New Yorkers, had heard Bull often. Another safe inference is that Whitman had heard most of the currently prominent artists by this time, since artists rarely appeared alone in concert in those days, but on highly diversified programs featuring many well-known individuals. For example, Leopold De Meyer had appeared with Burke in the concert mentioned above, though Whitman does not speak of him.[17] On October 13, 1846, another violin concert, this one by Ernesto Sivori, was the subject of comment.[18]

But popular music and concerts were by no means the extent of Whitman's experience in music in these days. Opera had already attracted his attention. His first reference to it occurs in a summary of the New York operatic stage of the time, which appeared in the *Daily Eagle* for February 24, 1847. The passage indicates his familiarity with performers and operas.

At the Olympic Theatre, they are giving a run, after the old sort, of the popular operas, very neatly got up on a small scale; Miss Taylor appears tonight as Zorlina in "Fra Diavolo" (the best played parts at this theatre are Diavolo's two fellow robbers). . . . At the opera house in Chambers street, they are continuing the representation of a narrow few—those not even the second best—of the Italian operas; tonight "Lucrezia Borgia." On Wednesday night it will be pleasanter to go, for then they give "Lombardi." Nor must we overlook the new musical corps, late from Havana, now giving operas at the Park, two evenings each week: after the next representation by this corps, our readers will get a plain man's opinion of them.[19]

Though it is certain that Whitman saw the productions by the great Havana company, for he later mentioned[20] several of the great singers of the organization, he never fulfilled his promise to review them.

In March, 1847, there appeared a short statement[21] declaring the cordial treatment accorded the representative of the *Daily Eagle* by members of Palmo's[22] opera company, about which another journal had complained. Possibly Whitman had now become known to some of the singers or managers, though there is little else from his pen to support such a belief.

The first of Whitman's critical reviews of opera appeared in the *Eagle* for March 23, 1847.[23] It is an evaluation of *The Barber of Seville* by Rossini, and the work of several singers is specifically mentioned, notably Benedetti,[24] Patti,[25] Beneventano,[26] Sanquirico,[27] and Pico. The tone of the review indicates that the critic had witnessed not only the opera but the work of the cast on many previous occasions. Another review appeared later in the year, on August 5,[28] when Whitman discussed the art of Mrs. Anna Bishop,[29] popular English singer, as it had been revealed in the English adaptation of the opera *Linda di Chamounix*.

During these years Whitman was naturally not unaware of the oratorio, a musical form closely related to the opera in structure and effectiveness, differing chiefly in the facts of sacred subject matter and presentation in concert form. On November 9, 1847, he published a review of *Elijah*, by Mendelssohn, which had been sung the night before for the first time in America.[30] The performance was by the Sacred Music Society of New York, which gave many presentations of oratorio, and on this occasion enlisted the services of Julia Northall, soprano, Rosina Pico, contralto, R. G. Paige, tenor, and Edward Shepherd, baritone, about the best oratorio soloists available at the time.[31] Whitman had previously heard the same composer's *St. Paul*, much like *Elijah* in that it makes use of dramatic episodes in the career of a Biblical personage, and had published a critical account in the Brooklyn *Evening Star*.[32]

That Whitman's interest in religious music, and his knowledge of it, were continuing and by no means superficial is suggested by an article he contributed to *Life Illustrated* of January 26, 1856,[33]

nearly ten years after the oratorio reviews mentioned above. The
comment begins: "Your correspondent's hungry musical sense was
delighted a day or two before Christmas just past at reading in the
daily papers the announcement that several pieces of sacred music
would be performed, with celebrated singers and organist, at Grace
Church, in this city."[33] The "hungry musical sense" must have been
very real, for the correspondent confesses he had to wait an hour in
the rain for the pew-holders to be seated. The list of pieces he wanted
to hear, which had been advertised in the New York Herald,[34] is
revealing. It included "Gloria in Excelsis," "Jubilate," and "Christmas Hymn," all arranged from Mozart; "Seventy-fifth Psalm," arranged from Beethoven; and "Show Me Thy Ways, O Lord," by
Torrente, to be sung by Julia Northall, one of the most admired
and widely heard singers of the day. It is worth noting that this
music is very different from that offered by the Hutchinson Family,
which had earlier attracted Whitman's interest.

But the interest in sacred music, which the references above show,
remained definitely subordinate to Whitman's interest in opera,
which had been developing apace. In August 14, 1851, he published
an essay on opera, called "Letter from Paumanok," in the New
York Evening Post.[35] It is an extended comment on the pleasures,
not to say raptures, of opera-going, particularly as they might be
experienced at a performance of La Favorita, an opera by Donizetti.
The essay establishes Whitman's detailed familiarity with the
opera as a work of art, and it analyzes his fondness for the singing
of the tenor, Bettini. There is also this significant statement: "After
traveling through the fifteen years display in this city of musical
celebrities, from Mrs. Austin up to Jenny Lind, from Ole Bull on
to the conductor Benedict,[36] with much fair enjoyment of the
talent of all; none have thoroughly satisfied, overwhelmed me but
this man [Bettini]."[37] By easy calculation this statement would
place his earliest musical experience in 1836, and it emphasizes his
active participation in musical affairs during all the following years.

In 1855, the year of the first edition of Leaves of Grass, appeared
the last of Whitman's published comments on music which were
written during the years when he was most attentive to music. It is
another relatively long essay on opera, called simply "The Opera,"
and appeared in Life Illustrated for November 10.[38] It discusses

many aspects of opera in general but specifically comments on Verdi's *Ernani* and the singing of several prominent artists of the time: Marini,[39] Steffanone,[40] La Grange,[41] Brignoli,[42] and Amodio.[43]

3

Fortunately it is not necessary to depend wholly on what Whitman wrote about opera while he was seeing so much of it during the forties and fifties. The memory of those days remained strong throughout his life, and he often referred to them in the writing of his later career. In these reminiscences are found many references to specific operatic works and specific singers, all of which add to our knowledge of his musical experience.

For example, on one occasion he said, "I remember Jenny Lind and heard her (1850 I think) several times."[44] Again in his "Diary in Canada," prepared while he was visiting his friend, Dr. Bucke, Whitman found occasion to declare, "Grisi[45] and Mario[46] arrived in N. Y. Aug. 19, 1854; I heard them that winter and in 1855."[47] Hearing the celebrated singers, during the significant years when he was preparing *Leaves of Grass*, seems to have been an occasion memorable enough to fix even its date in the poet's memory, or at least to have been worthy of a carefully preserved clipping.

In an essay called "The Old Bowery" Whitman recalls that he heard the tenor Mario, "many times, and at his best. In such parts as Gennaro in 'Lucrezia Borgia' he was inimitable."[48] Whitman also refers again to hearing the tenor's wife, Grisi, in *Norma*. She was, he says, "no longer first-class or young—a fine Norma though to the last." In the same passage Whitman refers to "the trumpet tones of Badiali's[49] baritone" and "Marini's bass in 'Faliero.' "[50] In another passage there is a mention of "the English opera of 'Cinderella'[51] (with Henry Placide[52] as the pompous old father), an unsurpassable bit of comedy and music."[53]

Later in the same statement Whitman enumerates many of the personalities he recalled from his younger days of devotion to great singers. Among the women listed are Mrs. Wood,[54] Mrs. Seguin,[55] Mrs. Austin, Grisi, La Grange, Steffanone, Bosio,[56] Truffi,[57] Parodi,[58] Vestvali,[59] Bertuca,[60] Jenny Lind, Gazzaniga,[61] and Laborde.[62] The roster of men includes Bettini, Badiali, Marini, Mario, Brignoli, Amodio, Beneventano, "and many, many others whose names I do not at the moment recall."[62a] To anyone who has examined the records of musical performances in New York in the forties and fifties, these lists constitute an amazing roll call of the leading artists of the time, all opera singers, of course, for these were the performers Whitman remembered. The inference is inescapable that he was devoted to their art with a remarkable intensity. It is also notable that most of these singers were most active in the early fifties, the very days when Whitman was planning and writing *Leaves of Grass*.

In *Specimen Days* Whitman again attempted to recall the musical pleasures of his young manhood. This time it was the individual operas which he called to mind.

I heard, these years, well render'd, all the Italian and other operas in vogue, "Sonnambula," "The Puritans," "Der Freischutz," "Huguenots," "Fille du Regiment," "Faust," "Etoile du Nord," "Poliuto," and others. Verdi's "Ernani," "Rigoletto," and "Trovatore" with Donizetti's "Lucia" or "Favorita" or "Lucrezia" and Auber's "Masaniello" or Rossini's "William Tell" and "Gazza Ladra" were among my special enjoyments.[63]

It is in the same passage that Whitman makes an unqualified statement which would prove his devotion to singers and opera if he had said little else on the subject: "I heard Alboni every time she sang in New York and vicinity."[63a] When one learns that this world-famous singer appeared as guest artist in one performance of Rossini's florid and operatic oratorio, *Stabat Mater*, that she gave twelve concerts of operatic selections, and that she sang leading roles in ten different operas, with sometimes as many as four performances of an individual role, all in the winter of 1852-53,[64] one realizes how constant was Whitman's absorption in the art of opera during these important years of his own development.

Another reference to opera-going, in *Specimen Days*, is of special interest for the somewhat dramatic if accidental way in which two of the greatest influences on Whitman's creative effort were linked together in his experience: opera and the Civil War.

News of the attack on fort Sumter and the flag at Charleston harbor, S. C., was received in New York City late at night (13th April, 1861) and was immediately sent out in extras of the newspapers. I had been to the opera in Fourteenth Street that night, and after the performance was walking down Broadway toward twelve o'clock. . . .[65]

4

With the coming of the Civil War the most important period of Whitman's musical experience ended. There were several reasons. First, his wartime activity occupied much of his time. Second, after 1861 he was in the New York area for only short periods of time and made his home first in Washington and then in Camden, New Jersey. Finally, in his later years his paralysis made it impossible for him to get about as he had once done.

But if his attendance at opera was less frequent after 1861 it did not stop altogether. There is considerable evidence that he continued to go until as late as 1872, and that as his opportunities for entertainment became less frequent he devoted himself exclusively to opera-going for recreation.

An entry in a diary which he kept for 1863, dated November 4, conveys the following information: "Opera (Lucrezia Borgia)— Medori,[66] Mazzoleni,[67] Biachi[68] very fine."[69] From other entries in the same diary we learn that he had arrived home in Brooklyn on the evening of November 2 for a short rest from strenuous duties in Washington, D.C.[70] He obviously wasted no time in availing himself of his favorite type of amusement, which he had doubtlessly missed while away.

Hearing this opera, after the busy months in Washington where he had no opportunities to hear such music, seems to have rekindled his enthusiasm. In any case, he wrote at once to one of his soldier friends in Washington, Lew Brown, a long and eloquent letter, which was to be passed around among other mutual friends. In it Whitman attempted to convey to his uninitiated comrades the peculiar charm of opera. The letter ends with an important sentence. ". . . opera is the only amusement I have gone to, for my own satisfaction for the last ten years."[71] The implications of the sentence are important. Since it was written in 1863, it means that by 1853, two years before Leaves of Grass appeared, Whitman found recreation exclusively in opera, and that during the important years when he was revising and adding to the book, he continued to find amusement in opera alone.

There are other references to opera in 1863. Whitman wrote to

Ellen O'Connor, the wife of a Washington friend, on November 15, 1863, as follows:

I have been several times to the opera & and to French Theatre. The opera here Maretzek's troupe is very fine. Medori, soprano, is pretty near perfection . . . Mazzoleni, tenor, ditto—Biachi, base, ditto. Miss Kellogg is also good. The pieces were Lucrezia, Sonnambula, etc.[72]

Another brief entry in the 1863 diary further testifies to his activities. Under the date of November 16, he stated briefly: "Opera.[73] Wrote to Ellen O'Connor."[74] Apparently he was making the most of his opportunities for opera-going while he was in New York for a time.

Such opportunities of course became increasingly rare for Whitman, chiefly because he was almost continuously away from New York. However, he did not miss what performances there were in Washington, where he was working. On January 8, 1867, he wrote his mother from Washington, "I went to the opera last night—went alone—I was much pleased—the piece was Ernani—first amusement I have been to in a year, except once to hear Ristori."[75] In another letter to his mother the next April he wrote, "I went to a concert last night—Brignoli and Parepa—nothing very great."[76]

Back in Brooklyn for a time in 1872, Whitman wrote to his friend, Peter Doyle, in Washington, "I have been to the Italian opera twice, heard Nilsson[77] both times,—she is very fine—one night Trovatore, and one, Robert,[78] with Brignoli—both good."[79] He was still not neglecting occasions when he could hear opera, though this is the last available mention by him of actual opera attendance.

After Whitman became partially paralyzed and left Washington to live in Camden, first with his brother George and later in his own home, his opportunities for hearing music were of course even rarer than they had been in the immediately preceding years. Even at this time, however, he managed to hear some of the music available in Philadelphia, just across the river. There is only one reference to such an experience from his own pen, however. In an entry in Specimen Days for February 11, 1880, he recalls having heard an orchestra concert in the foyer of the opera house (probably the Academy of Music) by a band "small but first rate."[80] He was particularly impressed by a septet of Beethoven,[81] and gives a somewhat extended and poetic account of his impression of the music. Further testimony to his concert-going in the Camden days is provided by the eminent music critic, James Gibbons Huneker, in his essay, "A Visit to Walt Whitman." He says, referring to Whitman, "I several times took him from the Carl Gaertner String Quartette concerts in the foyer of the Broad Street Academy of Music to the Market Street cars."[82] Possibly it was at one of these concerts that the Beethoven work had been heard. These musical experiences, late in the poet's career and after his greatest writing had been done, are important in showing that his love for music never vanished, though they can hardly be thought to bear an important relation to his creative efforts, as his earlier opera attendance undoubtedly had.

5

It might be expected that in the poems of so ardent and indefatigable an opera lover as Whitman there would be references to the masterworks he so much admired. Such is the case. Though he does not state positively that he witnessed performances of the works mentioned, the contexts in which the references are found make it seem altogether likely that he had, and knew them well.

In "Italian Music in Dakota"[83] La Sonnambula, Norma, and Poliuto are named. "Proud Music of the Storm"[84] includes references to leading characters in Lucia di Lammermoor, Norma, Ernani, I Puritani, La Favorita, and La Sonnambula. The same poem mentions William Tell, Huguenots, The Prophet, Robert, Faust, and Don Juan. In "The Dead Tenor"[85] Whitman mentions the leading tenor roles of Fernando in La Favorita, Manrico in Il Trovatore, Ernani in the opera of the same name, and Gennaro in Lucrezia Borgia. Two oratorios are also mentioned, Stabat Mater by Rossini and The Creation by Haydn.[86] Not identified by name but referred to are other oratorios by Beethoven and Handel. Probably no other poet has referred so many times to specific operatic works in the pages of his poems.

6

No mention has so far been made of Whitman's possible musical interests during the months he was in New Orleans in 1848. The

reason is that nowhere, either in his contributions to journals of the
time or in his later reminiscences, does he mention having attended
opera in the southern city. It would seem to be a safe assumption
that he did, however, for New Orleans was the operatic capital of
the country at the time, and regularly sent companies to New York
to perform, much as the present-day Metropolitan Opera Association takes to the road in post-season tours.

While Whitman was in New Orleans, four and five performances
of opera were being given each week at two houses, the Orleans
Theatre and the St. Charles Theatre.[87] At the latter, one of his
favorite singers from New York, Mrs. Anna Bishop, was appearing
in leading roles in operas much admired by Whitman such as
Norma, La Sonnambula, Lucrezia Borgia, and Linda di Chamounix.
It seems unlikely that Whitman could have foregone hearing them,
if only to compare the operatic standards of the New Orleans companies in their home theatres with those of New York, which by this
time he knew well.

7

By way of recapitulation, it may be helpful at this point to formulate a list of the various major works which Whitman indicated
specifically that he knew. The list will include all the titles that
he ever mentioned, though excepting the Beethoven Septet he had
heard them all before 1861, that is, during his most active musical
period. It will be noticed that the Beethoven is the only non-vocal
work in the list. The roster of twenty-five operas and four oratorios
is here prepared alphabetically by composer:

Auber	*Masaniello*
Beethoven	*Septet*
Bellini	*I Puritani; La Sonnambula; Norma*
Donizetti	*La Favorita; La Fille du Regiment; Linda di Chamounix; Lucia di Lammermoor; Lucrezia Borgia; Marino Faliero; Poliuto*
Gounod	*Faust*
Haydn	*The Creation*
Mendelssohn	*Elijah; St. Paul*
Meyerbeer	*Le Prophète; L'Etoile du Nord; Robert le Diable*
Mozart	*Don Giovanni*
Verdi	*Ernani; I Lombardi; Il Trovatore; Rigoletto*

Rossini   *Guillaume Tell; Il Barbiere di Siviglia; La*
               Cenerentola; La Gazza Ladra; Stabat Mater
Von Weber   *Der Freischütz*

NOTES—CHAPTER I

1. Marietta Alboni, Italian contralto, by all accounts one of the greatest who ever lived. Whitman's favorite singer. New York debut, 1852.

2. Allesandro Bettini, Italian tenor. New York debut, 1850.

3. "Good-Bye My Fancy," *The Complete Writings of Walt Whitman*, edd., Richard Maurice Bucke, Thomas B. Harned, Horace L. Traubel (New York and London, 1902), 10 vols., Prose IV, 49. Hereafter, only the Prose volumes of this work will be referred to. They will be identified as *Prose.*

4. Clifton J. Furness, *Walt Whitman's Workshop* (Cambridge: Harvard University Press, 1928), pp. 25-69. See also Thomas B. Harned, "Walt Whitman and Oratory," *Prose*, V., 244-60.

5. *Leaves of Grass* (Brooklyn, N. Y., 1855). *Leaves of Grass* (Brooklyn, N. Y., 1856). *Leaves of Grass* (Boston, 1860-61).

6. Richard Maurice Bucke, *Walt Whitman* (Philadelphia, 1883), p. 22.

7. Gay W. Allen, *Walt Whitman Handbook* (Chicago: Packard and Co., 1946), p. xii.

8. *The Uncollected Poetry and Prose of Walt Whitman*, ed. Emory Holloway, 2 vols. (Garden City, N. Y., 1921), I, 105.

9. *The Gathering of the Forces*, edd. Cleveland Rodgers, John Black, 2 vols. (New York, 1920), II, 346.

10. Philip D. Jordan, *Singin' Yankees* (Minneapolis: University of Minnesota Press, 1946), p. 55. See also Carol Brink, *Harps in the Wind* (New York: Macmillan, 1947).

11. *Gathering of the Forces*, II, 346.

12. George C. D. Odell, *Annals of the New York Stage*, 10 vols. (New York: Columbia University Press, 1927-38), V, 168.

13. New York debut, 1844.

14. "Specimen Days," *Prose*, I, 25.

15. *Gathering of the Forces*, II, 345-59.

16. *Ibid.*, II, 352-53.

17. Odell, *op. cit.*, V, 312.

18. *Gathering of the Forces*, II, 354-55.

19. *Uncollected Poetry and Prose*, I, 157.

20. "November Boughs," *Prose*, III, 186.

21. *Gathering of the Forces*, II, 359.

22. Ferdinand Palmo, director of Chambers Street opera house.

23. *Gathering of the Forces*, II, 349-50.

24. Sesto Benedetti, Italian tenor. New York debut, 1847.

25. Salvatore Patti, Italian tenor and impresario. New York debut, 1847.

26. Francesco Beneventano, Italian basso. New York debut, 1847.

27. Italian basso-buffo. New York debut, 1844.

28. *Gathering of the Forces*, II, 351-52.

29. English soprano. New York debut, 1847.

30. *Gathering of the Forces*, II, 353-54.

31. Odell, *op. cit.*, V, 403.

32. Quoted in Emory Holloway, "More Light on Whitman," *American Mercury*, I, 186 (January, 1924).

33. *New York Dissected*, edd. Emory Holloway, Ralph Adimari (New York: Rufus Rockwell Wilson, Inc., 1936), pp. 46-47.

34. *Ibid.*, p. 45.

35. *Uncollected Poetry and Prose*, I, 255-58.

36. English musician who conducted the orchestra for Lind's American concerts.

37. *Uncollected Poetry and Prose*, I, 257.

38. *New York Dissected*, pp. 18-23.

39. Ignazio Marini, Italian basso. New York debut, 1850.

40. Balbina Steffanone, Italian soprano. New York, debut, 1850.

41. Anna de La Grange, English soprano. New York debut, 1855.

42. Pasquale Brignoli, Italian tenor, subject of Whitman's poem, "The Dead Tenor," New York debut, 1855.

43. Amodio, Italian baritone. New York debut, 1855.

44. "Good-Bye My Fancy," *Prose*, IV, 53.

45. Giula Grisi, Italian soprano, with her husband, Mario, known for great successes at Covent Garden, London. New York debut, 1854.

46. Giuseppe Mario, Italian tenor. New York debut, 1854.

47. *Walt Whitman's Diary in Canada*, ed. William Sloane Kennedy (Boston, 1904), p. 64.

48. "November Boughs," *Prose*, III, 186.

49. Cesare Badiali, Italian baritone, perhaps the greatest in his day and one of Whitman's favorite singers. New York debut, 1850.

50. *Marino Faliero*, an opera by Donizetti.

51. Probably an adaptation of Rossini's opera, *La Cenerentola*.

52. Singer-actor, widely popular in New York for many years.

53. "Good-bye My Fancy," *Prose*, IV, 50.

54. Mrs. Joseph Wood, English soprano. New York debut, 1833.

55. Mrs. Edward Seguin, a soprano heard more than any other in her day in New York. New York debut, 1839.

56. Angiolina Bosio, Italian soprano, a very great favorite in her day. New York debut, 1850.

57. Teresa Truffi, Italian soprano. New York debut, 1847.

58. Teresa Parodi, Italian soprano, brought to New York to rival Jenny Lind. New York debut, 1850.

59. Felicita Vestvali, Italian contralto. New York debut, 1855.

60. Appolonia Bertucca, Italian soprano. New York debut, 1849.

61. Marietta Gazzaniga, Italian soprano. New York debut, 1858.

62. Mme Laborde, French soprano. New York debut, 1858.

62a. "Good-Bye My Fancy," *Prose*, IV, 56.

63. "Specimen Days," *Prose*, I, 26.

63a. *Ibid.*

64. Odell, *op. cit.*, VI, 263-340.

65. "Specimen Days," *Prose*, I, 28. The opera was probably Verdi's *Un Ballo in Maschera*. Odell, *op. cit.*, VII, 349.

MUSICAL EXPERIENCE 17

66. Josephine Medori, Italian soprano. New York debut, 1863.

67. Francesco Mazzoleni, Italian heroic tenor. New York debut, 1863.

68. Italian basso. New York debut, 1863.

69. Charles I. Glicksberg, *Walt Whitman and the Civil War* (Philadelphia: University of Pennsylvania Press, 1933), p. 139.

70. *Ibid.*, p. 139.

71. Horace Traubel, *With Walt Whitman in Camden*, 3 vols. (New York, 1914), III, 103.

72. Manuscript in the Berg Collection, New York Public Library. Quoted with permission.

73. Probably Clara Louise Kellogg in *La Sonnambula*, at the Academy of Music. Odell, *op. cit.*, VII, 581.

74. Glicksberg, *op. cit.*, p. 139.

75. *Letters Written by Walt Whitman to his Mother, 1866-1872*, ed. Thomas B. Harned (New York, 1902), p. 23. Ristori was a celebrated Italian actress of the time.

76. *Ibid.*, p. 42. Euphrosyne Parepa-Rosa, English soprano, best known for oratorio singing, subject of Whitman's poem, "The Singer in Prison."

77. Christine Nilsson, Swedish soprano. New York debut, 1870.

78. *Robert le Diable*, opera by Meyerbeer.

79. *Calamus*, ed., Richard Maurice Bucke (Boston, 1897), p. 91.

80. "Specimen Days," *Prose*, I, 287.

81. Septet, E Flat Major, Op. 20, for Violin, Viola, Cello, Bass, Clarinet, French Horn, and Bassoon.

82. James G. Huneker, "A Visit to Walt Whitman," *Essays* (New York: Scribner's, 1929), p. 419.

83. Walt Whitman, *Leaves of Grass*, Inclusive Edition, ed. Emory Holloway (Garden City, N. Y.: Doubleday and Company, 1946), pp. 334-35. Unless otherwise specified, all references to Whitman's poems are to this edition.

84. *Ibid.*, pp. 337-42.

85. *Ibid.*, p. 432.

86. "Proud Music of the Storm," *Ibid.*, p. 341.

87. New Orleans *Daily Delta*, New Orleans, La. (February, 1848).

Chapter II

Musical Climate

WHITMAN'S RECORD of his musical experiences is so completely unsystematic and fragmentary that at best the foregoing account, based strictly on his own testimony, can tell only part of the story. At various times the developing poet was steeped in operatic music. As he put it, "All through these years [his young manhood] off and on, I frequented the old Park, the Bowery, Broadway, and Chatham-Square theatres and the Italian operas at Chambers-street, Astor Place or the Battery."[1] Only by examining the quality of the opera seasons in New York during the forties and fifties can the student of Whitman achieve something like an understanding of the musical climate in which he matured. Even a brief summary is important, for present-day readers are inclined to feel that the musical scene in pre-Civil War New York must have been somewhat primitive and unrewarding, or at least hardly of a quality sufficiently impressive to be a major influence on the poet.

Artistically, the two decades were anything but primitive, for they witnessed some of the greatest triumphs in the history of music in America. Financially, of course, opera was then as now a risky business, and the forties and fifties saw the sad downfall of many an ambitious manager.

1

A summary[2] of the years can be most conveniently devised, perhaps, in terms of the different theatres presenting opera at the time, though it must be remembered that most of the houses varied their offerings with several different kinds of entertainment, including variety and the drama. First in the list of theatres, because the only one presenting opera in the season of 1841-42, is the Park Theatre, though the quality of opera given in that season and for several successive ones was not particularly notable. It presented a resident cast headed by Mr. and Mrs. Edward Seguin, well known because of their frequent appearances if not their excellence, in a few of the standard operas like *Norma* and *La Sonnambula*. There were also a good many performances in English of light operas like *Fra Diavolo* and Balfe's *The Bohemian Girl*, in which Mrs. Seguin scored her greatest personal success. Occasionally unusual items like Handel's opera, *Acis and Galatea*, and Rossini's oratorio, *The Israelites in Egypt* (staged in operatic form), were surprisingly successful. Often concerts were given at the Park, sometimes genuinely notable. For instance, in the fall of 1843 Mme Cinti-Damoreau, French prima donna, made her debut and became one of the celebrities of the season, and only two days later Ole Bull, the Norwegian violinist, performed there for the first time in America.

In June, 1845, a distinguished French opera company from New Orleans, headed by the great favorite Mme Julie Calvé, who had been heard earlier in New York, opened at the Park. The summer season of the company was one of great distinction, and operas of Meyerbeer, Auber, Rossini, and Donizetti were given productions equally notable for their polished style and perfection of ensemble. Two operas which were to become great favorites in New York were first presented there by this troupe: Donizetti's *La Favorita* and Meyerbeer's *Robert le Diable*, both performed in French.

The following winter the theatre returned to its former policy featuring the Seguins, varying light opera with Italian operas sung in English. In April, 1847, however, the Park Theatre figured in one of the most important events in the musical life of the decade in New York. At that time an Italian opera company from Havana, managed by Don Francesco Marty y Torrens, known usually as Señor Marty, opened at the Park. The organization was genuinely superior in both its soloists and ensemble, and it earned a pronounced success in performances throughout the summer of standard operas from the Italian repertory.

In the fall of 1847 the Park presented a new star in the person of Anna Bishop, wife of Sir Henry Bishop, the English composer. The coloratura artistry of Mme Bishop made her an overnight success, and she continued to head the opera casts at the Park until the theatre burned in December 1848, closing the record of one of the landmarks of music in New York.

2

The position of another house, Niblo's Garden Theatre, is perhaps quite as significant in the story of New York's music as that of the Park. For example, it was at Niblo's that the French opera company from New Orleans first appeared in New York, in May, 1843. In the fall of that year a resident Italian company was organized for the house, though without any success. The failure was probably due to poor artists and worse casting, for the same soprano would attempt to sing the coloratur. Lucia on one night and the mezzo-soprano Adalgisa in Norma on the following one. Naturally she could not have done either part very well.

Niblo's Garden was not conspicuous again for its musical offerings until April, 1850, when Señor Marty's Havana company, greatly enlarged and improved, once more invaded New York and opened at this theatre. The company now included not only a chorus and orchestra larger and finer than New Yorkers were accustomed to, but some of the finest soloists New York had ever heard. On the roster were Steffanone, Bosio, and Tedesco, sopranos; Bettini, Salvi, and Lorini, tenors; Badiali and Setti, baritones; and Marini and Coletti, bassos. Many of the singers ultimately left the company and remained in New York. At least three of them, Bosio, Badiali, and Marini, went on to later triumphs in Europe and to win international reputations as the finest artists of their day. The Havana performances at Niblo's ran into May when the company transferred to another theatre.

In January, 1852, several of the Havana singers who had in the meantime left the company returned to Niblo's for a season of two months, during which they presented Lucia, Norma, Don Pasquale, Lucrezia Borgia, I Puritani, La Sonnambula, and Don Giovanni. Bosio, Bettini, and Badiali were among the stars of the company.

During the great season of 1852-53, Niblo's took on new lustre. Opening in September, it varied French opera, presenting two well-known French sopranos, Mmes Thillon and Fleury-Jolly, with standard Italian items, sung by casts headed by Anna Bishop. In January, 1853, came the great coup. Henrietta Sontag, the celebrated

European diva, whose career was already legendary, made her operatic debut in *La Fille du Regiment*. Throughout January, February, and March, Sontag appeared with Pico, Badiali, and other great artists more than thirty times, singing works by Rossini and Donizetti. Following Sontag's remarkable incumbency, Niblo's was taken over by a new company headed by an even greater artist, though a less celebrated star, Marietta Alboni, the Italian contralto, who sang there regularly until May 6. Truly in 1853 Niblo's had become the most important opera house in the city.

In the fall the theatre presented regular performances of Italian operas with the best singers of the time, though without names of the magnitude of Sontag or Alboni. The series ended in December. Not until the season of 1854-55 did Niblo's again offer serious music; in the fall of that year there were occasional but unimpressive performances of opera, and in the spring a company of German singers performed through March and April without winning great success. By this time Niblo's had been thoroughly overshadowed by the opening of the Academy of Music.

3

A third establishment must stand with the Park Theatre and Niblo's Garden as an important home for opera during the years being discussed. This is Palmo's Opera House in Chambers Street, as notable for its stormy career of financial crises and managerial failures as the excellence of the opera produced there. Palmo's opened on February 3, 1844, with the first performance in New York of Bellini's *I Puritani*, and through March continued to produce standard Italian works with well-known singers. In April Ferdinand Palmo surrendered the management to Giuseppe de Begnis, the greatest *buffo* of his day, who for three months was both impresario and leading singer in such works as *The Barber of Seville*, *La Sonnambula*, *L'Elisir d'Amore*, *I Puritani*, and others. His regime ended with June, and through early July a different company, headed by Cinti-Damoreau, performed occasionally, yielding entirely to variety shows by the end of July.

In the fall, 1844, the house returned once more to opera, offering most of the standard Italian works with most of the popular singers of the time. Rosina Pico, a brilliant new contralto, was introduced during the season, and the first performance in New York of *Lucrezia Borgia* was a feature of November. By January, 1845, the management was no longer able to continue, however, and Italian opera ended at Palmo's for the season.

Two years later, after sporadic and unsuccessful performances of opera, two singers, Sanquirico, a *buffo*, and Salvatore Patti, a tenor whose greatest claim to fame is that he fathered the celebrated Adelina, took over the management of Palmo's, opening their season on January 4 with Donizetti's *Linda di Chamounix*, being given for the first time in New York. Their series included such works as *Lucia*, *The Barber of Seville*, *I Lombardi*, *Lucrezia Borgia*, and others and continued into June. The presentations were praised for their artistry but were not financially successful, and in June, 1847, opera at Palmo's was discontinued permanently, the house being later converted into Burton's Theatre.

4

Opera managers are not easily discouraged, apparently, for in November, 1847, a new and especially beautiful opera house, The Astor Place, opened with Sanquirico and Patti again managers. This was a relatively large house, with 1800 seats, and for some years was most important in New York's musical life. The opening season, presenting such favorite works as *Ernani*, *La Sonnambula*, *Lucia*, *I Puritani*, *Lucrezia Borgia*, and *The Barber of Seville*, along with novelties like Bellini's *Capuleti e Montecchi* and *Beatrice di Tenda*, Mercadante's *Il Giuramento* and Verdi's *Nabucco*, was artistically successful though there was an absence of any great stars in the casts. Financially, as usual, the season was less fortunate and ended in bankruptcy for the managers.

The second season at the Astor Place, 1848-49, was particularly important for the first appearances in America of the European conductor Max Maretzek,[3] who for many years was to be a leading figure in music in this country. During the first part of the season Maretzek merely conducted, but in March, 1849, after many difficulties, the manager of the house, E. R. Fry, retired, and the conductor became impresario as well. He finished out the season with respectable presentations of Italian opera.

The following season Maretzek reopened the Astor Place and

considerably enlarged the repertory of his company. He added such works as Rossini's *Otello*, Donizetti's *Maria di Rohan* and *Anna Bolena*, and Mozart's *Don Giovanni*. Following his season, the Havana company moved into the Astor Place from Palmo's where they had been singing, and through June and part of July gave superlative performances of standard Italian operas.

For the following winter, 1850-51, Maretzek engaged Teresa Parodi, whose professional reputation he elevated to the skies in an attempt to create a star to rival Jenny Lind, who was currently being so notoriously exploited. Parodi proved to be no Lind so far as popularity went, but she was greatly admired in dramatic soprano roles, particularly *Norma*. The remainder of Maretzek's company was not especially impressive, though he carried on throughout the year. By June he had corrected his deficiencies in personnel and had lured away from the Havana company most of its stars, including Steffanone, Bosio, Bettini, Salvi, Badiali, and Marini.

Maretzek's Astor Place season of 1851-52 was his most distinguished, for he was now able to offer unrivaled casts in all the great Italian operas. Troubles among the stars developed during the winter, however, and Bosio, Bettini, and Badiali withdrew from the company. Maretzek continued through February, however, when he ended his season. This was his last at the Astor Place, and with his departure the house no longer continued its important place in the musical life of the city.

5

Several other establishments, not primarily opera houses but all offering opera occasionally, are important in the story of operatic music in New York of the forties and fifties. One is Castle Garden, known often as simply "The Battery," where it was located. Its offerings were usually of a strictly popular sort, but it was also the summer home of various opera companies. The Havana troupe presented its standard repertory there in the summers of 1846 and 1849. In 1850 Maretzek took over the hall and offered four months of superior opera featuring the great artists he had succeeded in enticing away from the Havana company. In 1851 summer performances by a French company from New Orleans were given. Sontag and many other great names were featured in brilliant performances throughout the summer of 1853, while the following summer Maretzek returned, though with such poor casts this time that he earned small praise and less profit. In September of 1854 the hall was for a brief time the center of attraction for all opera lovers, when the internationally famed couple, Grisi, soprano, and Mario, tenor, made their debuts together in *Lucrezia Borgia*. They were more successful in later productions of *Norma*, but their appearances at Castle Garden in September were among the highlights of the theatre's history.

Another house which figured periodically in the musical life of New York was the Broadway Theatre, opened in 1847. Performances there in December of that year starred Anna Bishop in *Lucrezia Borgia*, *Linda di Chamounix*, and *La Sonnambula*. In October, 1848, Mr. and Mrs. Seguin were presented in a month of opera in English. During August and September of the following summer a repertory of Italian operas was given in Italian, usually starring the soprano Tedesco. In the winter of 1852 came the most notable opera performances at the Broadway, when Alboni sang a number of performances there.

6

All of the opera theatres were overshadowed after October 2, 1854, by the new Academy of Music, which opened then and remained for many years the most important home of opera in New York. The first year of the building's history was most successful artistically and must have been tremendously exciting to opera lovers of the area. But the managers had worse financial luck than usual, and there were three regimes during the first season. The Academy opened with Grisi and Mario in *Norma*, to be followed by the same pair in *La Sonnambula*, *Semiramide* (Grisi's greatest part) and *The Barber of Seville*. By the middle of December the the management was bankrupt, and the house closed.

In February it reopened, with Ole Bull as impresario, and offered many notable attractions, the chief being the first New York performance of Verdi's *Rigoletto*. Bull's regime did not last two months, but he was succeeded at once by another management which began auspiciously by introducing the tenor Brignoli to New York. In April the first New York performances of *William Tell* were given with the great Badiali as Tell, and on May 2 *Il Trovatore* was first heard in New York, with Steffanone, Brignoli, and a new baritone, Amodio, who quickly became established as one of the greatest artists of his day. In the same month a new soprano, de La Grange, made her debut in *The Barber of Seville*. She, too, earned quick fame. Performances of the favorite Italian operas ran through June, 1855, bringing to a close the first year of the Academy of Music, a year marked by much great music but also by constant financial and managerial troubles.

In succeeding seasons till the end of the decade, the Academy was rarely idle. All the well-known Italian operas were performed and some most important new ones, like Verdi's *La Traviata*, were introduced. Several important new artists made their bows at the Academy late in the fifties, too. Mmes Gazzaniga and Piccolomini were among them. On November 24, 1858, in *Lucia*, the sixteen-year-old singer who was to become the celebrated (though in the opinions of the best critics, never great) prima donna, Adelina Patti, made her operatic debut. In 1860 the two sopranos, Clara Louise Kellogg and Christine Nilsson, first appeared.

7

The foregoing summary of opera performances, though brief, indicates beyond question that Italian opera was one of the most significant types of musical entertainment available during the two decades, from 1840 to 1860. Though it completely overshadowed all other types of serious music, it was by no means alone in the field. Throughout the period concerts were very popular, almost invariably presenting several artists instead of one as is customary today. A few famous instrumentalists, like Bull, Sivori, and Vieuxtemps, violinists, and Strakosch, pianist, were heard but always in conjunction with great vocalists, of whom, at the time, there were far the greater number. It would have been impossible for an instrumentalist to have achieved the almost incredible popularity of a singer like Jenny Lind, who appeared at least twenty-five times in the single season of 1850-51. It was a day of singers, not players.

The popularity of singers is further exemplified by the early history of the Philharmonic Society orchestra, which was founded in 1842. Throughout the period it gave only four concerts each year, certainly a small number in comparison to the opera available. And for the orchestra's programs the featured soloists were almost invariably leading opera singers who performed generous quantities of operatic music.

With such an extravagant taste for singing on the part of audiences of the time, it is not surprising to find numerous performances of oratorio the rule. Often the great choral works were given with festival choruses of many hundred, sometimes merely with augmented church choirs. Occasionally the soloists were resident New Yorkers of more than average ability, but often the greatest Italian operatic singers were employed for leading parts. Two organizations were responsible for the greatest number of performances; in the forties the New York Sacred Music Society was the dominant group, while in the later years of the period the New York Harmonic Society performed most often.

Many of the greatest oratorios were given repeated hearings. The most common were Beethoven's *The Mount of Olives*, Handel's *The Messiah*, Haydn's *The Creation* and *The Seasons*, Mendelssohn's *St. Paul* and *Elijah*, and Rossini's *Stabat Mater*. Many other choral works were popular at the time, though since forgotten: such as Horn's *Seven Ages of Man* and Neukomm's *David and Goliah*.

8

Whitman declared that his interest in music was active all through the years which have just been summarized. One season was of special importance to him, however, for during it his favorite singer, Alboni, made all of her New York appearances, and during it he was quite certainly at work on *Leaves of Grass*. This was the season of 1852-53, and because of its significance to the poet its musical fare should be presented in some detail.[4]

To begin the season, or more exactly, to bring the preceding season to a close, were the three gala farewell concerts of Jenny Lind, by this time called Mme Otto Goldschmidt, on May 18, 21, and 24, 1852. Just about a month later came another event of greater artistic importance. It was the debut on June 23 of Alboni, called by some the greatest singer of mid-century, possibly the greatest singer of all time. At her first appearance, she offered arias from *Semiramide*, *Lucrezia Borgia*, *La Fille du Regiment*, *Don Pasquale*, and *La Cenerentola*, in the last of which she made her greatest success. She sang in concert again on June 28, but was not heard in opera until the following winter.

The opera season opened promptly in the fall at Niblo's Garden under the direction of Max Maretzek. A list of his performances with dates and principal singers will show the quality of his season, though it must be remembered that repeated performances of the individual works were the rule rather than the exception. The titles are given as they were advertised:

September 8   *Daughter of the Regiment* (Thillon, Hudson)
           11   *The Enchantress* (Thillon, Hudson)
           29   Zampa (Fleury-Jolly)
October   1   *Ne Touchez pas la Reine* (Fleury-Jolly)
November   1   *Martha*, first time in New York (Bishop)
           18   *Lucy of Lammermoor* (Braham)
           23   *La Sonnambula* (Bishop, Guidi)
           25   *Martha* (Bishop, Guidi)
           30   *Linda di Chamounix* (Bishop, Guidi)
December   6   *Crown Jewels* (Thillon)
           8   *Daughter of the Regiment* (Thillon)
           17   *The Basket-Maker's Wife*

On December 27, a company especially organized to star Alboni opened at the Broadway Theatre to give performances of the following operas. Note that Alboni chose to bow in the work which had served her so well at her summer recital:

December 27   *Cenerentola* (Alboni, Sangiovanni, Barili)
January   4   *La Figlia del Reggimento* (Alboni)
           10   *La Sonnambula* (Alboni)
           27   Norma (Alboni)

On January 10, Henrietta Sontag made her debut with Maretzek's company and in the next two and one-half months appeared thirty times as his star. It is worth noting that on the night of her debut, Alboni was also singing in New York at a rival house. Opera fans of the time must indeed have felt embarrassed with riches. Sontag's appearances were in the following operas:

January   10   *La Figlia del Reggimento*
           17   *The Barber of Seville*
           21   *Lucrezia Borgia*
           28   *L'Elisir d'Amore*

February   7   *Don Pasquale*
           14   *Lucia di Lammermoor*
           25   *Linda di Chamounix*
March   9   *Maria di Rohan*

On March 28, the special Alboni troupe and the Maretzek company joined forces and offered performances throughout the remainder of the season as follows (Sontag is noticeably absent from the casts):

March   28   *Don Pasquale* (Alboni, Salvi, Marini)
April   8   *La Favorita* (Alboni, Salvi, Marini)
            4   *The Barber of Seville* (Alboni)
           15   *La Sonnambula* (Alboni, Salvi, Rossi)
           20   *La Gazza Ladra* (Alboni, Vietti, Marini)
           22   *Lucrezia Borgia* (Alboni, deVries, Marini)
May   6   *Don Giovanni* (Alboni, Salvi)

At Castle Garden, for the usual summer performances, Sontag was again featured, along with many other first rate artists.

July   11   *Lucia* (Sontag, Salvi, Badiali)
           13   *Norma* (Steffanone, Salvi)
           16   *Lucia* (Sontag, Salvi)
           15   *Robert le Diable* (Sontag, Steffanone, Salvi)
           20   *L'Elisir d'Amore* (Sontag, Salvi, Badiali)
           22   *Don Giovanni* (Sontag, Steffanone, Amalia Patti)
           25   *La Sonnambula* (Sontag, Salvi, Badiali)
           29   *La Favorita* (Sontag, Salvi, Badiali)
August   3   *Lucrezia Borgia* (Steffanone, Salvi, Badiali)
            6   *La Figlia del Reggimento* (Sontag)
           10   *Lucia* (Sontag)
           12   *The Barber of Seville* (Sontag, Pozzolini)
           15   *Ernani* (Steffanone, Badiali, Marini)
           17   *I Puritani* (Sontag, Salvi, Badiali, Marini)

Like the opera houses, the concert field in 1852-53 was thoroughly dominated by the two reigning operatic stars, Alboni and Sontag. The former, assisted by other artists, gave eleven recitals in New York, all of them featuring operatic music exclusively. In addition to concerts, she appeared as soloist in one performance of Rossini's oratorio, *Stabat Mater*. Her farewell festival concert took place on May 26, 1853. She returned to Europe immediately and never revisited America. Thus all of her appearances in this country were confined to a period of less than a year. In that time, however, she was able to fix herself permanently in the memories of those who heard her. Richard Grant White, the leading music critic of the day, wrote in the New York *Courier and Enquirer*, following one recital, "Alboni's performances are as purely and absolutely beautiful as it is possible for anything earthly to be."[5] Walt Whitman was apparently not her only willing slave.

Sontag's concerts were probably even more numerous than Alboni's, though since she gave several series, it is difficult to establish the exact number. It is a testimony to her prestige, however, that in one series of four concerts she was assisted by an orchestra and a chorus of 600! Of Sontag, the critic White reported that her voice was "an absolute soprano, of full but not extraordinary compass or remarkable power."[6]

There were of course other concerts during the season. Anna Bishop sang, as did Rosina Pico and others. There were four regular concerts by the Philharmonic Society orchestra and four by the Eisfeld String Quartette. The instrumental groups did not attempt to appear without vocal soloists, however, so great was the popular taste for singers. And of these Sontag and Alboni overshadowed all the rest.

Writing of the 1852-53 season and of the debut of Alboni in particular, G. C. D. Odell, who has listed every recorded musical performance in New York to 1880 said, "New York had heard Bosio, Salvi, Badiali, Marini, Lind, and the little Patti; and now here was Alboni. We of later decades can but envy auditors so richly blest as those of 1852."[7] It is small wonder that Walt Whitman, a journalist with all these riches easily at his disposal, and with a poetic temperament just beginning to stir to life, should have found in these incredible outpourings of beautiful sound inspiration to last throughout his life.

9

Opera in Whitman's day, as the records clearly show, was predominantly Italian opera. According to the poet there was a good reason for it. In 1855 he stated positively, "By acknowledged consent, the music of the Italian composers and singers is at the head of all the rest; Germans, French, English, all bow down to the

Italian style."[8] Both the popularity of this kind of opera and Whitman's great preference for it make it important to examine briefly the essential marks of the Italian style as it was known in New York in the forties and fifties.

Exemplified principally by Gioacchino Rossini (1792-1868), Italian opera emphasized *singing* and the *voice* above everything else. Rich and beautiful melodies were devised in abundance and allotted to principal members of the casts. These so-called arias were ordinarily decorated with florid passages designed not only to enhance the effectiveness of the music as such and often to add to the characterization of the part and the emotion being portrayed, but as well to give the singer an opportunity to display the resources of his voice. Before Rossini, composers had been accustomed to permit singers to decorate their solo passages with vocal ornamentation of their own invention regardless of appropriateness. Rossini carefully composed all the notes he wished his interpreters to perform and attempted to give musical and dramatic significance to even the most coloratura passages.[9]

The most important followers of Rossini, Gaetano Donizetti (1798-1848), and Vincenzo Bellini (1802-35), as well as the early Giuseppe Verdi (1813-1901), also made extensive use of the flowing melody which we now associate with the Italian school. To interpret these taxing arias a style of singing was developed which is known as *bel canto*. One of the best descriptions of this singing method and the Italian operas which required it appears in a recent history of opera, in a passage devoted to Bellini.

He more than any other composer, summed up and displayed extravagantly, a style of singing that became at first impossible, and then unfashionable,—or *vice versa*. *Bel canto* is a phrase susceptible to several interpretations, but it is above all, and always, Bellinian. *Bel canto* relies primarily on purity of tone and ease of production and only secondarily, (sometimes never) on dramatic projection. *Bel canto* is partial to long passages of simple melody alternating with outbursts of vocal scrollwork, the latter usually for no better reason than that they illustrate the essence of *bel canto* itself. *Bel canto* really makes the voice a wind instrument. Its perfect practitioners make sounds of quite unearthly beauty and move the listener quite as a miracle would, so well do they do something it seems superhuman, or inhuman, to do at all.[10]

The same writers' description of the melodies of Italian opera clarifies our understanding of the kind of music Whitman liked.

A melodist [Bellini] of great originality, on not quite the highest level of inspiration, he introduced into music a note that was quickly taken up by his contemporaries, became an easy adjunct with the next generation, and is still echoing, sometimes in the most unlikely places, throughout the world. What was that note? It is a kind of hushed, neurotic ecstasy, a kind of gently languorous orgasm in moonlit, bloom pervaded gardens. Long before Verlaine, it was always crying in Bellini's heart. Chopin heard it, and it is the stuff of his sulphurous, elegant nocturnes.[11]

But the operas are by no means melody alone. Melody is reserved for the expression of emotions such as joy, sorrow, longing, and ecstasy, as lyrical passages occur in great poetic dramas. To carry on the dramatic action and to present conversational passages a kind of accompanied declamation was used, in which performers sang the words of the text, though with irregular rhythms, suggesting the timing of actual speech, and in musical patterns somewhat suggestive of the varying pitches of conversation. The composers attempted, of course, even in the recitatives, as such passages were called, to heighten the meaning and significance of the words by the added emotional effect of the music to which they were set. Recitative was not new to the Italian school, but particularly by Rossini it was made increasingly musical. In earlier operas it had been often mere recitation, unaccompanied or accompanied by only one instrument, such as the harpsichord. Rossini used the full orchestra for his recitative accompaniments and was thus able to treat scenes as musical wholes without calling attention to obviously different styles of musical writing.[12]

Most of the composers of the Italian school relied often upon the chorus for important musical effects. Rossini deserves credit for increasing the emphasis upon choral writing, but others, especially Verdi, came to allot to the chorus some of their most moving pages of music. The choruses from *Il Trovatore* are known to every school child today, but some of those from the earlier *Ernani* are musically even more effective. The Italian writers also experimented brilliantly with concerted numbers for the soloists, that is, duets, trios, quartettes and the like. Famous examples are the sextette from *Lucia*.

the quartette from *Rigoletto*, and the unsurpassed duet from Bellini's *Norma*.

One other important aspect of the operas by Rossini and his school should be noted briefly; it is the skillful handling of the orchestra. Though always deliberately subordinated to the voice throughout the opera itself, the orchestra was usually given at least one important moment in which to shine alone. Ordinarily this was the overture, and considerable attention was given to it by the composer. It was not always, as in the later nineteenth-century operas, compounded of main themes from the opera itself, woven together in a somewhat symphonic manner. It was, however, invariably composed of strongly contrasting sections and themes, put together with orginality in melody and skill in orchestration.

Of the principal composers, Donizetti and Bellini were less notable in their writing for orchestra than Rossini and Von Weber. That the latter two were conspicuously successful is proved by the fact that the overture to Von Weber's *Der Freischütz* and those to at least five of Rossini's operas are standard items in the symphonic repertory today. The Von Weber work is specially notable not only for its extraordinary charm but for the fact that it is in construction a miniature symphony, being built on the classic sonata form with themes drawn from the opera itself.[13]

The most famous of the Rossini overtures are of course those to *The Barber of Seville* and *William Tell*. The first of these has little to do with the opera so far as themes are concerned, since it was originally composed for another work, but it has always been praised for its sprightliness, its deft handling of interestingly contrasted subjects, and its pervasive, good-natured charm.[14] The overture to *William Tell*, though our taste for it has been somewhat dulled from hearing too many bad performances of it by school and village bands, is none the less a more impressive work. It is in effect a symphonic poem, opening with a pastoral *andante*, passing through a loud *allegro* section which portrays a violent storm, and closing with a return to the slow movement followed by a final lively galop. Within these main sections the principal themes are stated and restated with great skill, and all are made specially effective by the brilliant use of the instrumental coloring.[15]

The Rossini overtures, like most opera overtures of the time, are examples of the *pot-pourri* method of construction. That is to say that they do not follow an established pattern for the presentation of themes, such as the sonata form.

10

It is small wonder that Whitman frequented the Italian opera "all through these years," as he said. Opera was almost constantly available at one theatre or another, at the small and badly kept Palmo's, at the handsome Astor Place, or at the magnificent Academy of Music. Colorful managers like Palmo, Sanquirico, or the ebullient Maretzek, constantly on the verge of financial ruin and constantly plunging into new and risky ventures, kept the world of opera continually exciting to all who pretended to any sort of taste for it.

Furthermore, through this world there was a steady parade of the most glamorous celebrities of two continents. Some, like the fabulous Jenny Lind, were largely the creatures of clever publicity. Others, like the charming Bosio, came to New York wholly unknown and went on to become the toasts of Europe and the world. Some, like the greatest of them all, Alboni, came to New York at the height of their powers, and, for a brief but almost incredibly brilliant period, gave opera lovers a standard by which to judge singing ever afterward.

For these voices, as great as the world has ever known, there were available perfect vehicles like *Norma*, which today only the greatest vocalists dare approach, and *La Cenerentola*, which singers of today can no longer encompass. Furthermore, new operas from the pens of the great masters of the Italian style were constantly appearing, adding interest to practically every season. For lovers of music and the human voice, and their number certainly included Walt Whitman, the forties and fifties of the nineteenth century offered never-ending delights.

NOTES—CHAPTER II

1. "Specimen Days," *Prose*, I, 26.
2. Unless otherwise indicated, the following summary is based upon three sources: Odell, *op. cit.*, IV, V, VI; Richard Grant White, "Opera in New York," *The Century, Illustrated Monthly Magazine*, New Series, I, 686-703 (November, 1881); 864-82 (April, 1882); II, 31-43 (May, 1882);

193-210 (October, 1882); and Henry E. Krehbiel, *Chapters of Opera, The Lyric Stage in New York to 1909* (New York, 1909).

3. This persevering conductor-impresario has given a picturesque account of his career in his memoirs, *Crochets and Quavers, or The Revelations of an Opera Manager in America* (New York, 1855).

4. The details of this season are to be found in Odell, op. cit., VI, 185-277.

5. Quoted in White, op. cit., II, 38.

6. *Ibid.*, II, 41.

7. Odell, op. cit., VI, 186.

8. *Uncollected Poetry and Prose*, II, 97.

9. Francis Toye, *Rossini, A Study in Tragi-Comedy* (New York: Alfred A. Knopf, 1934), pp. 52-53.

10. Wallace Brockway, Herbert Weinstock, *The Opera, A History of its Creation and Performance: 1600-1941* (New York: Simon and Schuster, 1941), p. 155.

11. *Ibid.*, pp. 155-56.

12. Toye, op. cit., p. 52. Brockway, Weinstock, op. cit., pp. 136-37, 141.

13. Henry E. Krehbiel, *A Book of Operas* (Garden City, N. Y., 1916), p. 191.

14. Ernest Newman, *Stories of the Great Operas and their Composers*, 3 vols. (Garden City, N. Y.: Garden City Publishing Co., 1930), II, 208.

15. *Ibid.*, II, 237-39.

CHAPTER III

Development of Musical Taste

A TASTE FOR OPERA, like a taste for some unusual foods, must be acquired over a period of time. Walt Whitman was no exception to the rule. Though he came to be almost passionately fond of this art form in the years when his creative powers were most active, like others he passed through a period when it seemed meaningless and overrated and the profession of a taste for it an affectation. Furthermore, he was bothered at first by the fact that it seemed un-American and aristocratic, possibly even harmful to the development of a native American music.

1

Quite naturally, since he was wholly untrained in the technique of music, Whitman's early interest in music was in examples of a relatively simple sort, the performances of the family groups of singers who were so popular in the early forties and later. These troupes specialized in sentimental renditions of music which even, perhaps only, the most uncultivated listener could enjoy, music of which the words were simple, the melody wholly without complication or intricacy, and the accompaniment as unobtrusive as could be.

It was the simplicity of this music that Whitman liked, though he found its sentimentality agreeable too, and praised its 'heart' qualities as opposed to the 'art' qualities of much concert hall music. "At last we have found it!" he exclaimed after he had heard the Cheney family, meaning, as he explained, "something original and beautiful in the way of American musical execution." He further confessed, "The elegant simplicity of this style took us completely by surprise and our gratification was inexpressible."[1]

He found the Hutchinson family effective for the same reasons. Editorially, he praised their "elegant simplicity of manner" and referred to their "music of feeling." The editorial is of interest, however, not only because it praises the Hutchinsons, but quite as much because of its concern about Americans who professed to enjoy a kind of foreign music which they did not understand and which was fundamentally inappropriate for them.

A discriminating observer of the phases of humanity—particularly its affectations—propounded through his editorial voice, the other day, a query whether nineteen-twentieths of those who *appear* to be captured at the New York concerts with the florid Italian and French music, could really tell the difference, if they were blindfolded, between the playing of a tolerable amateur, and the "divine" execution of Sivori, DeMeyer, and so on. We trow not! Four-fifths of the enthusiasm for that kind of melody is unreal. We do not mean to say but that there *is* melody; but a man *here* might as well go into extatics at one of Cicero's orations, in its original Roman!

We do wish the good ladies and gentlemen of America would be truer to themselves and to legitimate refinement. With all honor and glory to the land of the olive tree and the vine, fair-skied Italy—with no turning up of noses at Germany, France, or England—we humbly demand whether we have not run after their beauties long enough. For nearly every nation has its peculiarities and its idioms which make its best intellectual efforts dearest to itself alone, so that hardly anything which comes to us in the music and songs of the old World, is strictly good and fitting to our nation. Except, indeed, that great scope of song which pictures love, hope, or mirth, in their most general aspect.

The music of feeling—heart music as distinguished from art music—is well exemplified in such singing as the Hutchinsons' and several other bands of American vocalists. With the richest physical power—with the guidance of discretion, and taste, and experience,—with the mellowing influence of discipline—it is marvellous that they do not *entirely* supplant the stale, second hand, foreign method, with its flourishes, its ridiculous sentimentality, its anti-republican spirit, and its sycophantic tainting the young taste of the nation! We allude to, and specially commend, all this school of singing—well exemplified as its beauty is in those "bands of brothers," whereof we have several now before the American public. Because whatever touches the heart is better than what is merely addressed to the ear. Elegant simplicity in manner is more judicious than the dancing school bows and curtsies, and inane smiles, and kissing of the tips of a kid glove a la Pico. Songs whose words you can hear and understand are preferable to a mass of unintelligible stuff, (for who makes out even the libretto of English opera, as now given on the stage?) which for all the sense you get out of it, might as well be in Arabic. Sensible sweetness is better than all distorted by unnatural nonsense . . . Such hints as the above, however, we throw out rather as suggestive of a train of thought to other and more deliberate thinkers than we—and not as the criticisms of a musical connoisseur. If they have pith in them well; if not, we at least know they are written in that true wish for benefitting the subject spoken of, which should characterize all such essays. We are absolutely sick to nausea of the patent-leather, curled hair, "japonicadom" style.—The real (not "artistes" but) singers are as much ahead of it as good real teeth are ahead of artificial ones.[2]

The reader will note at once that the editorial is the work of a writer whose own experience has by no means been limited to concerts by singers of heart songs. Unquestionably, by this time Whitman had availed himself of his free-list privileges and had heard many types of sophisticated music in New York. The various references to it would certainly lead us to think so. In any case, his opinions of such music as here expressed are pretty low. It is pointlessly florid and unintelligible. The performers are affected. The people who attend such concerts are hypocritical and insincere. The whole institution is foreign and un-American. What America needs is simple, heartfelt, American music.

Whitman never wholly outgrew his natural fondness for the kind of simple, affecting music that the Hutchinsons sang. His account of an episode in a Washington hospital during the Civil War shows that he could always be touched by "heart-music," performed with sincerity and joy.

The principal singer was a young lady—nurse of one of the wards, accompanying on a melodeon, and join'd by the lady—nurses of other wards. They sat there making a charming group, with their handsome, healthy faces, and standing up a little behind them were some ten or fifteen of the convalescent soldiers, young men, nurses, etc., with books in their hands, singing. Of course it was not such a performance as the great soloists at the New York opera house take a hand in, yet I am not sure but I received as much pleasure under the circumstances, sitting there, as I have had from the best Italian compositions, expressed by world-famous performers.[3]

Even in his old age Whitman did not forget his early pleasure at hearing popular music. In 1891 he wrote, "Yes; there were in New York and Brooklyn some fine non-technical singing performances, concerts, such as the Hutchinson band, three brothers, and the sister, the red-cheek'd New England carnation, sweet Abby; sometimes plaintive and balladic—sometimes anti-slavery, anti-calomel, and comic. There were concerts by Templeton, Russell, Dempster, the old Alleghenian band and many others."[4]

2

In the days when he was hearing the Hutchinsons and editorializing on their music, Whitman was not only explaining the virtues of popular singing; he was searching for a kind of music which he could champion as "American." It is more than likely that in his attacks on the foreign-sounding "art" music he was protesting too much, of course. In the light of his later development, it seems probable that by 1846 he was already beginning to come under the charm of Italian opera, though, as an ardently patriotic young writer, he was feeling pangs of guilt for enjoying too much something not home grown.

It had been the fashion of American writers for decades to urge Americans to recognize their own artists and develop an indigenous art.[5] Emerson's essay, "The American Scholar," one of the most important declarations of cultural independence, had appeared in 1837, and it is possible that Whitman had seen it. In any case, his journalistic writing, particularly in the middle forties while he was editing the Brooklyn *Daily Eagle*, was strongly nationalistic in tone, sometimes, as his most recent biographer feels, "too brashly patriotic, too smugly confident of the manifest destiny of the United States."[6] Much of his commentary on popular music was a part of this patriotic work. At the time, such music seemed to him most "American" and hence was to be championed, and played off against Italian opera, which he was at the moment suspicious of but beginning to find attractive.

Whitman expressed himself often on the topic of music in America, especially during the *Eagle* days. In one editorial on the subject of "Vocal Concerts by Children," inspired by a recent instance, he voiced his approval, for the reason that such activity would spread a fondness for music among the masses, and that, in turn, he believed would refine the general taste.[7] In fact, he argued that music should be made a regular branch of study in American schools, to improve not only the youth but the land generally. There is also a revealing reference to the "land of the sunny skies," in which

Whitman declared that though there was a real, national taste for music in America, it could not be compared to that in Italy.

Once more in the same journal, on September 8, 1847, Whitman editorialized on the topic. Again he urged Americans to develop their own music, and he complained that we were too willing to listen to music "made for a different state of society."

Great is the power of music over a people! As for us of America, we have long enough followed obedient and child-like in the track of the Old World. We have received her tenors and her buffos, her operatic troupes and her vocalists, of all grades and complexions; listened to and applauded the songs made for a different state of society—made perhaps by royal genius, but made to please royal ears likewise; and it is time that such listening and receiving should cease. The subtlest spirit of a nation is expressed through its music—and the music acts reciprocally upon the nation's very soul.—Its effects may not be seen in a day, or a year, and yet these effects are potent invisibly. They enter into religious feelings—they tinge the manners and morals—they are active even in the choice of legislators and magistrates. Tariff can be varied to fit circumstances—(though we don't believe it will ever be varied again in any way but a more free trade way,) bad laws obliterated and good ones formed; those enactments which relate to commerce or national policy, built up or taken away, stretched or concentrated, to suit the will of the government for the time being. But no human power can thoroughly suppress the spirit which lives in national lyrics, and sounds in the favorite melodies sung by high and low.[8]

It is probably natural, since opera was basically involved in Whitman's concern about American music, that he should ultimately be led away from matters of 'music and the national good' to speculation about the proper forms of American musical expression, particularly American opera. One of his conclusions is an ininteresting attempt to reconcile his early patriotic taste for simple music and an operatic form, which he was finding increasingly significant. He was still laboring under the conviction that Italian opera was too complicated and artificial, which it undoubtedly still was to him, and he betrayed his lack of understanding of what opera really attempts to be: drama emotionally heightened by music. But he had come to understand the importance of the voice as opposed to instrumentation, a consideration which was ultimately to attract him to the Italian masters so strongly. The fragmentary notation follows:

American opera—put three banjos (or more?) in the orchestra—and let them accompany (at times exclusively) the songs of the baritone or tenor—Let a considerable part of the performance be instrumental— by the orchestra only—Let a few words go a great ways—the plot not complicated but simple—Always one leading idea—as Friendship, Grati- tude, Courage, Love,—and always a distinct meaning—the story and libretto as now generally of no account—In the American opera the story and libretto must be in the *body* of the performance.

American Opera. When a song is sung the accompaniment to be by only one instrument or two instruments the rest silent—the vocal per- former to make far more of his song, or solo part, by by-play, attitudes, expression, movements, etc., than is at all made by the Italian opera singers—The American opera—to be far more simple, and give far more scope to the persons enacting the characters.[9]

In the incomplete sketch on language and words called *An American Primer*, Whitman also led himself into a comment on American opera and again revealed his interest in matters of oper- atic form. Discussing what he called the "nigger dialect," he called attention to the fact that the Negro pronunciation of most words was more "open" than standard usage: *yallah* for yellow, and *massah* for master. This characteristic he believed ideal for musical pur- poses, and he advocated a modification of English pronunciation for music, without changing the standard for spoken use. Pursuing the subject further, he declared, "America is to adopt the Italian method, and expand it to vaster, simpler, far superber effects. It is not to be satisfied till it comprehends the people and is compre- hended by them."[10] Thus he showed that by the time *An American Primer* was composed, probably in the early fifties,[11] he had acquired increased respect for Italian music, as well as an understanding of the 'open' and 'free' type of voice production in the Italian *bel canto* method. It is also important to notice here Whitman's in- sistence upon the fact that opera must become a 'people's' art. Later he was to make his own attempts to popularize the art form.[12]

Whitman's championship of the 'popular' in music, and his pro- fessed distaste for un-American and 'artistic' work, sometimes re- sulted in a serious inconsistency in his critical writing. In his review of *Elijah*, he found the music to be of the highest order judged by the rules of art, but too "elaborately scientific," "heavy," wanting the relief of "a proper proportion of lightness and melody." "There is scarcely a striking or pleasing air in it," he added.[13] Remembering passages like "If, With All Your Hearts," for tenor, "Hear Ye, Israel," for soprano, "O Rest in the Lord," for contralto, and "It Is Enough," for baritone, all airs as melodious and directly appealing as the operatic arias he was later to praise, and very much like them, one realizes that he was still mistaking art for artifice. Furthermore, he must have been following the 'popular' line primarily for journalistic purposes, for more than a year before the *Elijah* review he had published an almost rhapsodical account of the splendors of Mendelssohn's oratorio, *St. Paul*, a work which in general character and effectiveness almost exactly parallels *Elijah*. "It is utterly impossible to describe in words the effects produced by this fine composition," he had said, "for music, more subtle than words, laughs to scorn the lame attempts of an everyday medium."[14]

3

At the same time that Whitman was championing popular music and discussing various aspects of the topic of music in America, he was also writing occasionally about Italian opera, and by March 23, 1847, whether he had always approved of it or not, he had heard a good deal of it. On that date he published a critical review, his first, of *The Barber of Seville*. In it, his comments on the relative merits of members of the cast and his recommendations for substitutions show a familiarity with many of the leading operatic singers of the time which he could have gained only by having heard them sing. In particular, he insisted that the tenor, Sesto Benedetti, should in future performances take over the part sung by Signor Patti, and he praised the work of Beneventano, the baritone, as the Barber, and Rosina Pico as the heroine. The opera itself, he added, "is always heard with pleasure: the instrumentation is beautiful, and has that clean, though rather old-fashioned character, in which his [Rossini's] delicate ideas produce effect, and not any overpowering crash of instruments."[15]

This first critical comment on opera as such is considerably less enthusiastic than Whitman's later writings on the subject were to be, but it shows at least a working familiarity with operatic music and singers and, as all of his later comments were to do, it insists on preëminence for the voice.

Whitman's second review of opera concerns *Linda di Chamounix* by Donizetti, though it is largely devoted to the singing of the star, Mrs. Anna Bishop. Again, it reveals the writer's interest in the voice as an expressive instrument.

Her voice is the purest soprano—and of as silvery clearness as ever came from the human throat—rich but not massive—and of such flexibility that one is almost appalled at the way the most difficult passages are not only gone over with ease, but actually dallied with, and their difficulty redoubled. They put one in mind of the gyrations of a bird in the air.[16]

Though Whitman's own testimony to his musical tastes is too contradictory to permit a systematic account of growing appreciation, it is certain that by 1851 the whole-souled devotion to Italian opera which he demonstrated throughout his later life had been fully developed. There seem no longer to be any questions in his mind about the 'popular' versus the 'artistic' or the 'native' versus the 'foreign.' Italian opera had come to be a stimulation and a release to which he admitted his complete surrender. The evidence for such a conviction is to be found in "A Letter from Paumanok." This somewhat extended discussion concerning the importance of opera as an art form, illustrated by reference to *La Favorita* by Donizetti, calls opera "the sublimest and most spiritual of the arts," and again "the loftiest of the arts." The operatic composer is said to be the "limner of the spirit of life, of hope and peace; of the red fire of passion, the cavernous vacancy of despair, and the black pall of the grave."

In the "Letter" Whitman speaks of the inspirational quality of operatic music for him as follows:

Have you not . . . while listening to the well-played music of some band like Maretzek's, felt an overwhelming desire for measureless sound—a sublime orchestra of a myriad of orchestras—a colossal volume of harmony, in which the thunder might roll in its proper place; and above it, the vast, pure Tenor—identity of the Creative Power itself—rising through the universe, until the boundless and unspeakable capacities of that mystery, the human soul, should be filled to the uttermost, and the problem of human cravingness be satisfied and destroyed?

Of this sort are the promptings of good music upon me.[17]

These are the words of a mystic, for whom music had come to be the key capable of unlocking the deepest secrets of man and the universe, the force powerful enough to transform a man into a poet. All musical sounds are inspirational, but, said Whitman characteristically, it is "the vast, pure tenor," the human voice, which can best represent the creative power itself which at last solves mysteries.

Such quotations leave little doubt about the quality of Whitman's musical appreciation in 1851. If a final and specific statement of emancipation from his earlier concerns with popular and national music is needed, it can be found in the original manuscript version of his essay on opera-going of 1855. He called the original "A Visit to the Opera."

The English opera, the tunes and ballads, etc., sung by the various bands of "minstrels" and indeed all modern musical performances and compositions are, to all intents and purposes, but driblets from Italian music.—True there are bequeathed to us from other quarters, some fresh and original tunes, as the native songs of Scotland, Ireland, and one or two other lands; but as to a theory of the lyric art, and its practice too, there is really no other worth the attention of one who wishes to be a good musician, only that of Italy. That is the only large, fresh, free, magnificent method, and under its auspices alone, will there ever be great and perfect American singers, male and female.[18]

In the published version of the same passage, Whitman is even more specific in declaring the superiority of opera, as artistic music, over the popular forms so widely known, and he refers to the "artistic development" of the listener.

You listen to this music, and the songs, and choruses—all of the highest range of composition known to the world of melody. It is novel, of course, being far, very far different from what you were used to—the church choir, or the songs and playing on the piano or the nigger songs, or any performance of the Ethiopian minstrels, or the concerts of the different "families." A new world,—a liquid world—rushes like a torrent through you. If you have the true musical feeling in you, from this night you date a new era in your development, and, for the first time, receive your ideas of what the divine art of music really is.[19]

4

The development of these deeply felt convictions about Italian opera was by no means automatic for Whitman, as his early, scornful statements clearly reveal. He suggested the difficulties in acquiring a taste for opera and the need for study of the form in 1855, when he said, "Reader, perhaps you have been merely once to the Italian opera—and didn't like it.—If so the deficiency was in yourself.—So far-developed, and of course artificial a thing as Italian music cannot be understood or appreciated at once.—Then the flurry of a new scene distracts from your attention.—If the piece is unknown to you, it were better to procure the English translation of it beforehand and read it over once or twice."[20]

He went further in a later statement to say that even persons like himself, with natural inclinations toward a fondness for music, were often tempted to feel that simple forms of music were the best merely because they required least effort for comprehension. He was perhaps recalling his early championship of the popular singers and family troupes. He made the statement in reply to criticisms of his poem "A Child's Reminiscence," later called "Out of the Cradle Endlessly Rocking," explaining that critics had found the form of the poem crude and offensive because they had not understood it, just as most listeners did not at first comprehend the structure of operatic music.

Quite after the same token as the Italian opera, to most bold Americans, and all new persons, even of latent proclivities that very way, only accustomed to tunes, piano-noises and the performances of the negro bands—satisfied, (or rather fancying they are satisfied), with each and several thereof, from association and habit, until they pass utterly beyond them—which comes in good time, and cannot be deferred much longer, either, in such a race as yours, O bold American of the West![21]

It is interesting to speculate concerning the ways by which Whitman was himself able to overcome the handicaps he mentioned and arrive at his unqualified devotion to operatic music. Undoubtedly the answer lies largely in his "latent proclivities that very way," to use his own words. And there was of course his love of crowds and 'occasions,' of which a performance of opera, then as now, was one of the most glamorous. Furthermore, opera provided an opportunity for the display of all the resources of the human voice, that most musical of instruments, to which Whitman was always peculiarly sensitive. Not even the lecture platform, which once interested him partly because of its opportunities for vocal display, could call into use so many aspects of the voice in the portrayal of emotion as the opera.

But unquestionably a major influence upon Whitman's developing taste for operatic music was the novel *Consuelo* by George Sand.[22] Here, in what was to him a powerful and absorbing story about the career of a great singer, he found the appeal of lofty music explained and analyzed. Here, also, he encountered listeners to great music who, like himself, were curiously uplifted and inspired by what they heard. Through them he was helped to an understanding of what happened to him when he heard opera, and through them he learned the great importance of opera to him.

There is considerable evidence to support such a belief. In 1888, after one of his visits to Whitman, Horace Traubel recorded the following episode:

. . . On the table Consuelo. He had been repairing the loose covers: "I find I have all the volumes complete: five of them: three of the story proper: two of the sequel—The Countess of Rudolstadt." He had said to me in the summer that he was afraid one was missing. "I have had the books—or my mother—I think since '41—nearly fifty years. . . . I have always treasured it: read, read, read—never tiring. The book is a masterpiece: the noblest work left by George Sand—the noblest in many respects on its own field, in all literature." He desired that I should take and read it. "I can say it almost has an historic preciousness to me, now I have had it so long. It is very decrepit—the sheets often loose, ready to drop out. I have been minded to bind it—so to preserve it, if there can be any very great object in that."[23]

Several facts in the passage are important. The first is the poet's unswerving belief in the greatness of the novel, here declared only four years before his death. Perhaps even more important is his testimony to his continued interest in it and the fact that he had literally worn it out with repeated readings. There is also the fact that he began reading it at about 1841, near the time when he began to attend opera.

At least two other friends of Whitman have also left accounts of his enduring interest in this book. Helen E. Price, in whose home he sometimes visited, wrote in 1881, "In talking to him once about music I found he had read George Sand's 'Consuelo,' and enjoyed it thoroughly. One passage he liked best was where Consuelo sings in the church at the very beginning of her musical career. He said he had read it over many times."[24]

In his notes of conversations with Whitman, Herbert Gilchrist, son of Whitman's English friend and admirer, Mrs. Anne Gilchrist, recounted at some length a discussion he and Whitman held one day on the subject of Consuelo.[25] It was a subject which the poet often turned to, apparently, especially when matters of music were brought up.

Even a hurried examination of the book itself will show why Whitman's interest in it was inevitably related to his interest in vocal music. Shortly after the story opens, hints are given of the extraordinary beauty of the voice of Consuelo, a young music student. Soon she is called upon to perform a difficult sacred work in church and in the presence of the composer of the music, a genuine test of the young singer's mettle.

So soon as the first words of this lofty and brilliant production shone before her eyes, she felt as if wafted to another sphere. . . . Forgetting the spiteful glances of rivals . . . she thought only of God and of Marcello, who seemed to interpret those wondrous regions whose glory she was about to celebrate. . . .

A divine glow overspread her features, and the sacred fire of genius darted from her large black eyes, as the vaulted roof rang with that unequalled voice, and with those lofty accents which could only proceed from an elevated intellect, joined to a good heart. After he had listened a few instants, a torrent of delicious tears streamed from Marcello's eyes. The Count, unable to restrain his emotion, exclaimed—"By the Holy Rood, this woman is beautiful! She is Santa Cecelia, Santa Teresa, Santa Consuelo! She is poetry, she is music, she is faith personified!" . . .

It required all the respect due to the locality to prevent the numerous dilettanti in the crowd from bursting into applause.[26]

The florid passage must have made a strong impression on Whitman's mind, for in the days when he was considering a career as an orator and devising some precepts for himself, and possibly others, in the art of oratory, he toyed with the idea of "a *new school* of Declamation/Composition far more direct, close, animated and fuller of live tissue than any hitherto—entirely different (of course) from the old style—and acting as Consuelo's free and strong Italian style did in the singing of the respectable village church."[27] Whitman abandoned his interest in oratory as a career, but Consuelo and her Italian style undoubtedly led him to examine opera more intensively in order to discover its inspirational powers, and perhaps ultimately to poetry with an operatic method, as being the art form in the "new school" which should be most electrifying (like the voice in the village church) and appropriate for the communication of his ideas. Repeated readings of the passage must have permitted Whitman to turn individual phrases over in his mind. Some of them sound strangely like him. "Those lofty accents which could only proceed from an elevated intellect, joined to a good heart." "She is poetry, she is music, she is faith personified!"

Only a little further in the story, the mere act of singing is made dramatic when Consuelo, on an important occasion, performs an air of fearful difficulty, and completely confounds not only her listeners, but her teacher as well, by adding decorations of her own invention to the already trying score.[28]

Somewhat later Consuelo's lover analyzes his reactions to her singing:

She commenced to sing, and immediately the young Count, charmed or subdued, was consoled by tears, or animated with new enthusiasm. . . . "Consuelo," he exclaimed, "you know the paths to my soul; you possess the power refused to the common herd, and possess it more than any being in this world. You speak in language divine; you know how to express the most sublime emotions and communicate the impulse of your own inspired soul. Sing always when you see me downcast; the words of your songs have but little sense for me, they are but the theme, the imperfect indication on which the music turns and is developed. I hardly hear them: What alone I hear and what penetrates into my very soul, is your voice, your accent, your inspiration. Music expresses all that the mind dreams and foresees of mystery and grandeur. It is the manifestation of a higher order of ideas and sentiments than any to which human speech can give expression. It is the revelation of the infinite; and when you sing, I only belong to humanity in so far as humanity has drunk in what is divine and eternal in the bosom of the Creator.[29]

This is pretty much what Whitman came to think of operatic singing, and on occasion he used language quite as rhetorical and extreme to declare his enthusiasm. The language of such passages as that above even seems to have given him phrases for his own critical comments on music. For example, there is his already quoted

review of the oratorio *St. Paul*, in which he said, "Music, more
subtle than words, laughs to scorn the lame attempts of an every
day medium."[30] There is also the later discussion of *La Favorita*, in
which he exclaimed, "Ah, welcome that I know not the mere
language of the earthly words in which the melody is embodied; as
all words are mean before the language of true music."[31]

Thus it seems altogether probable that the novel which he read
so often, and to which he was so loyal, had much to do with forming
his taste and even with pointing the way toward his mystical appreciation of great operatic singing. It is also probable, of course, that
once he had acquired his passion for opera, the influence worked
both ways. If *Consuelo* helped to interest him in opera, opera
helped to keep alive his interest in *Consuelo*. And it is quite possible that in later years, when he could no longer hear great singers
so often, he could enjoy singing vicariously through the dramatic
and beautiful voice of George Sand's heroine.

The influence of *Consuelo* and its sequel, *The Countess of
Rudolstadt*, on Whitman has been exhaustively studied by Esther
Shephard in *Walt Whitman's Pose*.[32] The focus of her study, however, is on Whitman's developing conception of the heroic personality and function of the poet. The implication of the title is that in
George Sand's work Whitman encountered a mystic poet and pretended to be like him. Such a thesis can scarcely account for the
individual poetic masterpieces Whitman created; men cannot write
great poems by "posing" as poets. The most important function of
Consuelo, as has been pointed out, was that it taught him to appreciate great singing and to surrender to his mystical response to it.
Opera, in its turn, contributed immeasurably to his poetry. Shephard
does not discuss the influence of the book on Whitman's growing
appreciation for opera.

5

What Whitman's steadily developing appreciation for operatic
music led to when his taste was fully formed is shown best by the
list of musical works, presented at the close of Chapter I, which he
said he heard during the years of his most intensive devotion to
music. Perhaps the most important fact about the list is one which

is at once apparent: with one exception only vocal works are included and of these all but four are operas. Since the list includes all the major musical works mentioned by Whitman in the entire range of his work, his overwhelming preference for opera is at once established. It should also be remembered that the four other vocal works, oratorios, are constructed almost exactly like the Italian operas Whitman knew and were performed in his day chiefly by opera singers. In other words, a purely musical distinction between the operas and oratorios can scarcely be drawn.

The operas themselves include Italian works chiefly. French works are notable for their scarcity. The French operas fairly regularly performed by the New Orleans companies early in Whitman's opera-going days, such as Auber's The Bronze Horse, L'Ambassadrice, Le Domino Noir, Les Diamants de la Couronne, and La Perle de Savoie; Herold's Zampa, Le Pré aux Clercs; Adam's La Brasseur de Preston, Postillon de Longjumeau; Halevy's La Juive,[33] are nowhere mentioned by Whitman. To be sure Auber's Masaniello and Gounod's Faust appear in the list, but these works were often, even usually, performed with Italian artists and in the Italian manner. Meyerbeer's operas, with French titles, were written by a German for performance in Paris, but decidedly in the manner of Rossini and his school rather than in either the French or German tradition.[34] Only one German opera appears on the list, von Weber's Der Freischütz; it, too, is related to the Italian school in its broad melodies and romantic atmosphere.[35] Only one of Mozart's operas is mentioned, Don Giovanni, probably because others of this great master were not performed regularly by the Italian companies in New York in the forties and fifties.

Of the entire list of operas, four seem to stand out as Whitman's favorites, if we are to judge from the amount of comment he gave to them and the number of times he referred to them individually. These are Donizetti's Lucrezia Borgia and La Favorita; Bellini's Norma; and Verdi's Ernani. Not one of the operas is performed regularly today. The reason is probably less that our musical taste has changed than that today we lack the voices to sing the great scores satisfactorily. It was essentially the opportunities they gave for noble vocalism that endeared them to Whitman.

6

By the time Whitman had come to hear regularly and enjoy the great operatic masterpieces which have been listed, his taste and appreciation had come far from the days when he had referred with scorn to the "florid" music of Italy. It must not be supposed, however, that he ever came to be a musician in the technical sense. His interest was always appreciative and emotional, not technical. His use of music's technical words was usually managed with more pleasure than skill; just as his French terms were.[36] Certainly he never claimed to be technically informed. Early in Whitman's career, Edgar Allan Poe, the editor of the *Broadway Journal* when Whitman submitted his essay on "Art-Singing and Heart-Singing," added a footnote on the young writer's background when he published the manuscript:

The author desires us to say, for him, that he pretends to no scientific knowledge of music. He merely claims to appreciate so much of it (a sadly disdained department, just now) as affects, in the language of the deacons, 'the natural heart of man.' It is scarcely necessary to add that we agree with our correspondent throughout.[37]

Many years later the famed music critic, James Gibbons Huneker, said of Whitman, "I do recall that he said . . . that music was his chief recreation—of which art he knew nothing; it seemed to him as a sounding background for his pencilled improvisations."[38] First hand evidence of the poet's elementary technical knowledge may be found in a manuscript fragment which shows that Whitman at one stage of his career was not sure of the precise function of the violin in orchestral instrumentation.

The Violin. Talk with W. C. musician N. J. 6th Reg't Band—He said: 'the violin was one of the easiest instruments to begin on and the hardest to finish with in all music.' He spoke of some sensitive player who said an instrument badly out of tune 'tore the very flesh off his bones.' The first E-flat or B-flat cornet generally leads the band. Does the first violin lead . . .[39]

But if Whitman's technical information about music was meager, his response to it was none the less sensitive and his appreciation of it none the less significant to his own development. His feeling about music came close to religion with him. For example, when he was once devising some notes for a lecture on religion and was faced with the problem of exemplifying those moments when the soul is most sentient and worshipful, he turned to opera. The manuscript fragment is eloquent:

> *good moments*
>
> soul in high glee, *all out*
> exquisite state of feeling of happiness
> some moments at the opera
> in the woods. . . .[40]

But music, as he knew it in opera, came to have practical social values too, in Whitman's estimation, and he regretted that opera was so slow in becoming established in his own country.

A taste for music, when widely distributed among a people, is one of the surest indications of their moral purity, amiability, and refinement. It promotes sociality, represses the grosser manifestations of the passions, and substitutes in their place all that is beautiful and artistic. We find it to be so in families, in communities and in nations, and the reasons for so finding it are very plain.

We as a people are not musical. True, we have improved greatly of late years in this respect, but there is plenty of room for more. In New York we are afraid to say how many managers have been ruined in the expensive attempt to establish the Italian opera, and the nightly concerts which take place are mainly supported by foreigners. English opera succeeded pretty well for a time, when a pretty *prima donna* caught the public fancy, or a great cantatrice like Jenny Lind was announced with such a flourish of Barnumic trumpets that people crowded to see her as they would to see a wonderful performing elephant or a balloon ascent. But these musical furores were spasmodic in their nature and possessed nothing in common with the steady and unfailing love and reverence for music as an art—as a consoler—as an elevator—as a necessity of their very being, which distinguishes some of the European nationalities.[41]

Taken altogether, music, represented to him by opera, came to be pretty nearly all things to Walt Whitman. "Music, the combiner," he called it, "nothing more spiritual, nothing more sensuous, a god, yet completely human." For him, he confessed, music "advances, prevails, holds highest place; supplying in wants and quarters what nothing else could supply."[42]

7

In his old age, because of his infirmities and his residence in Camden, it was impossible for Whitman to hear opera. But he was sharply conscious of changing tastes and traditions in the opera house as the century wore on, and in theory he championed them because he believed they represented progress. He never knew the new operas well, however, and they were never an influence upon him.

His recognition of the changes in opera is to be seen in a comment in his essay on "Poetry Today in America." He wrote:

Character, a feature far above style or polish—a feature not absent at any time, but now first brought to the fore—gives predominant stamp to advancing poetry. Its born sister, music, already responds to the same influences. "The music of the present, Wagner's, Gounod's, even the later Verdi's, all tends toward this free expression of poetic emotion and demands a vocalism totally unlike that required for Rossini's splendid roulades, or Bellini's suave melodies."[43]

Whitman seemed instinctively to recognize the fact that the newer opera was less formal than the old. (The chief evidence of this was, of course, the tendency away from the set pieces of recitative and aria and toward a unified style of musical expression, suitable for all the needs of the score. The newer opera also tended to treat voices and orchestra together as parts of a whole composition, not to emphasize the voice so exclusively as had been the custom.) Once, in a conversation with his friend Traubel, Whitman explained his convictions. Traubel records the episode:

I had been seeing Verdi's Otello. "Is it our opera—the vocalism of the new sort? or is it still the old business lingering on?" It is both though mostly new. "Good, we have rather expected Verdi to do heroic things." I thought you liked the old operas—preferred them. "I do like them—at least I did—but their age is gone: We require larger measures in music as in literature, to express this spirit of the age."[44]

Naturally, the subject of Wagner and his revolutionary music came up often in the talk about music of Whitman and his friends. The poet's comments are of special interest because the work of the great German composer bears so many resemblances to his own. Of course the similarities are coincidental, for Whitman claimed very little knowledge of Wagnerian music. Though he never failed to defend the right of Wagner to make advances in musical art, he was not sure that he himself either understood or cared for the result of the experimentation. Again Traubel records a significant observation:

So many of my friends say Wagner is Leaves of Grass done into music that I begin to suspect there must be something in it. Dr. Bucke, who don't go much on operas, banks a lot on Wagner. I was never wholly convinced—there was always a remaining question. I have got rather off the field. The Wagner opera has had its vogue only in these later years since I got out of the way of going to the theatre. Do you figure out Wagner to be a force making for democracy or the opposite? O'Connor swears to the democracy—swears it with a big oath. Others have said to me that Wagner's art was distinctly the art of a caste—for the few. What am I to believe? I confess that I have heard bits here and there at concerts, from orchestras, bands, which have astonished, ravished, me, like the discovery of a new world. The masters keep on coming and coming again: Nature can always do better than her best: is prodigal, exhaustless.[45]

One stumbling block for Whitman in Wagner was the material. He told Traubel:

I question the wisdom of selecting Jack and the Beanstalk stories and putting them into this modern medium. Without a doubt there are points here which I have not considered—which are not quite familiar table talk with me—but my first impression, my original instinct, (I can only give that) is adverse, critical, though not, of course, absolutely negative.[46]

It would have been illogical for Whitman to deny the right of experimentation, and perhaps advance, to Wagner and Verdi, when he, in the field of poetry, had tried to accomplish so many new things. It is plain to see, however, that in music it was the old Italian opera which he knew and loved and understood. Furthermore, while the new operas might or might not be advances in dramatic art, Whitman would never have found the kind of singing they require a satisfactory substitute for the flowing melodies of Italian opera, which permitted great voices to be magnificently displayed. He had worked his way to a full appreciation of Italian opera, and during his most active years he had surrendered completely to its charms. He remained loyal to it as long as he lived.

NOTES—CHAPTER III

1. *Uncollected Poetry and Prose*, I, 105.

2. *Gathering of the Forces*, II, 346-47.

3. "Specimen Days," *Prose*, I, 69.

4. "Good-Bye My Fancy," *Prose*, IV, 52. Templeton, Henry Russell and W. R. Dempster were singers of popular songs, widely heard during the forties. The latter was probably the most popular solo vocalist of the day. The Alleghenians were a troupe of family singers.

5. Walter Fuller Taylor, *A History of American Letters* (New York: American Book Co., 1936), p. 88.

6. Henry Seidel Canby, *Walt Whitman, An American* (Boston: Houghton Mifflin Co., 1943), p. 51.

7. *Gathering of the Forces*, II, 358.

8. *Ibid.*, II, 345.

9. Manuscript quoted in *Workshop*, p. 201.

10. *An American Primer*, ed., Horace Traubel (Boston, 1904), p. 4.

11. *Ibid.*, p. vii.

12. Whitman was not alone in his eagerness to develop an American opera. In 1855 Ole Bull, then the new manager of the New York Academy of Music, offered a prize of $1000 for an American opera based on a strictly American subject. The prize was never awarded. Frederic Louis Ritter, *Music in America* (New York, 1883), p. 295.

13. *Gathering of the Forces*, II, 353-54.

14. Quoted in Emory Holloway, "More Light on Whitman," *American Mercury*, I, 186 (February, 1924).

15. *Gathering of the Forces*, II, 349-50.

16. *Ibid.*, II, 351-52.

17. *Uncollected Poetry and Prose*, I, 256.

18. *Ibid.*, II, 100.

19. *New York Dissected*, pp. 18-23.

20. *Uncollected Poetry and Prose*, II, 100.

21. *A Child's Reminiscence*, p. 20.

22. George Sand, *Consuelo*, translated by Fayette Robinson (Philadelphia, undated).

23. Traubel, *op. cit.*, III, 422-23.

24. Quoted in Bucke, *op. cit.*, p. 29.

25. Manuscript, Walt Whitman Collection, University of Pennsylvania Library.

26. *Consuelo*, p. 19.

27. *Workshop*, p. 34.

28. *Consuelo*, p. 23.

29. *Ibid.*, p. 109. Whitman once copied and kept a passage from *Consuelo* dealing with much the same idea, the possibility of direct inspiration. "Is it my fault that you have not understood me? You think I wished to speak to your senses, and it was my soul spoke to you. It was the soul of the whole of humanity that spoke to you through mine."—*Prose*, VI, 19.

30. Quoted in Holloway, "More Light on Whitman," *American Mercury*, I, 186 (February, 1924).

31. *Uncollected Poetry and Prose*, I, 258.

32. Esther Shephard, *Walt Whitman's Pose* (New York: Harcourt, Brace and Co., 1938).

33. *Odell, op. cit.*, IV, V, *passim.*

34. Brockway, Weinstock, *op. cit.*, p. 232.

35. *Ibid.*, p. 123.

36. Louise Pound, "Walt Whitman and the French Language," *American Speech*, I, 421-30 (May, 1926).

37. *Uncollected Poetry and Prose*, I, 104.

38. Huneker, *op. cit.*, p. 417.

39. Quoted in Clifton Joseph Furness, "Walt Whitman and Music," *News Bulletin*, Boston Chapter, Special Libraries Association, IV, No. 2, 2 (November, 1937).

40. *Workshop*, p. 51.

41. *I Sit and Look Out*, edd. Emory Holloway, Vernolian Schwartz (New York: Columbia University Press, 1932), p. 173.

42. "Democratic Vistas," *Prose*, II, 57.

43. "Collect," *Prose*, II, 216.

44. Traubel, *op. cit.*, I, 106.

45. *Ibid.*, II, 116.

46. *Ibid.*, II, 122.

CHAPTER IV

The Voice

1

IT WAS THE VOICES of great singers which enabled operatic music to capture the heart and the imagination of Walt Whitman, and his lifelong interest in vocalism is of fundamental importance in his work. He had been preoccupied with the voice early in his career. Before the development of his enthusiasm for opera he had speculated about the voice as it was employed both in oratory and on the dramatic stage.[1] He had apparently always been peculiarly sensitive to vocal sounds. The voice seemed to create in him not only an emotional response but a bodily one as well; the most intense and tumultuous feelings could be aroused in him by a beautiful and controlled voice. Lines from the poem "Vocalism" illustrate his reactions.

> O what is it in me that makes me tremble so at voices?
> Surely whoever speaks to me in the right voice, him or her
>   I shall follow,
> As the water follows the moon, silently, with fluid steps,
>   anywhere around the globe.[2]

He was always inclined to judge people by their voices. For example, in an article written while he was in New Orleans, he described meeting an enchanting girl. He pointed out that everything about her seemed perfectly desirable, and then, as a climax, added, "she was passionately fond of music . . . and by her musical voice I *knew* she could sing. I was happy in every sense of the word."[3]

Again, describing his friend William O'Connor, Whitman made it quite clear that much of the man's electrifying charm lay in his voice. "He was a gallant, handsome, gay-hearted, fine-voiced, glowing-eyed man. . . . He had a strange charm of physiologic voice. . . . There was always a little touch of pensive cadence in his superb voice. . . ."[4]

In *Specimen Days* a passage of particular tenderness also exemplifies Whitman's almost mystical sensitivity to the voice.

As I sat out front on the walk afterward, in the evening air, the church-choir and organ on the corner opposite gave Luther's hymn, *Ein feste berg* [sic] very finely. The air was borne by a rich contralto. For nearly half an hour there in the dark (there was a good string of English stanzas) came the music, firm and unhurried, with long pauses. The full silver star-beams of Lyra rose silently over the church's dim roof-ridge. Vari-color'd lights from the stain'd glass windows broke through the tree shadows. And under all—under the Northern Crown up there, and in the fresh breeze below, and the chiaroscuro of the night, that liquid-full contralto.[5]

Even in the less romantic surroundings, however, he could not fail to respond to a beautiful voice. In a letter to Ellen O'Connor, a friend in Washington, he once described his sister's voice. "She is walking in the other room, singing it [her baby] to sleep in her arms—she has a fine contralto voice & is singing beautifully, unconsciously—it does me good too."[6]

An evidence of *ease* and *strength*, as well as *richness*, was always important to Whitman in judging the voice, and on one occasion he advocated the cultivation of such qualities by all American young people.

What vocalism most needs in these States, not only in the few choicer words and phrases, but in our whole talk, is ease, sonorous strength, breadth, and openness. Boys and girls should practice daily in free loud reading—in the open air, if possible. Most of the conventional laws observed in the schools are unworthy any notice whatever. Open your mouth—sound copiously and often such rich sounds as *oi* and *wu*—let your organ sound loudly without screaming—don't specify each syllable or word, but let them flow—feel the sentiment of what you read or say, and follow where it leads.[7]

Whitman found this "openness" and freedom in voice production (*cantabile* or flowing, song-like, was his word), best exemplified in the voices of the Italian singers. On one occasion he attempted to analyze the technique by which they obtained this effect, "pure, strong, without being coarse,"[8] which so distinguished their voices. In achieving this "purest, and most perfect cantabile," the Italian voice, as he said, forms, or rather gathers the tone in the back of the mouth, and makes none of the fearful work with the mouth itself that gives such a distorted appearance to English singers. In the good Italian singer, the mouth, lips, cheek, etc., are at ease, perhaps illumined with a gentle smile even during astonishing vocal performances. What is done is draped, not evident to the hearer. The back of the mouth, the throat, great interior energy and muscular alertness are necessary, all under the espionage of a severe taste, permitting no extreme attempts, but pleasing and natural simple effects.[9]

Of course Whitman realized that while many Italians were gifted with naturally beautiful voices, the artistic use of the organ had to be cultivated.

Few realize the long and arduous study required to make a first class singer—years and years are to be occupied—precept upon precept—and, above all, practice upon practice.—In Italy there are conservatories of music, where young persons commence in time, under patient and competent teachers.[10]

Both natural gifts and cultivation seemed to Whitman to be required for the "perfect human voice," as he described it.

Stating it briefly and pointedly I should suggest that the human voice is a cultivation or form'd growth on a fair native foundation. This foundation probably exists in nine cases out of ten. Sometimes nature affords the vocal organ in perfection, or rather I would say near enough to whet one's appreciation and appetite for a voice that might be truly call'd perfection. To me the grand voice is mainly physiological—(by which I by no means ignore the mental help, but wish to keep the emphasis where it belongs). Emerson says *manners* form the representative apex and final charm and captivation of humanity: but he might as well have changed the typicality to voice.

Of course there is much taught and written about elocution, the best reading, speaking, etc., but it finally settles down to the *best* human vocalization. Beyond all other power and beauty, there is something in the quality and power of the right voice (*timbre* the schools call it) that touches the soul, the abysms. It was not for nothing that the Greeks depended, at their highest, on poetry's and wisdom's vocal utterance by *tete-a-tete* lectures—(indeed all the ancients did).

Of celebrated people possessing this wonderful vocal power, patent to me, in former days, I should specify the contralto Alboni, Elias Hicks, Father Taylor, the tenor Bettini, Fanny Kemble, and the old actor Booth, and in private life many cases, often women. I sometimes wonder whether the best philosophy and poetry, or sometimes like the best, after all these centuries, perhaps waits to be rous'd out yet, or suggested, by the perfect physiological voice.[11]

Such statements are extremely important to an understanding of the significance Whitman attached to vocalization, almost as an end in itself. For he believed it to be vocalization which made genuinely vital communication possible. In great orators and actors, and especially in singers, Whitman had experienced this ability to communicate, and even to inspire, through the resources of a magnificent voice.

2

In opera Whitman found the voice revealed at its absolute peak of effectiveness. After hearing his favorite tenor, Bettini, he once wrote, "Never before did I realize what an indescribable volume of delight the recesses of the soul can hear from the sound of the honied perfection of the human voice."[12] Whitman expressed himself often on the subject of singers and their voices, and only by collecting some of his comments can one fully appreciate the extent of his fascination.

His favorite of all singers was certainly Marietta Alboni, the contralto. His tributes to her voice and art are many.

The best songstress ever in America was Alboni.—Her voice is a contralto of large compass, high and low—and probably sweeter tones never issued from human lips. The mere sound of that voice was pleasure enough.— All persons appreciated Alboni—the common crowd quite as well as the connoisseurs.—We used to go in the upper tiers of the theatre, (the Broadway), on the nights of her performance, and remember seeing that part of the auditorium packed full of New York young men, mechanics, "roughs," etc., entirely oblivious of all except Alboni, from the time the great songstress came on the stage, till she left it again.—

Alboni is a fully developed woman, with perfect-shaped feet, arms, and hands.—Some thought her fat—we always thought her beautiful.—Her face is regular and pleasant—her forehead low—plentiful black hair, cut short like a boy's—a slow and graceful style of walk—attitudes of inimitable beauty, and large black eyes.—We have seen her in pathetic scenes, (as in Norma plann'g the death of her children,) with real tears, like rain, coursing each other down her cheeks.—Alboni is now in Paris, singing at the grand opera there.[13]

*   *   *   *

I doubt if ever the senses and emotions of the future will be thrill'd as were the auditors of a generation ago by the deep passion of Alboni's contralto.[14]

Such are the things, indeed, I lay away with my life's rare and blessed bits of hours, reminiscent, past—the wild sea storm I saw one winter day off Fire Island . . . or Alboni in the children's scene in Norma.[15]

Seems to me now when I look back, the Italian contralto Marietta Alboni . . . and the Italian singer Bettini, have had the greatest and most lasting effect upon me. I should like very well if Madame Alboni and the old composer Verdi . . . could know how much noble pleasure and happiness they gave me, and how deeply I always remember them and thank them to this day.[16]

> The teeming lady comes
> The lustrous orb, Venus contralto, the blooming mother,
> Sister of loftiest Gods, Alboni's self I hear.[17]

Two of Whitman's friends recorded his great admiration for the celebrated singer, also. Dr. Richard Maurice Bucke, in his biography of the poet said, "The climax of the opera to him was the singing of the famous contralto, Alboni. It is during the time of which I am now speaking that she came to New York and he did not miss hearing her one single night."[18] Another friend, Helen E. Price, in the same book, wrote, "Alboni he considered by far the greatest of them all, both as regards voice and artistic power. If I remember rightly, he told me that during her engagement in the city he heard her twenty nights."[19]

Incidentally, Whitman's judgment of Alboni was borne out by the leading music critic of the day, Richard Grant White, of the New York Courier and Enquirer. The morning after Alboni's debut White wrote as follows:

Madame Alboni's voice impresses the ear at once with its sumptuous quality. . . . In this voice is the chief power of the singer. And it is in the quality, the calibre, and the copiousness of the voice, rather than in its extent or flexibility that its charm is found. . . . She seems to give no thought to what she does, but merely to let the flood of song pour itself forth. . . . There seems to be nothing wanting in the concurrence of voice, style, and method to make every phrase she utters complete in its expression of richness of resource, and of elegance, and in its sensuous charm. Added to this there is an indefinable something, more delicate than expression, yet akin to it, which makes her song float like a seductive aroma around her hearer, penetrating to the most delicate fibres of his being, and pervading him with a dreamy delight.[20]

Many years later, recalling the art of Alboni, White wrote:

Alboni was probably the greatest singer the world has seen since Malibran. . . . As a vocalist, pure and simple, she was, both by her natural gifts and her art, first among the foremost of her generation.[21]

Next to Alboni in Whitman's affections stood Bettini, the tenor. Whitman often praised the art of this great vocalist, though he never referred to the gossip about him which the opera historian, H. E. Krehbiel, chose to perpetuate: "Bettini drank to excess and spent whole nights in the gambling room, rendering him unfit for duty ever and anon."[22] Whitman was more concerned with the communicativeness of Bettini's art.

The fresh vigorous tones of Bettini! I have often wished to know this man, for a minute, that I might tell him how much of the highest order of pleasure he has conferred upon me. His voice has often affected me to tears. Its clear, firm, wonderfully exalting notes, filling and expanding away; dwelling like a poised lark up in heaven; have made my very soul tremble.—Critics talk of others who are more perfectly artistical. But the singing of this man has breathing blood within it; the living soul, of which the lower stage they call art, is but the shell and the sham.[23]

The young and manly Ernani used to be well played by Bettini, now at the grand opera in Paris. Bettini was a beautiful, large, robust, friendly young man—a fine tenor.[24]

Bettini's pensive and incomparable tenor as Fernando in Favorita.[25]

Many other singers were mentioned with critical approval by Whitman. It is not necessary to list all his comments, but a few on outstanding artists should be noted.

Steffanone, the soprano, with her calm and finished style, and her delicious voice was always welcome as Elvira.[26]

The wonderful La Grange, the tenor Brignoli, and the baritone Amodio are all good.[27]

The baritone Badiali, the finest in the world.[28]

Badiali was the superbest of all superb baritones in my time—in my singing years. Badiali was a big, coarse, broad-chested feller, invested, however, with absolute ease of demeanor—a master of his art—confident, powerful, self-sufficient.[29]

I also heard Mario many times, and at his best. In such parts as Gennaro in *Lucrezia Borgia* he was inimitable—the sweetest of voices, a pure tenor, of considerable compass and respectable power.[30]

The principal lady singer, (her name is Medori) has a voice that would make you hold your breath with wonder and delight—it is like a miracle —no mocking bird or clearest flute can begin with it.[31]

Lest the reader think that all of Whitman's reactions to singers were extravagantly favorable, what he said about Jenny Lind should be recalled. Though Lind is of course better known by reputation today than any other singer Whitman mentioned, she does not deserve to be, if he is to be believed. In 1851, shortly after hearing her, he wrote as follows:

The Swedish Swan, with all her blandishments, never touched my heart in the least. I wondered at so much vocal dexterity; and indeed they were all very pretty, those leaps and double somersets. But even in the grandest religious airs, genuine masterpieces as they are, of the German composers, executed by this strangely overpraised woman in perfect scientific style, let critics say what they like, it was a failure; for there was a vacuum in the head of the performance. Beauty pervaded it no doubt, and that of a high order. It was the beauty of Adam before God breathed into his nostrils.[32]

In all of these descriptions of singing artists, including that of Jenny Lind, one is reminded of Whitman's statement, already quoted, concerning the Italian voice and singing method: "That is the only large, fresh, free, magnificent method."[33] White, the professional critic of Whitman's day, described the style as "the grand old Italian style of singing" and referred to "that large simplicity of manner, severe and yet not hard; that thoroughness, and completely present sense of the decorum in art."[34]

Whatever it was, Whitman missed it in the singing of Lind. Perhaps he missed it also in the singing of Henrietta Sontag, the celebrated soprano of Alboni's day, of whom he has left no personal criticism. White said of her style, "She rivalled the most skillful violin-players in the rapidity, exactness, and solidity of tone with which she ran scales. . . . Her style never grand, impressive or deeply pathetic, was always charming."[35] Whitman could sacrifice some perfection for a moving, communicative quality, which he always insisted upon. He fails to mention anywhere the great

French singers of his day, probably for this reason. Such names as Mmes Calvé, Fleury-Jolly, and Thillon, all celebrated divas, appeared in New York in the earlier of his opera-going days, principally with the French companies from New Orleans. It was unquestionably their singing tradition which kept Whitman from admiring or remembering them. Their style, according to White, was "the thin, throaty, French way of singing."[36]

3

Upon discovering Whitman's vital concern with voices of all sorts, trained and untrained, on the stage and in the home, the curious student cannot help wondering what Whitman's own voice may have been like. Many of his friends left testimonies to its character, some of which are of considerable interest.

One Thomas A. Gere, who had worked on a boat in the East River in 1852 and remembered Whitman in those days, recalled in 1882 that "Walt's musical ability was a very entertaining quality: he was devotedly fond of opera, and many were the pleasant scraps and airs with which he would enliven us in a round, manly voice, when passengers were few."[37] Whitman's friend, Dr. Bucke, also remembered the poet's singing. "He had a way of singing, generally in an undertone, wherever he was or whatever he was doing when alone. You would hear him the first thing in the morning while he was taking his bath and dressing (he would then perhaps sing out in full, ballads or martial songs), and a large part of the time that he sauntered outdoors during the day he sang, usually tunes without words, or a formless recitative."[38] Later Bucke added, "He is fond of singing to himself snatches of songs from the operas or oratorios, often a simple strain of recitative, a sort of musical murmur."[39] John Johnston, in his account of a visit to the poet, declared, "His voice is highly pitched and musical, with a *timbre* which is astonishing in an old man. There is none of the usual senile tremor, quaver, or shrillness, his utterance being clear, ringing and most sweetly musical."[40] Most of this testimony, though doubtless true in the main, must be accepted with reservations, for the accounts were published in Whitman's lifetime and the manuscripts approved by him before they appeared in print. Perhaps this is the way Whitman wanted the quality of his voice recorded. Hamlin

Garland, however, by no means a Whitman idolator, wrote after the poet's death, that a stack of manuscripts related to a visit to Whitman enabled him "to visualize the majestic head of the poet and to hear again his musical voice."[41]

4

The greatest beauties of voice were to be heard in singing, Whitman believed, and as his previously quoted comments on singers show, he had encountered the most electrifying and vital communicativeness in the great voices of opera. But at its best spoken utterance, too, could be inspiring, he thought. "A perfect reader," he once said, "must convey the same pleasure to his or her hearers that the best vocalism of the Italian singers does, just as much as the voice of Alboni, Bosio, Bettini or Brignoli does. There must be something in the very vibration of the sounds of the mouth, something in the movements of the lips and mouth, something in the spirituality and personality that produces full effects."[42]

A natural result of such deeply felt convictions was the belief that only by somehow getting into his poems something of the vibrancy of the human voice could he really expect to inspire and arouse his reader.

"Beyond all other power and beauty, there is something in the quality and power of the right voice . . . that touches the soul, the abysms,"[43] Whitman said, and went on to point out that the Greeks and other ancients were wise in depending on vocal utterance for their poetry. He referred to Homer as "the only chanting mouth that approaches our case near enough to raise a vibration, an echo."[44] And he speculated on the possibility that the greatest poetry of the future would be inspired by the voice, as doubtless much of his own was. In his discussion of words as entities in *An American Primer*, he explained how perfect, flexible vocal organs gave to all words spoken by them "deeper, sweeter sounds" and "new meanings, impossible on any less terms."[45] Late in his career he recalled with special approval a statement by the orator, Ingersoll, to the effect that "All great literature lends itself to the lips."[46] Perhaps all of these ideas on the subject were summarized in the 1876 Preface to *Leaves of Grass*, when Whitman wrote, "The real poems of the present, ever solidifying and expanding into the future, must vocalize the vastness and splendor and reality."[47]

Certain never completed projects indicate Whitman's interest in experimenting with vocal effects. In one fragmentary manuscript he outlined two projects: a poem on the strange power of the voice, using as material the voice as "the invisible demon of Socrates," and a treatment of the voices of Joan of Arc.[48]

Another undertaking was to be a series of songs, with actual notes written out for the voice and accompanied by dramatic activity, miniature operas really.[49] One suggested topic was the cutting down of a tree by wood cutters in the West and the pleasures of a "wood-life" in general. Still another idea which never materialized was an elaborate poem involving a series of different but presumably well-known "calls," each section of the poem to be based on one call.[50] The poem was planned especially for purposes of recitation.

These projects were doubtless rejected as being too obviously an exploitation of the voice and too closely related to oratory which he found unsuited to the effects he wanted. But his conception of poetry as a mystic chant, seeming to use the voice as its medium of expression, never altered from the time of its operatic beginnings. He described the rhapsodic effect he wanted literally hundreds of times. Two statements will serve our purposes here. One is from an early manuscript note in which he stated his ambition: "A song—a chant—which shall sing . . . with joyful bursts, lyric, exultant."[51] The second statement, suggesting matter as well as method, is from a preface to his poems. He never published the preface in this form, but many of these phrases he used again and again.

Therefore it comes, our New World, chords in diapason gathering. I chant with reference to original tastes, the flush and strength of things—chant materials, emanating spirituality—the human form surcharged through all its veins the same: chant from the point of view of my own land, and in the spirit of my own race and not other races—Chant the modern world and cities and farms and the sights and facts thereof—rejoicing.[52]

It should be noted in passing that the effect of this "singing" both in the opera house and in poetry is always jubilant. There seems to be an almost boundless buoyancy and happiness that is an inseparable part of the chant.

Whitman's countless references to his poems as songs and chants and his many allusions to vocalism and the voice show his constant preoccupation with the vocal quality of his work. The power of the communicative voice once even became the subject of the poem, "Vocalism." Some lines from an early version of the work show clearly why he wanted his poems to have the power of vocalism.

> Of a great vocalism, when you hear it, the merciless light
>   shall pour, and the storm rage around,
> Every flash shall be a revelation, an insult,
> The glaring flame turned on depths, on heights, on suns,
>   on stars,
> On the interior and exterior of man or woman,
> On the laws of nature—on passive materials,
> On what you called death—and what to you therefore was
>   death,
> As far as there can be death.[53]

There are many evidences in the poems of Whitman's conviction that through the voice meanings and implications could be achieved as in no other way. This was the special capability of the voice which he had discovered in the opera house. He had heard the great singers convey the emotions of anger, hate, love, heartbreak, all by the mere coloring and control of their expressive voices. The greatest virtue in poetry has always been that it conveys to a sensitive reader more than it says. Whitman believed that a vocal quality in poetry simply intensified this virtue. As he said in "Song of Myself":

> My voice goes after what my eyes cannot reach,
> With the twirl of my tongue I encompass worlds and
>   volumes of worlds.[54]

5

Whitman's poems are filled with references to the beauty and inspiration of singing voices as he had known them in opera. In his greatest lyrics, however, the singing voice, that most powerful of influences, is symbolized for the purposes of art. For the perfect symbol Whitman turned to nature and its sounds, to which he was always sharply sensitive. In the songs of birds he discovered nature's closest approach to the human voice,[55] and once hit upon, the bird songs were consistently his symbols for the singing which was so intimately involved with all his artistic endeavors.

His response to the bird songs was not casual or accidental, as he suggests in "Starting from Paumanok" at the close of the opening section:

> Having studied the mocking-bird's tones and the flight of
> the mountain hawk,
> And heard at dawn the unrivall'd one, the hermit thrush
> from the swamp cedars,
> Solitary, singing in the west, I strike up for a New World.[56]

That he was equally deliberate in his use of the songs as symbols is suggested by a comment he once made to a friend, to be later reported by her:

Her [Alboni's] mellow, powerful, delicate tones, so heartfelt in their expression, so spontaneous in their utterance, had deeply penetrated his spirit, and never, as when subsequently writing of the mocking-bird or any other bird song, on a fragrant, moonlit summer night, had he been able to free himself from the recollection of the deep emotion that had inspired and affected him while he listened to the singing of Marietta Alboni.[57]

Usually in the poems the relation of the symbol to human song is clear enough. For example, from "Song of Myself":

> And the jay in the woods never studied the gamut, yet
> trills pretty well to me. . . .[58]

And later in the same poem, the words "I hear the bravuras of birds"[59] recall unquestionably the coloratura gymnastics required in some of the operas Whitman knew.

The symbolism is especially important in the great lyric, "Out of the Cradle Endlessly Rocking."[60] Here Whitman chose the mockingbird to symbolize the voice of Alboni and the music which had so affected him in the opera house. He had probably read an account of an actual occurrence in which a mockingbird had been heard to sing nightly on a Long Island beach, blending its remarkable voice with the music of the ocean, producing an effect of genuine enchantment.[61] Recalling what he knew of the bird's song,

Whitman must have felt that here was a perfect duplication, in terms of the music of nature, of the vocal music which had meant so much to him.

Just as Whitman was always as much concerned with the effect of music as with the music itself, so in this poem he is more concerned with translating the bird's song, reading his own meaning into it, than he is with re-creating the mere sounds, the trills and warbles. To him the song is one of love, tragedy, and death, for which he provides the words, not the musical notes. It is to Whitman's credit, however, that the song, as he finally achieved it, does no violence to the general character of the mockingbird's actual kind of singing, though it was not the poet's first objective to reproduce the notes. In fact, a recent study has pointed out how remarkably close Whitman came to a duplication of the bird's phrases.[62] The perfection of the symbolism in the poem is thus at once a testimony to the sharpness of Whitman's response to the bird's song in nature and to its artistic counterpart in the opera house, the singing human voice.

In "Starting from Paumanok,"[63] a poem first published the year following "Out of the Cradle," in 1860, Whitman again used the mockingbird's song as the symbol for inspiring music.

> I have seen where the she-bird the mocking-bird sat on her
> nest in the briers hatching her brood.
> I have seen the he-bird also,
> I have paus'd to hear him near at hand inflating his throat
> and joyfully singing.
>
> And while I paus'd it came to me that what he really sang
> for was not there only,
> Not for his mate nor himself only, nor all sent back by the
> echoes,
> But subtle, clandestine, away beyond,
> A charge transmitted and gift occult for those being born.[64]

When he came to write his great tribute to Lincoln, "When Lilacs Last in the Dooryard Bloom'd,"[65] once more Whitman chose the song of a bird as one of his trinity of symbols, of which more will be said later. Here the song is an interpretation of death. It is not a song of tragedy, leading the poet to contemplate death, as

the song in "Out of the Cradle" had been. This is a lyric in praise
of death, at last fully comprehended and understood as the climax
of life, the great, natural, and universal deliveress, which must be
welcomed, not dreaded. Through the inspiration derived from the
mockingbird's song, of which the climax was an understanding of
death, the song of the thrush in the Lincoln poem is comprehensible. Here again we have an instance, rare in English poetry, where
a bird's song is not merely described and its listeners' moods interpreted, as in Shelley and Keats, but actually translated into words.
The stroke of artistic daring is a tribute not only to Whitman's
aesthetic instincts but to his great lyrical skill as well.[66]

Remembering that he declared the bird songs in these great
poems to have been directly inspired by the singing of Marietta
Alboni, the contralto, one looks for evidence of Whitman's association of the human with the bird in describing the song. Evidences are unmistakably present.

> Sing on dearest brother, warble your reedy song,
> Loud human song, with voice of uttermost woe.

Other lines of description recall the comments on Italian opera
singing and songs quoted previously. Whitman wrote:

> O liquid and free and tender!
> O wild and loose to my soul. . . .[67]

The historians of opera wrote: "*Bel canto* relies primarily on a
purity of tone and an ease of production . . . Its practitioners make
sounds of quite unearthly beauty . . ." The melodies were characterized by "a kind of hushed, neurotic ecstasy. . . ."[68] Clearly Whitman and the historians were writing about the same thing.

And exactly as Whitman had responded to the great Italian
singers by being caught up into a mystic reverie, so here

> And the charm of the carol rapt me,
> And I held as if by their hands my comrades in the night,
> And the voice of my spirit tallied the song of the bird.[69]
> . . . .
> To the tally of my soul
> Loud and strong kept up the gray-brown bird,
> With pure deliberate notes spreading filling the night.[70]

Once more Whitman was to turn to the thrush, nature's sweet singer, as the central symbol in an effective short poem, probably very close to its author's heart. In the dark days following the Civil War, when the champion of Democracy found evidence everywhere of corruption and evil rather than the honor and good which he had preached as the essentials of democratic life, the song bird reassured and cheered him, as singing could always do.

> Wandering at morn,
> Emerging from the night from gloomy thoughts, thee in
>   my thoughts,
> Yearning for thee harmonious Union! thee, singing bird
>   divine!
> Thee coil'd in evil times my country, with craft and black
>   dismay, with every meanness, treason thrust upon
>   thee,
> This common marvel I beheld—the parent thrush I
>   watch'd feeding its young,
> The singing thrush whose tones of joy and faith ecstatic,
> Fail not to certify and cheer my soul.
>
> There ponder'd, felt I,
> If worms, snakes, loathsome grubs, may to sweet spiritual
>   songs be turn'd,
> If vermin so transposed, so used and bless'd may be,
> Then may I trust in you, your fortunes, days, my country;
> Who knows but these may be the lessons fit for you?
> From these your future song may rise with joyous trills,
> Destin'd to fill the world.[71]

If the songbird could subsist on loathsome food, so could the Union, itself a "singing bird divine," transform its occasional treason and meanness into the good Democracy must ultimately produce. Here the bird fulfilled two functions. Its song, as always, inspired, and it, as an object lesson, reassured and helped to make possible the optimism which Whitman never abandoned.

Voices, it seems, whether in the opera house or in nature, never failed to stir Whitman deeply, and without a recognition of their importance to him readers can scarcely understand or appreciate many of his poems.

NOTES—CHAPTER IV

1. *Workshop*, pp. 25-69.
2. *Inclusive Edition*, p. 322.
3. Emory Holloway, "Walt Whitman in New Orleans," *Yale Review*, V (New Series), 181 (October, 1915).
4. "Good-Bye My Fancy," *Prose*, IV, 45-46.
5. "Specimen Days," *Prose*, I, 290.
6. Letter to Ellen O'Connor, Camden, N. J., May 15, 1874. Manuscript in Berg Collection, New York Public Library. Quoted with permission.
7. *New York Dissected*, p. 60.
8. "You speak of Neumayer as a true bass. Is he that? pure, strong, without being coarse? Oh! the true bass is the most precious of all voices because the rarest of all."—Traubel, *op. cit.*, II, 123.
9. *Prose*, V, 254. In another place Whitman wrote, "Everything these players and singers do is so much broader, sweeter, firmer. If you are a vocalist you see you did not previously know how to even open your mouth. You did not know how to express the simplest sounds properly. These singers do it all so much easier, and incomparably better. This is science! This is art!"—*New York Dissected*, p. 22.
10. *Uncollected Poetry and Prose*, II, 100.
11. "Good-Bye My Fancy," *Prose*, IV, 21.
12. *Uncollected Poetry and Prose*, I, 257.
13. *Faint Clews & Indirections: Manuscripts of Walt Whitman and His Family*, edd. Clarence Gohdes and Rollo G. Silver (Durham, N. C., 1949), p. 19.
14. "November Boughs," *Prose*, III, 186.
15. "Specimen Days," *Prose*, I, 292.
16. "Good-Bye My Fancy," *Prose*, IV, 49.
17. *Inclusive Edition*, p. 340. "To a Certain Cantatrice," p. 8, was ad dressed to Alboni.
18. Bucke, *op. cit.*, p. 22.
19. *Ibid.*, p. 29.
20. Quoted in White, *op. cit.*, II, 37.
21. *Ibid.*, II, 36.
22. Krehbiel, *Chapters of Opera*, p. 61.
23. *Uncollected Poetry and Prose*, I, 257.
24. *New York Dissected*, p. 22.
25. "November Boughs," *Prose*, III, 186.
26. *New York Dissected*, p. 22.
27. *Ibid.*, p. 23.
28. "Specimen Days," *Prose*, I, 26.
29. Traubel, *op. cit.*, II, 173.
30. "November Boughs," *Prose*, III, 186.
31. Traubel, *op. cit.*, III, 103.
32. *Uncollected Poetry and Prose*, I, 257.
33. *Ibid.*, II, 100.
34. White, *op. cit.*, II, 34.
35. *Ibid.*, II, 41.

36. *Ibid.*, I, 874.

37. Bucke, *op. cit.*, p. 34.

38. *Ibid.*, p. 53.

39. *Ibid.*, p. 70.

40. John Johnston, *Diary Notes of a Visit to Walt Whitman and Some of His Friends in 1890* (Manchester, 1898), p. 26.

41. Hamlin Garland, *Roadside Meetings* (New York: Macmillan, 1930), p. 143.

42. *Prose*, V, 248.

43. "Good-Bye My Fancy," *Prose*, IV, 21.

44. *A Child's Reminiscence*, p. 21.

45. *An American Primer*, p. 20.

46. Traubel, *op. cit.*, II, 162.

47. "Collect," *Prose*, II, 201.

48. Thomas Donaldson, *Walt Whitman, the Man* (New York: Francis P. Harper, 1896), p. 13. The original manuscript is reproduced in this volume.

49. *Prose*, VII, 25.

50. *Notes and Fragments*, ed. Richard Maurice Bucke (Privately Printed, 1899), p. 196.

51. *Ibid.*, p. 51.

52. *Workshop*, p. 133.

53. Inclusive Edition, p. 675.

54. *Ibid.*, p. 46.

55. An example of Whitman's response to bird songs is to be found in "Specimen Days." "There are blue-birds already flying about, and I hear much chirping and twittering and two or three real songs, sustain'd quite a while, in the mid-day brilliance and warmth. (There, that is a true carol, coming out boldly and repeatedly, as if the singer meant it.) Then as the noon strengthens, the reedy trill of the robin—to my ear the most cheering of bird notes."—*Prose*, I, 196.

56. Inclusive Edition, p. 12.

57. Statement by Mrs. Fanny Raymond Ritter, quoted in Bucke, *op. cit.*, p. 157.

58. Inclusive Edition, p. 34.

59. *Ibid.*, p. 47.

60. *Ibid.*, p. 210.

61. Courtland Y. White, "A Whitman Ornithology," *Cassinia*, XXXV, 16 (1945).

62. *Ibid.*, p. 17.

63. Inclusive Edition, p. 12.

64. *Ibid.*, p. 17.

65. *Ibid.*, p. 276.

66. See Louise Pound, "Walt Whitman and Bird Poetry," *English Journal*, XIX, 31-36 (January, 1930).

67. Inclusive Edition, p. 280.

68. Brockway, Weinstock, *op. cit.*, p. 155.

69. Inclusive Edition, p. 281.

70. *Ibid.*, p. 282.

71. "Wandering at Morn," *Ibid.*, p. 334.

Chapter V

Some Special Aspects of Opera

LIKE MOST DEVOTEES, Whitman found his greatest enjoyment in opera in the thrilling singing which he heard there. But there were at least three aspects of opera-going, not primarily concerned with vocal art, which contributed immeasurably to his interest and which increased his enjoyment of opera's first function, the presentation of great vocalism. These were the exciting 'occasion' which a night at the opera involved, the orchestral overture, and the drama.

1

The first of these aspects was unquestionably one of the most important to Whitman. He was always peculiarly sensitive to the kind of exhilaration persons feel when they are part of a crowd. At the opera house, the high spirits, the anticipation, and the general excitement of the assembly never failed to stir the poet especially deeply. He enjoyed the cosmopolitan nature of the audience, with its brilliant personages (sometimes more brilliant than appreciative, of course)[1] and its plainer music lovers who represented a cross section of Manhattan life. He loved the resplendent house, the tense moments just before the overture and curtain, the enraptured hush as a full-voiced singer held the great audience spellbound, the torrents of applause that gushed forth at the climax of a thrilling or much-loved vocal passage. All these things had a strong effect on Whitman, and he wrote eloquently about them in his essay on opera.

We invite you to spend an evening with us at the opera, and listen to the music, and look at the place and people. You there away so far from New York, perhaps in Ohio, or Wisconsin, or up toward Canada, or away up northeast or southwest, you need not travel hither; you can stop home and do your day's work, or at candlelight come into your own house and wash and put on some clean clothes, no matter how coarse, and then eat your supper, and sit down at the table by the fire, and we will bring the opera to you—even the Italian opera—in full bloom.

Up where Fourteenth Street crosses Broadway (and that is two miles and a half from the south end of our New York Battery), we turn the corner, and a few rods to the east is the Opera-house. It is the largest amusement building in New York, and one of the largest in the world. We see the rows of globe lamps outside on the balcony as we approach. The light falls softly, but plentifully, on the chocolate-colored walls, and on the iron railings, and on the dark painted sashes of the windows, and down over the four or five broad steps of the front, where the entrance lets in to the parquette and the boxes. Series of little crowds of people fill the corners, and along down the walks for some distance. There are plenty of policemen in blue frock-coats and caps, with brass stars on their breasts, and numerous loungers come to see the richly dressed women as they arrive in their carriages or on foot. Then, for a while before we reach the door, we are besought by half-grown youngsters to buy a "book of the opera, English and Italian"—that is, the original Italian words of the piece on one page, and an English translation off against them.

It is nearly eight o'clock, and the arrivals are full and hurried. At the crossings there is a steady stream, sometimes dammed up and heaped into great masses by the obstructing carriages. These latter are constantly driving up—sometimes they are in crowds also. What beautiful, proud, fat, pampered horses! The gas shines upon their polished harness—the liveried coachman pulls taut on the reins—the footman jumps down from his seat beside the coachman and opens the door—out steps a gentleman in full dress, and out step the ladies in full dress. Fast and plenty they succeed each other—these carriages and their contents. We are in the midst of the show of the high life of New York—the aristoc-racy—the "upper ten." Look at that woman just stepping to the pave-ment! With what sinewy and supple grace she descended at one light leap from the carriage, and pausing, with a slight, proud motion of her limbs, as if to shake off the confinement of a few moments' sitting; she pays no attention to the offered arm of the gentleman (it is her hus-band), but walks by herself on and up the steps. What a face! Light hair, large round features, complexion perfect, figure tall, dress dazzling. A half indifferent look she gave to the crowd, every one of whom renders to her his mute admiration, and then she passed on. The gentle-man, her husband, is a mean-looking man forty-five or fifty years old, a very rich banker and capitalist. She was of poor family, and married him for his wealth, and has no love or respect for him. You can see many such couples at the opera.

Amid all this crowd, and dazzle, and elegance there is very little speak-ing. It shines here—it is rich—but somehow do we not feel cold, estranged, mocked? Are we not in this place as in a heartless place?

Would not a commoner gathering of every-day people, with friendship, and jokes, and plenty of fun and laughter, be more of a satisfaction?

We enter the vestibule, take our place in the procession so steadily and silently squeezed through the aperture where the ticket-taker sits—in due time get squeezed through also, and are in the ample lobby. The white vested ushers are showing the various parties to their seats. Without any guidance, however, we descend through the dress circle and take ours in the middle of the parquette. Imagine an immense church (we are talking now to a country reader, or young person, who has no experience at all in theatre-going), a church vastly widened, and lengthened, and heightened, and a far extension back of the pulpit—this extension has the floor raised six or eight feet, and is "the stage," or place of performances. The main floor of your church corresponds with this parquette, which is not level, but slopes upward from the stage. Between the latter and the parquette is a space partitioned off for the band, or orchestra—a platform and high-legged chair in the middle for the leader; he comes in with white vest and white gloves (orchestras at the opera all do alike), and parts his coat-tails and takes his seat, and seizes his baton (a round stick about eight inches long and an inch thick), and looks around to see if the players are ready before he gives a couple of short, quick taps on the tin screen before him, as a signal to commence.

Back and around the parquette, spreading from it in the shape of a horse-shoe, is the first gallery or tier—the "dress circle." Above it again, supported in front by iron pillars, is the second tier; and above that another tier, called at the opera-house the amphitheatre. The seats, except in the amphitheatre, are velvet arm-chairs, having a pivot and spring, so that unless sat upon, the seats turn up and lay flat to the back of the chairs—a very useful arrangement for the exit or entrance of the audience.

From our place in the middle of the parquette,[2] let us occupy the few minutes before the performance begins by looking around us. It is a full house—it is splendid! What costly and fashionable dresses! What jewelry! What a novel sight to you—those white-gloved hands, lifting or holding the large opera glasses! What an odor of the different perfumes —the whole combined and floating in one faint, not unpleasant stream into one's nostrils! What an air of polished, high-bred, deliberate, heartless, bland, superb, chilling, smiling, repelling fashion! How the copious yet softened gas-light streams down from the hundreds and hundreds of burners! What a rim of fire up overhead encircling the base of the dome! What a rich and gay aspect from the profusion of gilt ornaments on the iron pillars and on the white ground! What a magnificent spectacle to see so many human beings—such elegant and beautiful women—such evidences of wealth and refinement in costume and behavior! Why, if there were no opera, we could just spend the three hours looking around the house, and studying the wonders of the auditorium, and drawing inferences from what we see.[3]

It can be seen quite obviously in the extended quotation that Whitman is in a sense attempting by popularization to "bring opera to the people." The magnificent and complicated art form which he had come to enjoy must be shared and interpreted. He wishes that the audience, brilliant to be sure, might also include the "en-masse" for whom he wanted to be spokesman. Also to be noted is the writer's almost boastful indication of his own great familiarity with the opera house, based of course on his frequent experiences there. But most important, in the quoted passage, is the extended attempt to communicate to persons who had never known it, the thrill and excitement which make an 'occasion' of opera-going.

In his old age, though he had long since ceased attending, Whitman remembered well the excitement of the opera house, especially the exhilarating sense of communication between performer and audience, and when he came to suggest a farewell to his own audience of readers, whom he had always thought of as listeners to a vocal performance, it was in terms of just this situation.

And so let us turn off the gas. Out in the brilliancy of the footlights— filling the attention of perhaps a crowded audience and making many a breath swell and rise—O so much passion and imparted life!—over and over again, the season through—walking, gesticulating, singing, reciting, his or her part—But sooner or later inevitably wending to the flies or exit doors—vanishing to sight and ear—and never materializing on this earth's stage again![4]

2

Preoccupied as he was with the voice and singing, Whitman was none the less aware of the importance to opera of the orchestra, especially as it was heard in the opening overture. This instrumental piece occurred at a moment when the tension of the waiting audience had reached its height, and to Whitman, as the composers intended, it served a particularly important function of bridging the gap from the real to the unreal world. For these psychological reasons he listened to it with particular intensity, responding with excitement to the conductor's first rap for attention until the crashing finale brought the opening of the stage curtain. As he listened, Whitman studied not only the effectiveness of the various instruments but also the composition itself, with its successive passages strongly contrasting in rhythm, tempo, and dynamics.

Many of Whitman's poems show the result of his interest in the opera overture, but he also discussed his impressions in his essay on the opera. His most revealing comment is to be found in the original manuscript version of the essay.

Now, to the tap-tap of the conductor, the orchestra begins.—What honeyed smoothness! How exact! How true and clear! How inimitable the manner of the conductor quietly signing with slight waves of his wand, to the right hand or the left. How delicious the proportion between the kinds of instruments—rarely met with in ordinary bands, but here perfect.—The violins, the bugles, the flutes, the drums, the base-fiddles, the violincello—all, all so balanced and their results merging with each other.—

Now a rapid passage full of semiquavers given without the least discord by fifteen or twenty violins—Now the clear warble of the flute—and now a passage in which advances the elephantine tread of the trombones. Now a solo on the fagotto, relieved by the low, soothing, gulping notes of the base-viols.—And now, a long, tumultuous, crowded finale ending with a grand crash of all the instruments together, every one, it would seem, making as much noise as it possibly can—an effect which we perceive you don't like at all, but which we privately confess in your ear is one of the greatest treats we obtain from a visit to the opera.[5]

Clearly a feeling for the structure of orchestral writing was present to the writer of the passage, though the structure is analyzed in terms of contrasts and theatrical effects (which were, in reality, the stock in trade of the Italian overtures). There is also to be noticed an awareness of the possibilities for variety of tone color in the orchestra through the use of various instruments, and of the emotional effects of these different instrumental colorings. Whitman was always excited by great masses of sound, and he did not overlook the orchestra's possibilities for such stirring effects. He speaks of that aspect of orchestral music a little apologetically, perhaps realizing that he is confessing a taste for the obvious, when he says that the mounting crescendo and crashing climax of the overture is one of the biggest moments in the whole opera for him.

3

A third essential quality of opera which increased its fascination for Whitman was its drama. Even before he had fully cultivated his fondness for the lyric stage he had been a regular theatre-goer and had heard with a pleasure that he recalled all his life the great actors of his time in most of the classic roles.[6] It is only natural that he should have found a constant interest in the dramatic aspects of opera and to have responded with the most intense feelings to the high tragedy most of the operas involved.[7] Incidentally, it was the tragic operas which he seemed to prefer. Comedies, even so great a one as *The Barber of Seville*, never stirred him so deeply as dramatic moments from the great tragedies, a fact which shows that in part his response to music was conditioned by its dramatic content.

Whitman has given many indications of his understanding of the central importance of drama to opera. One of the most interesting is the letter he sent to his Washington friends about a performance of *Lucrezia Borgia*, in which he tried to re-create for them the excitement he had felt in the theatre. The letter shows him to have remembered the plot in elaborate detail, and he repeatedly calls attention to the fact that the music so heightened the drama that the situations became almost overwhelming in their power.

Two or three nights ago I went to the N. Y. Academy of Music, to the Italian Opera. I suppose you know that is a performance, a play, all in music and singing, in the Italian language, very sweet and beautiful. There is a large company of singers and a large band, altogether two or three hundred. It is a splendid great house, four or five tiers high, and a broad parquette on the main floor. The opera here now has some of the greatest singers in the world. . . . Boys, I must tell you just one scene in the opera I saw—things have worked so in the piece that this lady is compelled, although she tries very hard to avoid it, to give the cup of poisoned wine to her lover—the king her husband forces her to do it—she pleads hard, but her husband threatens to take both their lives (all this is in the singing and music, very fine)—so the lover is brought in as a prisoner, and the king pretends to pardon him and make up, and asks the young man to drink a cup of wine, and orders the lady to pour it out. The lover drinks it, then the king gives her and him a look, and walks off the stage. And now came as good a piece of performance as I ever saw in my life. The lady as she saw that her husband was really gone, she sprang to her lover, clutched him by the arm, and poured out the greatest singing you ever heard—it poured like a raging river more than anything else I could compare it to—she tells him he is poisoned—he tries to inquire, etc., and hardly knows what to make of it—she breaks in trying to pacify him and explain etc—all this goes on very rapid indeed—and the band accompanying—she quickly draws out from her bosom a little vial, to neutralize the poison, then the young man in his desperation abuses her and tells her perhaps it is to poison him still more as she has already poisoned him once—this puts her in such agony, she begs and pleads with him to take the antidote at once before it is too late—her voice is so wild and high that it goes through one like a knife, yet it is delicious—she holds the little vial to his mouth with one hand and with the other springs open a little secret door in the wall for him to escape from the palace—he swallows the antidote, and as she pushes him through the door, the husband returns with some armed guards, but she slams the door to, and stands back up against the door, and her arms spread wide open across it, one fist clenched, and her eyes glaring like a wildcat so they dare not touch her—and that ends the scene. Comrades, recollect all this is in singing and music, and lots of it too, on a big scale, in the band, every instrument you can think of, and the best players in the world, and sometimes the whole band and the whole men's chorus and the women's chorus putting on the steam together—and all in a vast house, light as day, and with a crowded audience of ladies and men. Such singing and strong rich music always give me the greatest pleasure . . .[8]

In his longer discussions of opera Whitman never failed to devote some attention to the plots of the dramas and to comment upon them. For example, discussing Donizetti's La Favorita he said, "I always thought the plot of the 'Favorite' a peculiarly well-proportioned and charming story. It is a type of the experience of the human kind, and, like Shakespeare's dramas, its moral is worldwide."[9] There follow several paragraphs of a detailed summary of the plot in which young Ferdinand leaves the priesthood to marry Leonora, only to discover too late that she was the mistress of the king. Ferdinand rejoins his order and the 'Favorite' dies. Like the stories of all Whitman's favorite operas, this one is stormy and emotional with many of the effects of melodrama. The more violent the emotion, of course, the more passionate the vocal utterance demanded, and this is what Whitman enjoyed. His description of the

close of the opera calls attention to both music and dramatic situation, each heightening the other, though there can be no question
of which is the more important to him.

Now we approach the close of the legend. We see again the dark groves
of the convent. Up through the venerable trees peal the strains of the
chanting voices. Oh, sweet music of Donizetti, how can men hesitate
what rank to give you!

With his pale face at the foot of the cross kneels the returned novice,
his breast filled with a devouring anguish, his eyes showing the death
that has fallen upon his soul. The strains of death, too, come plaintively
from his lips. Never before did you hear such wonderful gushing sorrow,
poured forth like ebbing blood from a murdered heart. Is it for peace
he prays with that appealing passion? Is it the story of his own sad wreck
he utters?

Listen. Pure and vast, that voice now rises, as on clouds, to the heaven
where it claims audience. Now, firm and unbroken, it spreads like an
ocean around us. Ah, welcome that I know not the mere language of the
earthly words in which the melody is embodied; as all words are mean
before the language of true music.[10]

Much of the same sort of recognition of the important union of
drama and music is revealed in sentences from Whitman's essay,
"The Opera." Here the piece is Verdi's early work, *Ernani*, a setting
of Victor Hugo's play. Again it is passionate, elemental music
which arouses the poet's sensibilities.

With the rise of the curtain you are transported afar—such power has
music. You behold the mountains of Aragon, and the bandits in their
secure retreat, feasting, drinking, gaming, and singing. And such singing,
and such an instrumental accompaniment! Their wild, rollicking spirits
pour themselves out in that opening chorus.

We will not repeat the story of the opera of Ernani, with its passions
of love, jealousy, pride, and faith. De Sylva, the proud old Spaniard—
how well it is represented by Marini, a magnificent artist! The haughty
attitudes, the fiery breath, the hate, despair, and fiendish revenge—never
did we realize an old Spanish hidalgo till we saw Marini play Ruy Gomez
de Sylva.[11]

Undoubtedly Whitman's understanding of the plots of operas
and their dramatic significance, even though most of them were
performed in Italian, came from his habit of familiarizing himself
with the operas in translation before going to the theater. For ex-

ample, on one occasion he said, "As a young fellow, when possible I always studied a play or libretto quite carefully over, by myself (sometimes twice through), before seeing it on the stage. . . . Tried both ways—not reading some beforehand; but I found I gain'd most by getting that sort of mastery first, if the piece had depth. (Surface effects and glitter were much less thought of, I am sure, those times.)"[12] Doubtless it was this systematic study which accounted for the growth of his appreciation since the day when he had said, "The story and libretto are now generally of no account."[13] In his early experience, he simply didn't understand the stories.

It seems unquestionable that these three aspects of opera-going, the 'occasion,' the overture, and the drama, were essential parts of Whitman's great devotion to the lyric stage. He could have found each of them elsewhere, in the concert hall and in the theatre. But it was only when they were joined together and united with great singing that the appeal of all became irresistible and inspiring.

NOTES—CHAPTER V

1. "Come, I will not talk to you as one of the superficial crowd who saunter here because it is in the fashion; who take opera glasses with them, and make you sick with shallow words, upon the sublimest and most spiritual of the arts." "Letter from Paumanok," *Uncollected Poetry and Prose*, I, 256.

2. "Mr. Whitman was an appreciative lover of the drama and music. In early life he was a constant theatre and opera goer. Any place in the house did him so long as he could see and hear. He was as frequently in the gallery with the gods as with the boys in the pit, or the upper crust in the boxes, or orchestra seats. Here he studied life."—Thomas Donaldson, *Walt Whitman, the Man* (New York, 1896), p. 60.

3. *New York Dissected*, pp. 18-21.

4. "Good-Bye My Fancy," *Prose*, IV, 57.

5. *Uncollected Poetry and Prose*, II, 99.

6. "This musical passion followed my theatrical one."—"Specimen Days," *Prose*, I, 26.

7. Canby's statement (*op. cit.*, p. 63) that "it is questionable whether he gave it [the drama in opera] much attention" is scarcely borne out by the facts, though of course the drama was secondary to the music with him.

8. Traubel, *op. cit.*, III, 103.

9. *Uncollected Poetry and Prose*, I, 258.

10. *Ibid.*, p. 258.

11. *New York Dissected*, p. 21.

12. "Good-Bye My Fancy," *Prose*, IV, 50.

13. Quoted in *Workshop*, p. 202.

CHAPTER VI

A Source of Poetry

PERHAPS THE MOST basic influence of grand opera upon
Walt Whitman was that it made a poet of him. One of the
topics which Whitman's biographers and critics have speculated
about with greatest zeal and least profit is the mysterious circumstance which in the early fifties seemed to develop the competent
but uninspired and not especially promising young journalist into a
major poet.[1] Every writer has realized that there must have been
some conditioning experience, some "long foreground,"[2] as Emerson put it, to account for Leaves of Grass. The Whitman of the
forties could not suddenly have put pen to paper and turned out
such a book as that.

The conditioning experience, in very large part, was his passionate and mystical devotion to operatic music, in which he was almost
literally immersed during the days when he was planning and writing the early Leaves. Whitman himself freely admitted the part
opera played, and though he discussed it more often in his later
days than during his early career, he never denied it.

1

In one of his conversations with his friend Horace Traubel, Whitman said, "My younger life was so saturated with the emotions,
raptures, and uplifts of such musical experiences that it would be
surprising indeed if all my future work had not been colored by
them. A real musician running through Leaves of Grass—a philosopher-musician—could put his finger on this and that anywhere in
the text no doubt as indicating the activity of the influence I have
spoken of."[3] The "musical experiences" of which he was speaking
were the singing of Alboni, the contralto, and Badiali, the baritone,
in particular, as well as opera in general. He added, "No one can
tell, know, ever suspect, how much they had to do with Leaves of
Grass."

In *Specimen Days* the poet had also declared the importance of music and singers to him during what he called the "gestation of *Leaves of Grass*," though on this occasion he admitted that the critics would probably be amused at the idea and not understand what he was talking about. Critics or no critics, he insisted that certain singers "had a good deal to do with the business,"[4] and this time he mentioned Alboni and Bettini, the tenor.

In the very last year of his life, in a declaration of unusual terseness, Whitman said, "I was fed and bred under the Italian dispensation, and absorbed it and doubtless show it."[5]

Significant corroboration of these professions of indebtedness to operatic music came from a good many of Whitman's friends, writers with whom he doubtless often discussed his work and its origins and technique. These friends, in manuscripts which Whitman saw before publication and approved, commented on the musical background of the poetry at some length. For example, Richard Maurice Bucke, in his biography, quoted with approval an article on Whitman which had appeared in a New York paper in 1873. "I claim that in these verses Walt Whitman follows the method of the tone poets, and that what you call vagueness and obscurity is simply the art of the musician, the only art that transcends the art of the poets."[6] In the same volume a quotation from a newspaper article prepared by William D. O'Connor, the poet's friend and champion, referred to "A Woman Waits for Me" as "oratorio music." "Nothing that the poet has ever written, either in signification or splendid oratorio music, has more the character of a sanctus."[7]

O'Connor further wrote in his famous essay championing Whitman, whom he called "The Good Gray Poet," "For music, perfect and vast, subtle and more than auricular—woven not alone from the verbal sounds and rhythmic cadences, but educed by the thought and feeling of the verse from the reader's soul by the power of a spell few hold—I know of nothing superior to 'By the Bivouac's Fitful Flame.'. . . If these are not examples of great structural harmony as well as of the highest poetry there are none now in literature."[8]

Even more striking than these quotations, however, is a memorandum by Mrs. Fanny Raymond Ritter, the wife of a prominent musicologist of the day, Dr. Frederic Louis Ritter, director of the School of Music at Vassar College. Whitman often visited in their home. Mrs. Ritter's statement follows:

Those readers who possess a musical mind cannot fail to have been struck by a peculiar characteristic of some of Whitman's grandest poems. It is apparently, but only superficially, a contradiction. A fault that critics have most insisted upon in his poetry is his independence of, or contempt for, the canons of musico-poetical art, in its intermittent, irregular structure and flow. Yet the characteristic alluded to which always impressed me as inherent in these—especially in some of the Pindaric "Drum-Taps"—was a sense of strong, rhythmical pulsing, *musical* power. . . . Therefore on a certain memorable Olympian day at the Ritter-house, when Whitman and Burroughs visited us together, I told Whitman of my belief in the presence of an overwhelming musical pulse, behind an apparent absence of musical form in his poems. He answered with as much sincerity as geniality, that it would indeed be strange if there were no music at the heart of his poems, for more of these were actually inspired by music than he himself could remember. Moods awakened by music in the streets, the theatre, and in private, had originated poems apparently far removed in feeling from the scenes and feelings of the moment. But above all, he said, while he was yet brooding over poems still to come, he was touched and inspired by the glorious, golden, soul-smiting voice of one of the greatest of Italian contralto singers, Marietta Alboni.[9]

This document is thoroughly enlightening. Music was at the heart of his poems, said Whitman, and more had been inspired by music than he could recall. His whole poetic creation, he confessed, was tempered by the inspiration of music.

There are other kinds of references to opera in the work of Whitman's friends. For example, John Burroughs, in a book the poet helped him write, said, "Many passages of his poetry were composed in the gallery of the New York Academy of Music during the opera performances."[10] But perhaps John T. Trowbridge best summed up the whole matter in his "Reminiscences of Walt Whitman" when he quoted the poet directly. " 'But for the opera,' he declared, that day on Prospect Hill, 'I could never have written *Leaves of Grass*.' "[11]

Why not? There are many answers, but an important one is that by opera Whitman was first lifted to the heights of mystical rapture wherein he realized that he was a poet with a poet's message for the world. Following this inspiration came the recognition that in opera lay the elements of a technique which would enable the "outsetting bard" to present his message in a manner which could preserve its largeness and naturalness, which would not destroy its inspirational power by cloaking it with forms of artificiality and pettiness, and which, incidentally, would be exactly appropriate for the great new land which he was to celebrate.

Once Whitman had overcome his prejudices against opera, he almost invariably spoke of it in terms of mystical rapture. He remembered his opera-going days themselves with almost boundless pleasure, as when he said to Traubel, "My singing years. Oh! those great days! great, great days!"[12] But most significant are the passages in which he spoke of music's value and meaning, in the days when he was almost constantly in the midst of it. At first he was unable to describe satisfactorily, or even understand, the strange emotional power which he felt in great vocal masterpieces, and which he had read about in *Consuelo*. "It is utterly impossible to describe in words the effects produced by this fine composition," he wrote in 1846 about Mendelssohn's oratorio, *St. Paul*. He went on, ". . . for who shall tell the how and the why of the singular passion caused by melodious vibrations?"[13]

By 1851 he was much closer to an understanding of what happened to him when he heard great singing. Describing Bettini's performance in *La Favorita*, he first characterized the meaning of the song and then the voice. "The strains of death, too, come plaintively from his lips. Never before did you hear such wonderful gushing sorrow, poured forth like ebbing blood from a murdered heart. Pure and vast, that voice now rises, as on clouds, to heaven where it claims an audience." Then he proceeded to a suggestion of what the music did to him. "Now, firm and unbroken, it spreads like an ocean around us." The words of the aria have dropped their significance and the poet has lost himself in the ocean of sound until, at last, "the boundless and unspeakable capacities of that mystery, the human soul, shall be filled to the uttermost, and the problem of human cravingness be satisfied and destroyed."[14] Here is a description of a mystical experience in which, literally on wings of song, the poet's soul is so filled with ecstasy that truth is directly and almost blindingly revealed to him.

Whitman went even further to explain how music was more than mere enjoyment to him in an entry in one of his manuscript notebooks, written probably after the above comment but before 1855, and later revised for a part of "Song of Myself":

I want that tenor, large and fresh as the creation, the orbed parting of whose mouth shall lift over my head the sluices of all the delight yet discovered for our race.—I want the soprano that lithely overleaps the stars and convulses me like the love-grips of her in whose arms I lay last night.—I want an infinite chorus and orchestrium, wide as the orbit of Uranus, true as the hours of the day, and filling my capacities to receive, as thoroughly as the sea fills its scooped out sands.—I want the chanted Hymn whose tremendous sentiment shall uncage in my breast a thousand wide-winged strengths and unknown ardors and terrible ecstasies, putting me through the flights of all the passions—dilating me beyond time and air—startling me with the overture of some unnamable horror—calmly sailing me all day on a bright river with lazy slapping waves—stabbing my heart with myriads of forked distractions more furious than hail or lightning—lulling me drowsily with honeyed morphine—tightening the fakes of death about my throat, and awakening me again to know by that comparison, the most positive wonder in the world, and that's what we call life.[15]

Here can be seen clearly the almost terrifying intensity and wide variety of the responses which Whitman gave to operatic music with its singers, chorus, and overture, responses which were at the same time sexual in their bodiliness and mystical in their spirituality. The climax of the passage, with its implication of mystical revelation of the meaning of life itself, is especially important to an understanding of the origins of Whitman's inspiration. The entire fragment is an impressive testimony to the power of music as Whitman knew it in grand opera in the days before Leaves of Grass appeared. Opera was indeed an important aspect of the "long foreground" of the book. The overwhelming impact of operatic music on a soul of sufficient sensitiveness and mysticism to respond, had awakened it to new ideas, aspirations, and ambitions.

Whitman's great masterpiece, "Out of the Cradle Endlessly Rocking,"[16] contains a symbolical presentation of these shaking and transforming experiences of his young manhood, and in itself, properly understood, the poem explains most of the questions about his poetic growth and serves as the most unquestionable proof of the fundamental importance of opera to his artistry. In looking at the poem one must remember, of course, the poet's specific statement that the song of the mockingbird, which is so prominent in it, is really a symbol for the song of Alboni, the great contralto who sang in New York in 1852, three years before the first edition of *Leaves of Grass*, the singer who was for Whitman a representative of and a climax to Italian operatic singing in general. Following the mockingbird's lyric in the poem come these significant words:

> The aria sinking
> . . . .
> The boy ecstatic. . . .
> The love in the heart long pent, now loose, now at last
>   tumultuously bursting,
> The aria's meaning, the ears, the soul, swiftly depositing,
> The strange tears down the cheeks coursing,
> . . . .
> To the boy's soul's questions sullenly timing, some
>   drown'd secret hissing,
> To the outsetting bard.
>
> Demon or bird! (said the boy's soul,)
> Is it indeed toward your mate you sing? or is it really to
>   me?
> For I, that was a child, my tongue's use sleeping, now I
>   have heard you,
> Now in a moment I know what I am for, I awake,
> And already a thousand singers, a thousand songs, clearer,
>   louder, and more sorrowful than yours,
> A thousand warbling echoes have started to life within me,
>   never to die.
> . . . .
> My own songs awaked from that hour,
> And with them the key, the word up from the waves,
> The word of the sweetest song and all songs,
> That strong and delicious word [death]. . . .[17]

In other words, though this is not the entire meaning of the poem, Whitman is here re-creating through the symbol of a bird's song a moment of opera with its tragically beautiful and powerful music. As the bird's song broke through the boy's reserve and penetrated his innermost soul, mystically firing his imagination and at the same time producing a violent physical response, so opera touched and awakened the young Whitman, leaving him never again "the peaceful child," or workaday young journalist, which he had been before. Whitman shows in the poem, through beautifully appropriate symbolism, how opera awoke in him not only his ideas, or songs, which were mystically derived under the spell of great singing, but also the realization that he was a dedicated soul, destined inescapably to the role of poet and bard.

The close of the quoted passage is important also. To Whitman the highest capability of the human mind and soul was the ability to understand fully the meaning of death in the universal scheme of things and to accept it not with fear but with joy and trust. He felt that one of the fundamental purposes of his poetry was to explain death by suggesting in various indirect ways all of its aspects and meanings. Only a true poet could accomplish this mission, he believed, and only an inspired poet could himself possess the requisite knowledge. In his own case it was opera which provided the inspiration necessary for his understanding.

Naturally, Whitman made the bird's song, the symbol, a song of tragic love, for this was the emotion, tremendously heightened by the communicativeness of great voices, which had stirred him so deeply in the opera house. Even the presentation of the tragedy in song is operatic in method, with its opening song of ecstatic love, its central lyric of waiting, and its final outburst of passionate grief. It was such tragic and unrestrained love-music, such "cries of unsatisfied love," which had made a poet of Whitman and elevated him to a plane whereon he could contemplate death itself. In this poem he declares that once the inspirational music had awakened him, he could never cease perpetuating it (or its inspirations and revelations) in his poems.

> O you singer solitary, singing by yourself, projecting me,
> O solitary me listening, never more shall I cease perpetuating you,
> Never more shall I escape, never more the reverberations,
> Never more the cries of unsatisfied love be absent from me,
> Never again leave me to be the peaceful child I was before what there in the night,

By the sea under the yellow and sagging moon,
The messenger there arous'd, the fire, the sweet hell within,
The unknown want, the destiny of me.[18]

The last lines quoted suggest an important fact, which must not be overlooked. It is that in the poem, as in Whitman's career, there were other influences in addition to those of opera, predominantly those of nature, which contributed to the mystical experience, the great emotional climax. The ocean, for example, the old mother with her husky music, was always an especially powerful influence, as the poet often confessed. But as the poem makes clear, it was the music, the aria, which started to life the thousand songs within him, and it was the aria which he vowed never to cease projecting.

Once Whitman had encountered these tremendous impulses in opera, his immediate response was to create, to fashion something which might enable him to convey to the world the mysteries which had been revealed to him. Inspired as he was, however, he could not immediately reach the rare artistic heights of "Out of the Cradle." At first he turned to American opera, in ways already described, and he concerned himself with this project over a period of time. But he was not a musician, and he could find small satisfaction in urging others to compose and in helping them devise proper operatic forms. A more likely medium of expression was oratory. He had been interested in it for some time anyhow, and in it the human voice, that musical instrument which so moved him at the opera, was also the prime agent. Little by little, however, oratory, too, came to seem unsatisfactory; it was too earthbound, too limited in suitable subject matter, too prosy. The kind of subtleties Whitman needed to express were not the province of the orator; they were suitable only for poems, great rhapsodies in which he could *sing*, as he had been sung to, reveal truth as it had been revealed to him. He needed now not to speak persuasively on political issues, but to go behind politics and reveal America to itself, to chant, in terms of a perceptive and representative man, the glories and virtues of the great, new land. This could be done only in poetry.

He explained it all to Horace Traubel.

When I was younger—way back: in the Brooklyn days—and even behind Brooklyn—I was to be an orator—to go about the country spouting my pieces, proclaiming my faith. . . . I was afraid I would get no chance to say it through books: so I was to lecture and get myself delivered that way. . . . For a while I speechified in politics, but that of course would not satisfy me—that was only come-day-go-day palaver: what I really had to give out was something more serious, more off from politics and towards the general life. But the Leaves got out after all—in spite of the howl and slander of the opposition, got out under far better conditions than I expected.[19]

The same sequence of ambitions is mentioned in a rejected poem beginning "Long I thought that knowledge alone would suffice me."[20] Here the poet explains that he first sought knowledge; then patriotism engrossed him and he determined to be an orator; then heroism attracted him; finally he determined to "sing songs" as his crowning function. The point of the poem is that all the ambitions had been put aside for love. Probably written in a fit of dejection, the poem was later discarded as unrepresentative or perhaps too personally revealing.

"Proud Music of the Storm"[21] showed why the 'faith' of which the poet had spoken demanded an expression more subtle and more lyrical than oratory, and of what the 'faith' was compounded and how it arrived. In the poem, after a magnificent recital of the effects of all music, natural and man-created, as they are heard in a dream, the poet wakes and for a moment recalls the musical splendors. Then he addresses his soul:

> Come, for I have found the clew I sought so long,
> Let us go forth refresh'd amid the day,
> Cheerfully tallying life, walking the world, the real,
> Nourish'd henceforth by our celestial dream.
>
> . . . .
>
> Haply what thou hast heard O soul was not the sound of
>   winds
>
> . . . .
>
> Nor vocalism of sun-bright Italy,
> Nor German organ majestic. . . .
>
> . . . .

> But to a new rhythmus fitted for thee,
> Poems bridging the way from Life to Death, vaguely
>   wafted in night air, uncaught, unwritten,
> Which let us go forth in the bold day and write.[22]

In other words, the clue by which Whitman came to understand that poems, in a new rhythmus, a musical one, were to be the way for him to express "the way from Life to Death," was music itself.

Some of Whitman's tentative and fragmentary jottings reveal how he tried at times to translate opera directly into poetry, or at least to employ obviously the methods and materials of opera. They show us that he did not easily reach the pinnacles of the two poems quoted from. For example, there was a projected "Poem of Musicians—tenor—soprano—baritone—basso."[23] Other fragments of lines, composed early, were in some instances reworked and included in later poems. They show his preoccupation with operatic effects:

> A soprano heard at intervals over the immense waves
> Audible there from the underlying chorus[24]
> A clear and transparent base [sic] that lusciously shudders
>   the universe
> A tenor strong and ascending, with glad notes of morning
>   —with power and health[25]
> The heavy base [sic], the great hum and harshness, composite and musical[26]

Even during or following the Civil War, in the years when some of his finest and subtlest work was being produced, Whitman still attempted to achieve a poem which might have the effectiveness of opera and almost the exact form of the lyric drama. The project is outlined in a manuscript now in the possession of the Library at Duke University. The entire outline follows:

Theme for piece poem An Opera

An opera in a dream—different singers and characters—the suggestions, associations. Some old songs? hymn? Rock me to sleep mother? Rock'd in the cradle of the deep?—With its memories, associations—or where I last heard it, in Hospital? some typical appropriate? tune, or? hymn—or? something played by the band (? some dirge or? opera passage or dead? march) Calling up the whole dead of the war. The march in last act of La Gazza Ladra. One stanza must describe a strong triumphal instrumental & vocal chorus as of triumphant man—triumphant over temptation & all weakness.[27]

It is interesting to discover the poet attempting to combine popular songs and hymns with operatic music in this melange of effects. However, it must finally have seemed a hopeless, or at least at inartistic project, if, indeed, he gave it much attention at all. Certainly the manuscript is in the crudest, initial stages of jotting. At any rate, Whitman never wrote the poem, "An Opera."

Ultimately in his artistic development Whitman realized that he would have to "translate" opera into his poetry in more subtle ways, and he never abandoned the figure of speech. Indeed, throughout his poetic career he continued to think of his poetry as "translation" of the kind of music he loved. If poetry to Wordsworth was powerful feelings recollected in tranquillity, to Whitman it was music so recollected. His greatest creative excitement was the result of his musical experience, and, in one way or another, it was this which he attempted to get into his poetry.

Two poems indicate clearly what he meant by this "translation." One is "The Dead Tenor,"[28] a memorial tribute to Brignoli, a singer whom Whitman had often admired.[29] In the short poem he confesses touchingly how deeply the singer's voice had moved him and how all his creative effort had been an attempt to translate music's inspiration into words. Written late in the poet's career, in 1884, when he was no longer able to hear the opera which had so charmed and uplifted him as a young man, the lyric has a peculiar, nostalgic beauty.

> As down the stage again,
> With Spanish hat and plumes, and gait inimitable,
> Back from the fading lessons of the past, I'd call, I'd tell
> and own,
> How much from thee! the revelation of the singing voice
> from thee!
> (So firm—so liquid-soft—again that tremulous, manly
> timbre!
> The perfect singing voice—deepest of all to me the lesson
> —trial and test of all:)
> How through those strains distill'd—how the rapt ears, the
> soul of me absorbing
> Fernando's heart, Manrico's passionate call, Ernani's, sweet
> Gennaro's,
> I fold thenceforth, or seek to fold, within my chants
> transmuting,

Freedom's and Love's and Faith's unloos'd cantabile,
(As perfume's, color's, sunlight's correlation:)
From these, for these, with these, a hurried line, dead
    tenor,
A wafted autumn leaf, dropt in the closing grave, the
    shovel'd earth,
To memory of thee.[30]

In many other places Whitman refers to "translations" of music, by which he meant getting into his poetry the inspiring quality of music as well as the actual inspirations which came to him from music. Usually it was opera which he made the basis of such references. In one splendid lyric, however, "The Mystic Trumpeter," it is the trumpet which he uses to symbolize the exaltation music can induce. The poem opens with a short section establishing an unreal atmosphere:

Hark, some wild trumpeter, some strange musician,
Hovering unseen in air, vibrates capricious tunes tonight.
I hear thee trumpeter, listening alert I catch thy notes,
Now pouring, whirling like a tempest round me,
Now low, subdued, now in the distance lost.[31]

The poet continues to address the trumpeter, urging him closer so that the music may be caught which

Gives out to no one's ears but mine, but freely gives to
    mine,
That I may thee translate.[32]

In successive stanzas the trumpeter is called upon to provide music in various moods so that the responding poet may share them. The inspirational magic worked by the trumpet's tones becomes the body of each stanza. With the opening 'prelude' of music, the poet confesses:

Thy song expands my numb'd imbonded spirit, thou
    freest, launchest me,
Floating and basking upon heaven's lake.[32]

The trumpet re-creates medieval atmosphere, and the poet envisions knights, tournaments, crusaders on the march. The trumpet sounds the theme of love, and the poet sees

> . . . the vast alembic ever working, I see and know the
> flames that heat the world.[32]

The call to war is blown, and the poet sees the spectacle of conflict
and hears the noise of battle. Then occurs a most important section
in which the poet comments on music as inspiration:

> O trumpeter, methinks I am myself the instrument thou
> playest,
> Thou melt'st my heart, my brain—thou movest, drawest,
> changest them at will. . . .[33]

A last section calls upon the trumpeter for a joyful sound.

> Now trumpeter for thy close,
> Vouchsafe a higher strain than any yet,
> Sing to my soul, renew its languishing faith and hope,
> Rouse up my slow belief, give me some vision of the future,
> Give me for once its prophecy and joy.[34]

The joyful strain comes, and the poem closes in exclamations of
joy and rapture.

Thus does Whitman affirm unequivocally the power of music
as an inspiring force. It can induce all the emotions; it can elevate
and it can cast down. Most important of all, it gives the poet material which he may "translate" into poetry.

2

Just as positively as he claimed opera as his inspiration, Whitman
declared that it gave him his method. As early as 1860, when critics
were finding his poems formless and crude, he gave them an important clue to the source of this strange kind of poetic art, and to
an understanding of its formal aspects when he said, "Walt Whitman's method in the construction of his songs is strictly the method
of the Italian Opera."[35] He knew instinctively, however, that such
a pronouncement would not immediately clear up all misgivings
about the poems in the critics' minds. He remembered too well his
own struggles to appreciate opera, a highly complicated, foreign,
art form in a field where his taste had long since been formed on
simple, sentimental fare. So he reminded the critics that just as a
taste for opera must be cultivated by a patient attempt to understand the form and most of all by repeated hearings, so his poems

ought to be approached. "In the ardor of youth," he told his dogmatic critics, "commit not yourself too irretrievably that there is nothing in the Italian composers, and nothing in the Mocking Bird's chants. But pursue them awhile—listen—yield yourself—persevere."[36]

Whitman had earlier attempted to put readers on the right track without being quite so obvious, at the time "A Child's Reminiscence," the poem commented on above, was originally published. In an editorial comment he had said, "Like Leaves of Grass, the purport of this wild and plaintive song, well enveloped, and eluding definition, is positive and unquestionable, like the effect of music. The piece will bear reading many times—perhaps, indeed, only comes forth, as from recesses, by many repetitions."[37] However, he had obviously failed to make his theoretical ideas clear. And rarely again, during the height of his productive years, did he explain so candidly the relationship between opera and his poems. Perhaps if he had continued to point out the parallels, critical appreciation of his individual kind of poetry would not have lagged so far behind its composition.

The most obvious contribution of opera to Whitman's poetic method was that it caused him to abandon traditional and conventional techniques. As John Townsend Trowbridge declared in writing his recollections of talks with the poet, "To the music of the opera, for which he had a passion, more than to anything else, was due his emancipation from what he called the 'ballad-style' of poetry by which he meant poetry hampered by rhyme and metre."[38]

Whitman's case against such conventionalities was well stated by John Burroughs, probably with the assistance of the poet himself, in one of the Burroughs books on Whitman. It is important to notice in the statement the reference to music, and what were felt to be its boldness and freedom, as the ideal means of artistic communication.

Modern verse does not express the great liberating power of art but only its conventional limitations, and the elegant finish of details to which society runs. It never once ceases to appeal directly to that part of the mind which is cognizant with mere form—form denoted by regular lines. It is never so bold as music, which in the analysis is discord, but in the synthesis harmony. . . .

To accuse Walt Whitman, therefore, of want of art, is to overlook his generic quality, and shows ignorance of the ends for which Nature and Time exist to the mind. He has the art which surrounds all art, as the sphere holds all form.[39]

Whitman himself repeatedly stated the weaknesses of traditional verse forms. "The clink of words is empty and offensive . . . the poetic quality blooms simple and earnest as the laws of the world. The audible rhyme soon nauseates . . . The inaudible rhyme is delicious without end."[40] "The poetic quality is not marshal'd in rhyme and uniformity, or abstract addresses to things, nor in melancholy complaints or good precepts, but it is the life of these and much else and is in the soul."[41] "Nature seems to look on all fixed-up poetry as something almost impertinent."[42] "America needs her own poems in her own body and spirit and different from all hitherto —freer—more muscular, comprehending more and unspeakably grander. . . . Not the current products of imaginative persons, with tropes, likenesses, piano music and smooth rhymes."[43]

To Whitman, poetry was an organic thing,[44] as music seemed to him to be. The idea was first to be achieved, then allowed to develop fully. The idea should never be crammed into a preëstablished mold. The form of expression must grow with the idea; then the product would be forever fresh and vital. Whitman said of Lowell, he "was not a grower—he was a builder. He built poems: he didn't put in the seed, and water the seed and send down his sun letting the rest take care of itself; he measured his poems—kept them within the formula."[45] Of another poet of his day he said, "Poe's verses illustrate an intense faculty for technical and abstract beauty, with the rhyming art to excess . . . and by final judgment, probably belong among the electric lights of imaginative literature, brilliant and dazzling, but with no heat."[46]

Regularity and traditional forms seemed to Whitman to prevent the achievement of richness in poetry. In discussing the work of Burns, he put the matter in musical terms, "He gives melodies, now and then the simplest and sweetest ones; but harmonies, complications, oratorios in words, never."[47] It was the richness of the oratorio, with its masses of vocal sound and soaring melody, which he wanted in his own poems. And once speaking of Lanier, he made the same point, fundamentally. "He had genius—a delicate, clairvoyant genius: but this over tuning of the ear, this extreme deference paid to oral nicety, reduced the majesty, the solid worth of his rhythms."[48]

In any case, Whitman, for himself, wanted freedom rather than restriction; nature, not artifice; massive chants, not pretty ballads. "I will be also a master after my own kind, making the poems of the emotions, as they pass or stay, the poems of freedom, and the expose of personality—singing in high tones Democracy and the new world of it through these States."[49] He wanted "our own song, free, joyous, and masterful. Our own music, raised on the soil, carrying with it all the subtle analogies of our own associations."[50] And he was determined to be original in his new, operatic songs. "Finally," he wrote, "as I have lived in fresh lands, inchoate, and in a revolutionary age, future founding, I have felt to identify the points of that age, these lands, in my recitatives, altogether in my own way."[51]

In his poems themselves, Whitman repeatedly emphasized the fact that they were to escape dulcet rhymes and pretty effects. He wanted power, crude and violent perhaps but irresistible, and always with the effect of operatic music. "To a Locomotive in Winter" is a good example of such poems. Here he calls upon the roaring engine to serve him as a model:

> Thee for my recitative,
> . . . .
> Type of the modern—emblem of motion and power—pulse
>   of the continent,
> For once come serve the Muse and merge in verse, even as
>   here I see thee,
> With storm and buffeting gusts of wind and falling snow,
> By day thy warning ringing bell to sound its note,
> By night thy silent signal lamps to swing.
>
> Fierce-throated beauty!
> Roll through my chant with all thy lawless music . . .
> . . . .
> Law of thyself complete, thine own track firmly holding,
> (No sweetness debonair of tearful harp or glib piano
>   thine,)
> Thy trills of shrieks by rocks and hills return'd,
> Launch'd o'er the prairies wide, across the lakes,
> To the free skies unpent and glad and strong.[52]

Whitman realized that what to him were the emancipations of

operatic music had made his poetry seem formless to his critics. He never worried too much about it, however, for he was perfectly aware of his own formal objectives and it did not make too much difference whether the critics fully appreciated his attempts or not. Occasionally he spoke out. "Of course my poetry isn't formless," he told W. R. Thayer, who recalled it in his book about Whitman. "Nobody could write in my way unless he had the melody singing in his ears. I don't often contrive to catch the best musical combination nowadays; but in the older pieces I always had a tune before I began to write."[53]

He might have added that the "tune" was opera, for opera had not only started him on his poetic way, but had also provided many suggestions as to how he might proceed in the creation of poems which would in themselves possess the inspirational power of opera.

NOTES—CHAPTER VI

1. Allen, *Handbook*, p. 85.
2. *Ibid.*, p. 128.
3. Traubel, *op. cit.*, II, 173.
4. "Specimen Days," *Prose*, I, 24.
5. "Good-Bye My Fancy," *Prose*, IV, 50.
6. Article by "Matador" in New York *Graphic*, Nov. 25, 1873. Quoted in Bucke, *op. cit.*, p. 209.
7. William D. O'Connor, "Letter to Editor," New York *Tribune*, May 25, 1882. Quoted in Bucke, *op. cit.*, p. 160.
8. William D. O'Connor, "The Good Gray Poet," quoted in Bucke, *op. cit.*, p. 120. Other poems mentioned are: "Out of the Rolling Ocean," "Out of the Cradle," "Elemental Drifts," "Splendor of Falling Day."
9. Bucke, *op. cit.*, pp. 156-57.
10. John Burroughs, *Notes on Walt Whitman as Poet and Person* (New York, 1867), p. 82.
11. John Townsend Trowbridge, "Reminiscences of Walt Whitman," *Atlantic Monthly*, LXXXIX, 166 (February, 1902).
12. Traubel, *op. cit.*, II, 173.
13. Emory Holloway, "More Light on Whitman," *American Mercury*, I, 186 (February, 1924).
14. *Uncollected Poetry and Prose*, I, 256-58.
15. *Ibid.*, II, 85.
16. Inclusive Edition, p. 210.
17. *Ibid.*, p. 214.
18. *Ibid.*, p. 214.
19. Traubel, *op. cit.*, I, 5.
20. Inclusive Edition, p. 477.
21. *Ibid.*, pp. 337-42.

22. *Ibid.*, p. 342.

23. *Prose*, VII, 21.

24. *Notes and Fragments*, p. 11.

25. *Ibid.*, p. 11.

26. *Ibid.*, p. 40.

27. *Faint Clews & Indirections: Manuscripts of Walt Whitman and His Family*, p. 13.

28. Inclusive Edition, p. 431.

29. So identified in Whitman's handwriting on the envelope in which the poem was mailed to William D. O'Connor. Manuscript in Berg Collection, New York Public Library.

30. Inclusive Edition, p. 431.

31. *Ibid.*, p. 389.

32. *Ibid.*, p. 390.

33. *Ibid.*, p. 391.

34. *Ibid.*, p. 391.

35. *A Child's Reminiscence*, p. 20.

36. *Ibid.*, p. 20.

37. *Ibid.*, p. 10.

38. Trowbridge, *op. cit.*, p. 166.

39. Burroughs, *op. cit.*, p. 46.

40. *Notes and Fragments*, p. 124.

41. "Collect," *Prose*, II, 166.

42. "Specimen Days," *Prose*, II, 42.

43. *Notes and Fragments*, p. 67.

44. "The idea must always come first—is indispensable. Take my own method—if you can call it that. I have the idea clearly and fully realized before I attempt to express it. Then I let it go."—Traubel, *op. cit.*, I, 64.

45. *Ibid.*, I, 215.

46. "Specimen Days," *Prose*, I, 285.

47. "November Boughs," *Prose*, III, 137.

48. Traubel, *op. cit.*, I, 170.

49. *Notes and Fragments*, p. 92.

50. *A Child's Reminiscence*, p. 21.

51. Inclusive Edition, p. 521.

52. *Ibid.*, p. 392.

53. W. R. Thayer, "Personal Recollections of Walt Whitman," *Scribner's*, LXV, 682 (June, 1919).

Part 2

ANALYSIS

CHAPTER I

Subject Matter

I F THE MUSIC OF OPERA is at the heart of Whitman's
poetry, as he insisted it is, it would seem to be fair to look for
some outward evidence of that musical center in the material of the
poems themselves. To be sure, as Whitman explained, the thoughts
that thronged his mind when uplifted by the sound of great voices
were not necessarily concerned with music. Usually the reverse was
true, and music led him into contemplation of truths not outwardly
connected with music in any way. It was probably for this reason
that Whitman himself confessed that he could not remember how
many or which of his poems had musical origins. Neither can a
reader expect to discover in every poem musically inspired a mark
of origin. It is possible, however, to find unmistakable evidence in
many of the poems of the tremendous importance of music in his
life and thought, and many poems are specifically on the subject of
music.

Perhaps the most objective statement of this importance to be
found in the poems is Section 3 of "Proud Music of the Storm,"[1]
which reads like a musical autobiography. First the musical impressions of childhood and early boyhood are recounted.

> Ah from a little child,
> Thou knowest soul how to me all sounds became music,
> My mother's voice in lullaby or hymn,
> (The voice, O tender voices, memory's loving voices,
> Last miracle of all, O dearest mother's, sister's, voices;)
> The rain, the growing corn, the breeze among the long-
>   leav'd corn,
> The measur'd sea-surf beating on the sand,
> The twittering bird, the hawk's sharp scream,
> The wild-fowl's notes at night as flying low migrating north
>   or south,
> The psalm in the country church or mid the clustering
>   trees, the open air camp-meeting,

The fiddler in the tavern, the glee, the long-strung sailor-
      song,
The lowing cattle, bleating sheep, the crowing cock at
      dawn.

Next comes the popular music of young manhood, leading to the
climax of grand opera, a progression which has already been followed
in terms of Whitman's journalistic writing.

All songs of current lands come sounding round me,
The German airs of friendship, wine and love,
Irish ballads, merry jigs and dances, English warbles,
Chansons of France, Scotch tunes, and o'er the rest,
Italia's peerless compositions.

The last line leads logically into a remarkable series of operatic
vignettes, stirring scenes from six different operas etched with remarkable sharpness and capturing the emotional tension of the
moment portrayed. First the climax from *Norma:*

Across the stage with pallor on her face, yet lurid passion,
Stalks Norma brandishing the dagger in her hand.

Next the Mad Scene from *Lucia di Lammermoor:*

I see poor crazed Lucia's eyes' unnatural gleam,
Her hair down her back falls loose and dishevel'd.

From *Ernani* the tragic moment of separation:

I see where Ernani walking the bridal garden,
Amid the scent of night-roses, radiant, holding his bride
      by the hand,
Hears the infernal call, the death-pledge of the horn.

The great Trombone Duet from *I Puritani:*

To crossing swords and gray hairs bared to heaven,
The clear electric base and baritone of the world,
The trombone duo, Libertad forever!

One of the poet's favorite scenes in all opera, from *La Favorita:*

From Spanish chestnut trees' dense shade,
By old and heavy convent walls a wailing song,
Song of lost love, the torch of youth and life quench'd in
      despair,
Song of the dying swan, Fernando's heart is breaking.

And finally, the joyful awakening scene from *La Sonnambula:*

> Awaking from her woes at last retriev'd Amina sings,
> Copious as stars and glad as morning light the torrents of
>   her joy.[2]

As a climax to these vivid impressions of the opera stage (only *Lucrezia Borgia* of Whitman's favorite operas is missing) comes the only reference to a singer by name in the poems:

> The teeming lady comes,
> The lustrous orb, Venus contralto, the blooming mother,
> Sister of loftiest gods, Alboni's self I hear.

These are not Whitman's greatest lines, but his intention is clear: Alboni was the absolute zenith of all his musical experiences.

Other types of music which had influenced the poet are by no means omitted in the poem. For example, the violin is significantly mentioned:

> The tongues of violins,
> (I think O tongues ye tell this heart, that cannot tell itself,
> This brooding yearning heart, that cannot tell itself.)[3]

And religious music, the great oratorios and masses sung by great festival choirs, the thunder of great organs, these sounds are re-created as the poet yearns to assimilate them all.

> To organs huge and bands I hear as from vast concourses
>   of voices,
> Luther's strong hymn *Eine feste Burg ist unser Gott,*
> Rossini's *Stabat Mater dolorosa.*
> Or floating in some high cathedral dim with gorgeous
>   color'd windows,
> The passionate *Agnus Dei* or *Gloria in Excelsis.*[4]

The most important aspect of the poem has already been pointed out: Its conclusion to the effect that music was poetry of a new kind to Whitman. That is the conclusion to which most of the poems on musical subjects ultimately point.

An illuminating comment on the influence of music on Whitman in the days just before the outbreak of the Civil War, the days when he was writing and publishing his first three editions of *Leaves of Grass,* is "That Music Always Round Me,"[5] which first appeared in 1860.

> That music always round me, unceasing, unbeginning, yet
>   long untaught I did not hear,
> But now the chorus I hear and am elated,
> A tenor, strong, ascending with power and health, with
>   glad notes of daybreak I hear,
> A soprano at intervals sailing buoyantly over the tops of
>   immense waves,
> A transparent base shuddering lusciously under and
>   through the universe,
> The triumphant tutti, the funeral wailings with sweet flutes
>   and violins, all these I fill myself with,
> I hear not the volumes of sound merely, I am moved by
>   the exquisite meanings,
> I listen to the different voices winding in and out, striving,
>   contending with fiery vehemence to excel each other
>   in emotion;
> I do not think the performers know themselves—but now
>   I think I begin to know them.

There are a good many important implications here which substantiate what we have already noted in the background section of this study. Great music had not always been inspiring to Whitman because he had not always understood it. Once it became comprehensible to him he was elated by it and felt himself in the midst of it almost constantly. What kind of music was it which so moved him? The opera with its chorus, its powerful and jubilant tenor, its soaring soprano, its organ-point bass, and its great climaxes where voices and orchestra combine to stir the soul. But it is not only the 'volume of sound' that is important; it is the meanings which the poet realizes under the influence of sound which are important to him, important in mystical ways of which not even the singers themselves are aware. We could scarcely ask for a more forthright confession of inspiration than this brief poem.

Other poems present the same idea somewhat less obviously. Most important is "Out of the Cradle Endlessly Rocking,"[6] which has already been examined for its important contribution to our knowledge of how Whitman became a poet. Furthermore, one entire section of "Song of Myself"[7] is important for what it shows of the significance of music to Whitman. It is devoted to suggesting, in detail, ways in which a wide variety of sounds have entered into the personality and character of the poet and thence into his poem.

Now I will do nothing but listen,
To accrue what I hear into this song, to let sounds contribute toward it. . . .

The sounds are varied in the extreme; there are bird songs, city noises, and workers' calls. As always, music is given the position of greatest importance. First, two instruments are mentioned, the violoncello and the cornet, and the poet's physical response noted:

It shakes mad-sweet pangs through my belly and breast. . . .

Then comes the climax of music, opera.

I hear the chorus, it is a grand opera,
Ah this indeed is music—this suits me.

A tenor large and fresh as the creation fills me,
The orbic flex of his mouth is pouring and filling me full.

I hear the train'd soprano (what work with hers is this?)
The orchestra whirls me wider than Uranus flies,
It wrenches such ardors from me I did not know I pos-
sess'd them,
It sails me, I dab with bare feet, they are lick'd by the
indolent waves,
I am cut by bitter and angry hail, I lose my breath,
Steep'd amid honey'd morphine, my windpipe throttled in
fakes of death,
At length let up again to feel the puzzle of puzzles,
And that we call Being.

This is, of course, the poetic version of the manuscript note already examined. It explains somewhat less literally than the manuscript the effects of a mystical absorption in operatic music, effects which were always related in terms of physical sensations, but it is quite as suggestive as the original. And it is important to observe the important position Whitman gave it in its final form.

In another poem, the short "I Heard You Solemn-Sweet Pipes of the Organ,"[8] Whitman again listed musical sounds with opera as the climax. This time the list provides the material for a love poem; the highest tribute to the loved one is that her voice is re-called by this wonderful music. The solemn-sweet pipes of the organ are heard, and the sighing of the winds. Then:

> I heard the perfect Italian tenor singing at the opera,
>   I heard the soprano in the midst of the quartet singing;
> Heart of my love! you too I heard murmuring low. . . .[9]

Another poem concerning the music of the opera, is "Italian Music in Dakota."[10] In the evening the poet hears a military band on a Dakota post play operatic airs. Strangely, there is no incongruity; the music is still inspiring and even yields "meanings unknown before." Strains from *Sonnambula*, *Norma*, and *Poliuto* seem perfectly appropriate in this far-away place. Nature, "sovereign of this gnarl'd realm," seems to listen and approve, attesting the universality of the well-loved melodies.

This example of Whitman's poetic treatment of instrumental music leads to a mention of a few of the many other passages. "The Mystic Trumpeter,"[11] already referred to, is the most notable example, but there is also the shrill and excited "Beat! Beat! Drums!"[12] with its loud and irresistible bugle calls to war. Beside it may be noticed the same drums and bugles playing low-keyed music of slow and somber rhythm in "Dirge for Two Veterans."[13]

> The moon gives you light,
> And the bugles and the drums give you music,
> And my heart, O my soldiers, my veterans,
> My heart gives you love.

And of course there are such revealing lines as those in "Song of Myself" where the poet characterizes the music of so much of his work, lines beginning:

> With music strong I come, with my cornets and drums,
> I play not marches for accepted victors only,
>   I play marches for conquer'd and slain persons. . . .[14]

It has been pointed out that Whitman was devoted to musical personalities as such, great vocal artists whose gifts and skill he felt he could never sufficiently praise. His poems reflect this trait, of course. Three compositions concern singers whom he had often heard and admired. One, "To A Certain Cantatrice,"[15] is directed to Alboni and found its place among the Inscriptions in the poet's final arrangement of *Leaves of Grass*. In it he dedicates his poems to her. He explains that he had supposed he would reserve the dedication for some renowned public figure who had served the progress and freedom of the race. But he has discovered that the dedication belongs to the singer as much as to any. Through her inspiring effect upon the poet, an effect he often confessed, she, too, had advanced "the good old cause."

The second poem to a singer is the memorial tribute to Brignoli, "The Dead Tenor."[16] The third work, "The Singer in Prison,"[17] is longer than the others and quite different from them. It is based upon an incident in which Parepa-Rosa, the famous singer, visited a prison and sang for its inmates. The poem makes of the dramatic moment when the singer performed with great conviction and beauty of tone a simple and moving hymn of the heavenly pardoner, death, an instance showing the strange power of music to electrify and inspire. On hearing the beautiful hymn, the hardened criminals recall better days in their youth:

> The long-pent spirit rous'd to reminiscence;
> A wondrous minute then—but after in the solitary night,
>   to many, many there,
> Years after, even in the hour of death, the sad refrain, the
>   tune, the voice, the words,
> Resumed, the large calm lady walks the narrow aisle,
> The wailing melody again, the singer in the prison sings,
>   *O sight of pity, shame and dole!*
>   *O fearful thought—a convict soul.*[18]

It was not only the music of the trained artist, of the opera house and concert hall, that Whitman sought to interpret and present in his poems, however. The irregular and undisciplined but impressive music of nature and the world about him appealed strongly to him, and his poetry is continually enriched by his references to it. Often he is simply responsive, as any music-lover would be, to the noises about him which in some way or other seemed musical to him, as in the rich fabric of city sounds he re-creates in "Song of Myself."

> I hear all sounds running together, combined, fused or
>   following,
> Sounds of the city and sounds out of the city, sounds of the
>   day and night,
> Talkative young ones to those that like them, the loud
>   laugh of work-people at their meals,

The angry base of disjointed friendship, the faint tones of
    the sick,
The judge with hands tight to the desk, his pallid lips
    pronouncing a death sentence,
The heave'e'yo of stevedores unlading ships by the wharves,
    the refrain of anchor-lifters,
The ring of alarm-bells, the cry of fire, the whirr of swift-
    streaking engines, and hose-carts with premonitory
    tinkles and colored lights,
The steam-whistle, the solid roll of the train of approach-
    ing cars,
The slow march play'd at the head of the association
    marching two and two,
(They go to guard some corpse, the flag-tops are draped
    with black muslin.) [19]

Of course one cannot help noticing that even in a passage such as
this the sounds of the human voice emerge prominently, always
claiming first interest from Whitman.

It will be recalled how the sounds of the city, cacophonous to
some but musical to him, drew Whitman finally away from the
quieter charm of the country in "Give Me the Splendid Silent
Sun."[20]

The endless and noisy chorus, the rustle and clank of
    muskets, (even the sight of the wounded,)
Manhattan crowds, with their turbulent musical chorus!
Manhattan faces and eyes forever for me. . . .

The progress of a company of soldiers was sometimes described
in terms of music.

They take a serpentine course, their arms flash in the sun—
    hark to the musical clank. . . .[21]

Even the sounds of workers had the ingredients of a kind of
primitive music, sometimes described with an exactness which
could have resulted only from a keen ear and first-hand experience.

The carpenter dresses his plank, the tongue of his fore-
    plane whistles its wild ascending lisp. . . .[22]

And the woodsmen of the West Coast were presented as existing
in a kind of intricate pattern of sound.

In the echo of teamsters' calls and the clinking chains, and
    the music of choppers' axes,
The falling trunk and limbs, the crash, the muffled shriek,
    the groan. . . .[23]

Of course Whitman was particularly sensitive to the scraps of
actual music which any city-dweller is bound to hear. He wove these
snatches of musical sound into his lines frequently.

Pleas'd with the tune of the choir of the whitewash'd
    church. . . .[24]

The pure contralto sings in the organ loft. . . .[25]

The parades, processions, bugles playing, flags flying,
    drums beating. . . .[26]

The boy I love. . . .
First-rate to ride, to fight, to hit the bull's eye, to sail a
    skiff, to sing a song or play a banjo. . . .[27]

The music falling in where it is wanted, and stopping
    where it is not wanted,
The cheerful voice of the public road, the gay fresh senti-
    ment of the road. . . .[28]

Fitted for only banquets of the night where dancers to
    late music slide. . . .[29]

They fill their hour, the dancers dance, the musicians play
    for them. . . .[30]

Fingers of the organist skipping staccato over the keys of
    the great organ. . . .[31]

The dim-lit churches and the shuddering organs. . . .[32]

The glad clear sound of one's own voice, the merry
    song. . . .[33]

Whitman was by no means insensitive to the music of nature,
however, and though we often think of him as having drawn his
imagery largely from the city, this is not entirely the case. Indeed,
he was fascinated by storms, and "Proud Music of the Storm"
opens with a magnificent statement of splendid musical effects as
a furious gale lashes the world and thrills a sensitive beholder. The
varied tone colors and vast volumes of sound of the orchestra are
there, as well as the vibrant and thrilling chorus of voices, all blending in pulsing rhythms of compelling power. But the milder forms
of nature were musical, too.

> The youth lies awake in the cedar-roof'd garret and harks
>   to the musical rain. . . .[34]

And even the lowly katy-did on summer evenings suggested a wood-
wind instrument and its rapid scales.

> Where the katy-did works her chromatic reed on the
>   walnut-tree over the well. . . .[35]

There was also for Whitman an especially deep and suggestive
music in the ocean, which he often re-created in his poetry.

> With whistling winds and music of the waves, the large
>   imperious waves. . . .[36]

> The tones of unseen mystery, the vague and vast sugges-
>   tions of the briny world, the liquid-flowing syllables,
> The perfume, the faint creaking of the cordage, the mel-
>   ancholy rhythm. . . .[37]

> The heaving sea, the waves upon the shore, the musical,
>   strong waves. . . .[38]

> As I walked where the ripples continually wash you
>   Paumanok,
> Where they rustle up hoarse and sibilant. . . .[39]

It is important to notice in such passages as these how Whitman
translated the sounds of nature into music, often employing musical
terms in so doing. Music was of course the most moving force in
his emotional make-up, and it was natural for him to discover music
in sounds that affected him deeply, at least to speak of these sounds
in terms of music.

One final poem should be mentioned in this chapter which calls
attention to Whitman's poetic work devoted to music. It is "On
the Beach at Night Alone,"[40] ordinarily thought of as primarily a
sea poem. Indeed, Whitman placed it in the section of his book
called "Sea-Drift." But a clue to the poem's real significance is gained
from its original title, "Clef Poem."[41] In successive editions of the
book the poem was much edited, the principal change being the
omission of a score or so of lines on immortality. The real meaning
was not changed, however. As the poet stands alone on the beach,
listening to the haunting and almost hypnotic sound of the sea,
he reflects upon the organization of the universe. He realizes that
in spite of outward differences which seem to divide the world, bar-

riers of geography, biology, civilization, even time itself which seems to give the past, the present, and the future independent existences, in spite of all these differences "a vast similitude interlocks all . . . and shall forever span them and compactly hold and enclose them." The central and focusing image for this universal organization which insures everlasting and fundamental harmony in the world comes from music.

> On the beach at night alone,
> As the old mother sways her to and fro singing her husky song,
> As I watch the bright stars shining, I think a thought of the clef of the universes and of the future.[42]

Just as in music an underlying principle brings beauty to tones that would otherwise be harsh and dissonant, so a principle, or clef, in the universe organizes its parts into permanent system.

Only an ardent devotee, to whom music was much more than pleasant amusement, would have written so many poems devoted to music entirely. And only a writer for whom music was a constant inspiration would have turned so consistently to music for help in conveying his ideas to others.

NOTES—CHAPTER I

1. Inclusive Edition, p. 339.
2. Ibid., p. 340.
3. Ibid., p. 338.
4. Ibid., p. 341. Alice L. Cooke has pointed out that the Handel-Haydn oratorio festivals of 1868 may have inspired these particular references. The poem first appeared in that year. "Ein Feste Burg" was sung by a chorus of 10,000 voices in the Boston Peace Jubilee of 1869, and preparation for the event may have led to the reference here.—Alice L. Cooke, "Notes on Whitman's Musical Background," New England Quarterly, XIX, 224-35 (June, 1946).
5. Inclusive Edition, p. 374.
6. Ibid., p. 210.
7. Ibid., p. 47.
8. Ibid., p. 93.
9. Ibid., p. 94.
10. Ibid., p. 334.
11. Ibid., p. 389.
12. Ibid., p. 240.
13. Ibid., p. 265.
14. Ibid., p. 38.

15. *Ibid.*, p. 8.
16. *Ibid.*, p. 431.
17. *Ibid.*, p. 316.
18. *Ibid.*, p. 317.
19. *Ibid.*, p. 47.
20. *Ibid.*, p. 265.
21. Cavalry Crossing a Ford," *Ibid.*, p. 254.
22. "Song of Myself," *Ibid.*, p. 34.
23. "Song of the Redwood-Tree," *Ibid.*, p. 177.
24. "Song of Myself," *Ibid.*, p. 54.
25. "Song of Myself," *Ibid.*, p. 34.
26. "Manhattan," *Ibid.*, p. 694.
27. "Song of Myself," *Ibid.*, p. 72.
28. "Song of the Open Road," *Ibid.*, p. 125.
29. "Song of the Exposition," *Ibid.*, p. 171.
30. "Song of the Broad-Axe," *Ibid.*, p. 160.
31. *Ibid.*, p. 156.
32. "When Lilacs Last in the Dooryard Bloom'd," *Ibid.*, p. 277.
33. "Song of the Broad-Axe," *Ibid.*, p. 157.
34. "Song of Myself," *Ibid.*, p. 35.
35. "Song of Myself," *Ibid.*, p. 54. A remarkable passage in *Specimen Days* shows further Whitman's close observation of outdoor sounds and tendency to speak of them in terms of music. "A single locust is now heard near noon from a tree two hundred feet off, as I write—a long, whirring, continued, quite loud noise graded in distinct whirls, or swinging circles, increasing in strength and rapidity up to a certain point, and then a fluttering, quietly tapering fall. Each strain is continued from one to two minutes. The locust song is very appropriate to the scene—gushes, has meaning, is masculine. . . ."

"A long, chromatic, tremulous crescendo, like a brass disc whirling round and round, emitting wave after wave of notes, beginning with a certain moderate beat or measure, rapidly increasing in speed and emphasis, reaching a point of great energy and significance, and then quickly and gracefully dropping down and out. Not the melody of the singing bird—far from it; the common musician might think without melody, but surely having to the finer ear a harmony of its own; monotonous, but what a swing there is in that brassy drone, round and round, cymbal-like—or like the whirling of brass quoits."—*Prose*, I, 196.
36. "In Cabin'd Ships at Sea," Inclusive Edition, p. 2.
37. *Ibid.*
38. "The Return of the Heroes," *Ibid.*, p. 301.
39. "As I ebb'd with the Ocean of life," *Ibid.*, p. 216.
40. *Ibid.*, p. 221.
41. See Variorum Readings, *Ibid.*, p. 641.
42. *Ibid.*, p. 221.

CHAPTER II

Diction

IT IS A LOGICAL FACT that creative writers usually betray their deep and consuming interests as well as the cultural background that conditioned their development by the words to which they resort in the expression of their ideas and in the creation of their moods and effects. We should be surprised indeed if a writer who spent his impressionable years at sea could wholly outgrow his background and never fall back on reference to the ocean to intensify an image or sea-talk to clarify an idea. For the same reason we should be surprised to find no musical terms in Walt Whitman's poems, or references to the opera house and its glories in the work of this man who matured artistically under its spell.

The most casual glancing through *Leaves of Grass* yields evidence that there are musical terms in abundance, and an only slightly more intensive study shows the preponderance of words associated with vocal music, especially opera. But in Whitman we note almost at once a circumstance different from that in which a writer naturally uses the language of his own background in conveying to others ideas on universal topics. Whitman seems to have been attracted to the language of the world of music for its own sake and to have attempted to use technical words in nontechnical ways, believing that the words would prove valuable additions to the general vocabulary.

In his fragmentary study of language, *An American Primer*, he wrote, "Music has many good words, now technical, but of such rich and juicy character that they ought to be taken for common use in writing and speaking."[1] Whitman was particularly fond of words which gave the articulator an opportunity for vocal display and naturally found the Italian and French musical terms much to his liking.[2]

An example of the mouth-filling technical musical term employed by Whitman in a general sense is *romanza*. Technically the term

115

is applied to a relatively short aria, usually employing only one musical subject and presenting highly romantic material. That Whitman probably knew its strict operatic meaning is suggested by his use of it in "A Song for Occupations,"[3] in which he speaks of "the baritone singer singing his sweet romanza."[4] In "Song of the Answerer,"[5] however, he uses it much more loosely to mean simply song.

> Now list to my morning's romanza, I tell the signs of the
>   Answerer,
> To the cities and farms I sing as they spread in the sunshine before me.

He uses it again in the same poem with the same meaning. Clearly, he simply liked the sound of the word and decided to use it, whether it applied technically or not.

Another term for which he had something of the same feeling was cantabile. Strictly speaking, the word is an adjective and means "having the qualities of song" or "in a flowing style." Whitman used it invariably as a noun, roughly synonymous with "melodious song." He was doubtless quite deliberate in his loose usage, feeling that the musical sound of the word was sufficient justification for almost any usage. In "A Broadway Pageant"[6] he addressed his "song," or composition, as some poets have addressed their muse: "See my cantabile! these and more are flashing to us from the procession."[7] In "Proud Music of the Storm"[8] the word is used to indicate a kind of melodious accompaniment: "A festival song . . . to flutes' clear notes and sounding harps' cantabile." In "The Dead Tenor"[9] cantabile means simply song:

> I fold thenceforth, or seek to fold, within my chants transmuting,
> Freedom's and Love's and Faith's unloos'd cantabile. . . .[10]

Still another word of a character sufficiently "rich and juicy" to encourage Whitman to use it in both technical and nontechnical meanings was the word finale. In the strictest sense the term refers to the closing section of a large, formal work of music, usually characterized by a considerable flourish. Whitman used it with a variety of meanings, all related to its origin but all figurative departures from it.

In "The Base of All Metaphysics"[11] the term seems to mean "a final or definitive word":

> A word I give to remain in your memories and minds,
> As base and finalè too for all metaphysics. . . .

Elsewhere *finale* means *end*, but in the sense of "reason for being." Speaking of "Faces"[12] in the poem of that name, Whitman said,

> Do you suppose I could be content with all if I thought
>   them their own finalè?

In "Song at Sunset"[13] the word occurs in an interesting paradox, "I sing the endless finalés of things,"[14] suggesting closing climaxes which seem to go on forever. Perhaps the widest deviation from the original meaning comes in "Now Finalè to the Shore," where it means an end of association or farewell:

> Now finalè to the shore,
> Now land and life finalè and farewell. . . .[15]

Clearly it is the sound of the word Whitman wanted, as in its alliterative use in the last quoted line, rather than a word of strict meaning. In all of the words just mentioned, of course, the matter of associations for the poet must be considered. All of the words sounded glamorous and romantic to him. Their backgrounds in opera gave them a peculiar richness which seemed to impart itself to the context in which they appeared. A *finale* to the shore, or to life, was more moving and heartbreaking than a farewell, just as the lofty and tragic conclusion of an opera with its sweeping and torrential passion was more memorable than a mere good-bye.

Sometimes, inevitably, if the reader's feeling for the word from opera is less than the poet's, if its connotations are fewer for him than for the poet, the line does not gain so much as its author hoped for. In "Passage to India"[16] we come to the lines,

> As the chief histrion,
> Down to the footlights walks in some great scena . . .[17]

If the reader knows that in opera a *scena* is a great soul-shaking moment, composed of a "contrasting succession of solo recitatives and formal airs which represent a character as actuated by a series of varied moods that eventually lead to an emotional climax,"[18] the figure quoted becomes connotative in the extreme. Without that technical knowledge on the reader's part the image is simply that of a stage player in a scene, something considerably less imposing. But writers must always take chances with the backgrounds and perceptions of their readers and enrich their work as best they can, by language which means most to them. In so doing, of course they reveal themselves to their students.

There are many other instances of technical terms in Whitman's poetry. In the significant short poem "That Music Always Round Me,"[19] he used such a term in a position of climax. Having detailed the sound of a variety of voices he described a climactic ensemble as "the triumphant tutti," an expression which he of course learned at the opera house and which suggested cascades of sound pouring from many throats. A particularly effective image combining opera and bird songs, as Whitman was wont to do, was evolved for "Song of Myself."[20] To describe the showy brilliance and highly decorated musical runs and trills of the bird song he referred to the "bravuras of birds."[21] In the opera house the term was used to describe just such florid, coloratura song, such music as that written for the heroine of La Sonnambula, for example.

While not exclusively an operatic word, bacchanal would certainly be richly suggestive to an opera devotee who had seen a frenzied ballet. "Riotous laughing bacchanals fill'd with joy!"[22] was the way Whitman used the word in "The Mystic Trumpeter"[23] to suggest the overthrow of restraint, care, and sorrow. And in "Out of the Cradle,"[24] a term which at first looks gauche indeed is discovered to be singularly appropriate in its technical meaning.

> Shake out carols!
> Solitary here, the night's carols. . . .[25]

In one sense, the verb to shake means to execute a musical trill, and though it is rarely used in that sense today, it was commonly heard in Whitman's opera-going years. As it appears in the bird's song, the term which was an almost perfect synonym for trill gives exactly the effect the poet wanted.

All of the words discussed so far are related to opera or singing, though there are many technical terms not strictly from this field of music in Leaves of Grass, and they suggest, as we know to be

the case, that Whitman's knowledge of music was not limited exclusively to opera. Such words as *bolero, cadenza, chromatic, clef,
diapason, dolce affetuoso, embouchure,* and *staccato* show his familiarity with music generally. So does his mention of twenty-five
different musical instruments. The list includes banjo, bells, bugle,
castanets, cornet, cymbal, drum, fife, flageolet, flute, guitar, harp,
horn, lyre, oboe, piano, rebeck, reed, trombone, trumpet, tympanum,
vina, violin, and violoncello.

As in the instances of the technical words from opera, Whitman
often resorted to the special language of general music to create
an image that to him was especially effective. For example, in "Starting from Paumanok,"[26] when he wished to identify himself as
rugged and robust, he declared:

No dainty dolce affettuoso I. . . .[27]

The fact that the Italian terms were adjectives meaning *sweet* and
emotional bothered him not in the least. He had encountered them
to describe a certain kind of delicate, precious music, which he dis-
liked, and he turned them together into a noun for his purpose.

This usage is another example of his love for and loose usage of
especially "vocal" words; usually he was more accurate. In describing the sound of a katy-did, for instance, he spoke of her "chromatic
reed,"[28] which is an exact description of a sound and a precise use
of *chromatic,* which means "giving all the tones of the chromatic
scale." The line

I blow through my embouchures my loudest and gayest
   for them. . . .[29]

shows that he knew and could use exactly if a little ostentatiously
the terminology of wind instruments. Another line

Fingers of the organist skipping staccato over the keys of
   the great organ. . . .[30]

is a similarly exact usage of a word describing a manner of performing musical notes.

In the matter of musical instruments themselves, he was particularly skillful in referring to various ones to help in the establishment of a precise mood. He had heard most of the instruments
he mentioned, and he was keenly sensitive to the special emotional

effect of the various instrumental tone colors. The trumpet and
bugle figure most largely in his verse, and appropriately enough,
for there are stirring, rousing, and richly emotional qualities in the
bright tones of these instruments when they are well played, qualities which Whitman sought for his verse. The pipe-organ also appears often. The poet needed not only brilliant, ringing tones, but
also the deep rumbling of the organ, with its capabilities for immense, encompassing volume and somber, dark coloring.

> Now the great organ sounds,
> Tremulous, while underneath, . . .
> . . . .
>
> The strong base stands, and its pulsations intermits not,
> Bathing, supporting, merging all the rest. . . .[31]

The piano is also introduced into Whitman's lines, but invariably
with scorn. He found its effect tinkling and small, the very opposite
to what he wanted in his great rhapsodies. He once admitted preju-
dice to his friend, Horace Traubel, and agreed that he had probably
never heard the instrument properly played.[32] Furthermore, his
English friend and admirer, Mrs. Anne Gilchrist, complained to
him about his blind spot. She wrote him in 1876:

By the bye, I feel a little sulky at your always taking a fling at the poor
piano. I see that I have got to try to show you it too is capable of waking
deep chords in the human soul when it is the vehicle of a great master's
thought and emotion—if only my poor fingers prove equal to the task.[33]

The instrument remained, however, one of his most consistently
used symbols for shallow, inconsequential, traditional poetry.

> And go lull yourself with what you can understand, and
>   with piano-tunes,
> For I lull nobody, and you will never understand me.[34]
>
> (No sweetness debonair of tearful harp or glib piano
>   thine)[35]

On one occasion he employed the term in its strictly Italian sense
as an adjective meaning *soft*, but he was quite as scornful as in
other instances:

> Not you as some pale poetling seated at a desk lisping
>   cadenzas piano. . . .[36]

Only a few lines need be cited to reveal Whitman's skillful handling of the qualities of minor instruments.

The bolero to tinkling guitars and clattering castanets . . .[37]

I hear the Spanish dance with castanets in the chestnut
     shade, to the rebeck and guitar. . . .[38]

I see the Roman youth to the shrill sound of flageolets
     throwing and catching their weapons . . .[39]

. . . the funeral wailings of sweet flutes and violins. . . .[40]

Perhaps the most interesting of Whitman's uses of the words of music are not to be found in lines dealing with the material of music, but in passages where he resorted to such words to convey ideas which he found difficult to present in any other way. Attention has already been called to the way in which the term *clef* provided him with a central focus for his important reflection "On the Beach at Night Alone." And his consistent use of the terms *song, chant, recitative* for his own bardic poems is known even to casual readers. But there are many other examples which explain themselves.

The melodious character of the earth . . .[41]

Why are there trees I never walk under but large melodious
     thoughts descend upon me?[42]

O such themes—equalities! . . .
Strains musical flowing through ages, now reaching hither
I take to your reckless and composite chords, add to them,
     and cheerfully pass them forward.[43]

I, chanter of Adamic songs . . .
Deliriate, thus prelude what is generated, offering these,
     offering myself. . . .[44]

Whispers of heavenly death murmur'd I hear,
Labial gossip of night, sibilant chorals. . . .[45]

Many, many more lines could be listed to show the important fact that the language of music was indispensable to Whitman for the communication of ideas. He seemed often to think in terms of music, just as he was inspired by it; and when he came to present some of his most significant "meanings," to use his word, music gave him the required language.

When a list of all the words related to music found in *Leaves of Grass* is compiled, some most revealing deductions about Whitman's vocabulary may be made. First, upon examination of the diction of the titles exclusively, it is discovered that twenty-two different musical terms appear, used forty-seven times. Of these terms, fourteen refer specifically to vocal music: ballad, cantatrice, carol, chant, chanting, finale, prelude, sing, singer, singing, song, tenor, vocalism, warble. The word *song* alone occurs seventeen times. Surely few other poets have felt impelled so often to entitle their creations in terms of music.

In the poems, two hundred and six different musical words can be found. Of these, omitting general terms like *music* and *notes*, as well as the names of musical instruments, one hundred twenty-three words have to do with vocal music. Of this list, in turn, eighty-three are specifically related to opera. In other words, considerably more than one-third of all the musical usages are derived from opera. It is also important to notice that within the list of opera terms, six are the names of composers; thirteen are the titles of operas; six are the names of characters in opera, and one is the name of a great opera singer.

Most of the different terms ordinarily encountered in discussing opera performance can be found. For example, there are score, conductor, orchestra, baton, overture, prelude, recitative, aria, scena, chorus, ensemble, duet, trio, quartette, soprano, contralto, tenor, baritone, bass. These are in addition to such technical words as have already been noticed, like *romanza*, *shake*, *tutti*, and the like.

However, while the greatest number of words related to an individual department of music concern opera, as might be expected, the words which occur most frequently are general in nature. Six terms appear more than thirty times each. It is important to note that all but one of these, *music*, have to do with singing. The list and the number of usages follow: *song*, 154; *sing* (all forms except singing) 117; *singing*, 45; *singers*, 36; *music*, 30. Thus it seems quite clear that Whitman was greatly concerned with "singing songs," as far as music in general was concerned, and that opera and its effects and departments were his particular interest in music.

To be sure, lists of words such as we have been compiling and analyzing prove nothing. They are suggestive, however, and Whitman's repeated confession that music had been the greatest influence on his poetry seems amply borne out by the great number of words it contributed to his vocabulary. A list of all such words is here provided.

Music Vocabulary in *Leaves of Grass*
(Numbers indicate frequency of appearance)

Titles

1 ballad	1 lilt
2 beat	3 music
1 bells	1 organ
1 cantatrice	1 prelude
2 carols	4 sing
2 chant	1 singer
1 chanting	2 singing
1 dirge	17 song
1 drum-taps	1 tenor
1 drums	1 vocalism
1 finale	1 warble

Poems

1 accompaniment	1 cadenza
2 airs	3 cantabile
1 Alboni	16 carol
1 anthems	3 caroling
2 aria	2 castanets
2 audience	2 chansonnier
	1 chansons
	77 chant
1 bacchanals	4 chanter
5 ballad	8 chanting
4 band	1 choir
1 banjo	1 chorals
2 baritone	6 chord
6 base (bass)	10 chorus
1 bassi	1 chromatic
1 baton	1 clang
7 beat	1 clef
1 bells	3 composer
1 blare	8 composers by name
14 blow	1 conductor
1 bolero	2 contralto
1 bravura	5 cornet
12 bugles	2 cymbals

Poems

1 dance music	1 maestros
2 dead-march	8 marches
2 diapason	1 masses
8 dirge	1 measure
1 dolce affetuoso	6 melodious
19 drum	2 melody
2 drummer	1 minnesingers
1 duet	2 minstrels
2 dulcet	1 minstrelsy
1 duo	30 music
	14 musical
1 embouchures	1 music-house
1 ensemble	6 musicians
	1 music-song
1 fiddler	
1 fife	15 notes
6 finale	
1 flageolets	
6 flue	1 oboe
1 full-key'd	1 odes
	6 opera
	6 opera characters by name
1 glee	1 opera house
1 gleemen	1 opera-music
1 grand-opera	13 opera titles by name
2 guitar	1 oratorio
	1 orotund
1 harmony	5 orchestra
4 harp	12 organ
1 harper	1 organist
1 heart-chants	3 overture
1 horn	
2 hum	2 piano
10 hymn	1 piano-tunes
	5 play
8 instruments	1 players
	1 playing
1 jiggs	7 prelude
	2 programme
1 key	3 psalm
1 lays	1 quartette
2 lilt	
2 lullaby	2 rattle
1 lyre	1 rebeck

Poems

8 recitative	1 timbre
2 reed	1 toll
1 reedy	2 tolling
6 refrain	4 tones
1 reverberation	1 tremulous
1 resonant	4 trill
1 roll	1 trilling
3 romanza	1 trombone
	1 trio
5 sacred music by title	3 troubadour
1 sailor song	4 trumpet
1 scena	10 trumpeter
1 score	1 trumpet-note
2 serenades	1 trumpet-voice
1 shake	5 tune
117 sing (all forms)	1 tuning
36 singers	1 tutti
45 singing	1 tympanum
2 singing voice	
154 song	1 valved
1 soprani	1 vina
5 soprano	3 violin
1 staccato	1 violoncello
13 strain	2 vocalist
1 strophe	
3 symphonies	1 waltz
5 tenor	1 wind (trumpet)
1 tenori	9 warble
5 theme	3 warbling
1 thrum	1 wardrum

NOTES—CHAPTER II

1. *An American Primer*, p. 7.
2. See Louise Pound, "Walt Whitman and the French Language," *American Speech*, I, 421-30 (May, 1926).
3. Inclusive Edition, p. 179.
4. *Ibid.*, p. 183.
5. *Ibid.*, p. 140.
6. *Ibid.*, p. 206.
7. *Ibid.*, p. 207.
8. *Ibid.*, p. 337.
9. *Ibid.*, p. 431.
10. *Ibid.*, p. 432.
11. *Ibid.*, p. 101.

12. *Ibid.*, p. 386.
13. *Ibid.*, p. 410.
14. *Ibid.*, p. 411.
15. *Ibid.*, p. 416.
16. *Ibid.*, p. 343.
17. *Ibid.*, p. 348.
18. Clarence W. Hamilton, *Music Appreciation, Based on Methods of Literary Criticism* (Boston, 1920), p. 375.
19. Inclusive Edition, p. 374.
20. *Ibid.*, p. 24.
21. *Ibid.*, p. 47.
22. *Ibid.*, p. 392.
23. *Ibid.*, p. 389.
24. *Ibid.*, p. 210.
25. *Ibid.*, p. 213.
26. *Ibid.*, p. 12.
27. *Ibid.*, p. 21.
28. *Ibid.*, p. 54.
29. *Ibid.*, p. 39.
30. *Ibid.*, p. 156.
31. *Ibid.*, p. 338.
32. Traubel, *op. cit.*, I, 223.
33. *The Letters of Anne Gilchrist and Walt Whitman*, ed. Thomas B. Harned (Garden City, N. Y., 1918), p. 143.
34. Inclusive Edition, p. 272.
35. *Ibid.*, p. 393.
36. *Ibid.*, p. 239.
37. *Ibid.*, p. 340.
38. *Ibid.*, p. 115.
39. *Ibid.*, p. 340.
40. *Ibid.*, p. 374.
41. *Ibid.*, p. 389.
42. *Ibid.*, p. 128.
43. *Ibid.*, p. 17.
44. *Ibid.*, p. 91.
45. *Ibid.*, p. 369.

CHAPTER III

Suggestiveness

W HEN WHITMAN became fired with the impulse to compose poems, poems which should "sing" and throb with the sound of the voice, it is natural that he should have conceived as his poetic goal the same kind of inspiration or "suggestiveness," to use his own word, which he had felt under the spell of great vocal music. Over and over again he had felt electrified and roused, to the depths of his emotional nature. These rapturous moments came when a great performer, stirred emotionally by sensing the appreciative response of attentive listeners, would catch fire suddenly and, quite beyond his own ability to explain or analyze, would transcend himself and create art that was not the product of technique or rule alone, but of inspiration. Such moments were the significant ones in the world of art, Whitman believed, for to him art at its best was never a product of the intellect, always of the heart. But this moment of inspiration was a two-way process; the listener had to be present. The singer could never closet himself in his practice room and turn phrases of such haunting beauty or color the tones of his voice with such warmth and splendor as when he felt the existence of this electric current of communication between him and his listener. Then, the bond of common understanding and excitement would elevate both and great art could be achieved.

Whitman pushed this aesthetic conception even further and claimed that great art simply could not exist in a vacuum. Masterpieces of artistic creation are so only when they communicate something to a beholder, when they become "suggestive." He expressed the idea in "A Song for Occupations":[1]

> All architecture is what you do to it when you look upon it,
> (Did you think it was in the white or gray stone? or the
>   lines of the arches and cornices?)

> All music is what awakes from you when you are reminded
>   by the instruments,
> It is not the violins and the cornets, it is not the oboe nor
>   the beating drums, nor the score of the baritone singer
>   singing his sweet romanza, nor that of the men's
>   chorus, nor that of the women's chorus,
> It is nearer and farther than they.[2]

The music of great voices, of course, was more insistent and direct in its appeal to the listener than an artistic edifice to a beholder, and one listening to music could readily experience the exhilaration of communication. The musical performer could feel it, too. Whitman felt himself to be such a performer. His songs, which were in so many ways like the great recitatives and arias in the theatre, needed the listener, the audience. He was singing in his poems, and he could never sing in the practice room. His great, soaring voice was to sound over the roofs of the world, and for its songs to be perfectly effective the audience must always be there, listening. At least the poet could proceed as if it were listening. He could address himself to it, sometimes as if it were the great darkened mass of humanity on the other side of the footlights, unrecognized individually, but there, applauding, laughing, perhaps sighing. Sometimes it might be a single individual, particularly interested and responsive, to whom the singer could unburden his soul.

Whether composed of the many or the one, however, the listening audience is always there in Whitman's poetry, and his conception of art as a process of communication is always apparent. It is most obviously so in his earlier poems, possibly because these were most closely under the influence of opera, possibly because as an inexperienced poet he needed the inspiration of a sense of his listener always at hand. And it is obvious, of course, that the rhapsodical manner is more youthful than the reflective manner, which is natural to age. In any case, all of the poems which best illustrate this artistic conviction were composed before 1860.

Before these poems are examined, however, it will be helpful to notice some of Whitman's discussions of the almost magical situation in the theatre when a performance suddenly becomes electric, and both performer and hearer are carried to heights difficult to explain except in terms of inspiration. Whitman experienced his first such moments at performances of drama, particularly when witnessing the great tragedian, Edwin Booth. "Yes," he wrote, recalling such a performance, "although Booth must be classed in that antique, almost extinct school, inflated, stagy[3]. . . his genius was to me . . . a lesson of artistic expression. The words *fire, energy, abandon,* found in him unprecedented meanings. I never heard a speaker or actor who could give such a sting to hauteur or the taunt."[4] And of the audience at such an occasion he wrote, "The Old Bowery, packed from ceiling to pit with its audience mainly of alert, well dress'd, full-blooded young and middle-aged men . . . the emotional nature of the whole mass arous'd by the power and magnetism of as mighty mimes as ever trod the stage—the whole crowded auditorium and what seethed in it, and flashed from its faces and eyes—bursting forth in one of those tempests of hand clapping peculiar to the Bowery."[5] Again, and still of Booth, Whitman wrote, "I never saw an actor who could make more of the hush or wait, and hold the audience in an indescribable, half-delicious, half-irritating suspense . . . Especially was the dream scene impressive. A shudder went through every nervous system in the audience; it certainly did through mine."[6]

It was because of such possibilities for communicating with the listener, even to the point of "sending a shudder through the nervous system," that Whitman was attracted early in his career to the arts of both drama and oratory. But as he found music loftier than either as an artistic medium, and as his own mystical rapture was far more revealing under the stimulus of music, it is logical to believe that principally, though by no means exclusively, from his devotion to opera came the important ingredient in his literary theory: the belief that creative art involves both performance and response. It is scarcely necessary to repeat here the many quotations already advanced showing his moments of exaltation in the opera house.

The almost abstract emotional *power* of operatic music was to be duplicated in poetry if it was to be of the highest sort, Whitman thought. To achieve such power, poetry, like music, should not attempt to portray, depict, explain; it should inspire, or to use Whitman's own word, it should *suggest.* So his poems were to suggest meanings and truth rather than explain or present them, and they were to do so by communicating directly and inspiringly with the reader, as the opera singer did with the listener.

It was proper that a poet should so regard his function, Whitman believed, for he could not hope to explain nature by commenting on it, and he ought not to try to interpose any artificial interpretation of nature between it and the beholder. Natural objects are themselves the truest poems.[7] Thus it was to be the poet's job merely to call attention to natural things, to suggest meanings, to give clues to understandings. "I put not in the following leaves melodious narratives, or pictures for you to con at leisure, or bright creations all outside yourself," Whitman said. "But of suggestiveness alone out of the things around us, with steady reference to the life to come, and to the miracles of everyday this is the song."[8] Again he said, "I do not propose to school man in virtues nor prove anything to his intellect . . . The ordinary critic . . . likely sees not the only valuable part of these leaves, namely, not what they state, but what they infer—scornfully wants to know what the Mocking-Bird means, who can tell? gives credit only for what is proved on the surface—ear—and makes up a very fine criticism, not out of the soul, to which these poems altogether appeal, and by which only they can be interpreted, but out of the intellect."[9] In other words Whitman wanted the appeal of his poems to be exactly the appeal of music.

Of course this expansive and mystical view of poetry had its dangers, just as musical composition could not be fool-proof, and Whitman was aware of the risks. He was quite willing to take them, however, as he explained in the preface to the 1876 edition of Leaves of Grass.

I have not been afraid of the charge of obscurity . . . because human thought, poetry or melody, must leave dim escapes and outlets—must possess a certain fluid, aerial character, akin to space itself, obscure to those of little or no imagination, but indispensable to the highest purposes. Poetic style when address'd to the soul is less definite form, outline, sculpture, and becomes vista, music, half-tints, and even less than half-tints.[10]

Even he was sometimes baffled by his own inspirations. "Has not the chaos of my pages its purpose enclosing it? its clue or formulation? No—no more than nature has. Or, if it has, Reader dear, it

is not in the usual way. . . . Upon the whole, it puzzles me and
evades me more than anybody."[11] This is certainly the confession
of the mystic, the seer, obediently following his inspiration.

Whatever the risks, it was this kind of poetry which would appeal to the reader in a vital moving way, like music, and it was
important to Whitman that it should. In his poems there is always
an awareness of the poet speaking directly to the reader. And in his
comments on his poems, over and over again, Whitman attempted
to take the reader into his confidence with the most personal sort
of intimacy, for this was part of the poetic as well as the musical
experience. One passage from a preface may serve to illustrate the
point.

For you, O friend whoe'er you are, journeying, at last arriving thither,
accept from me, as one in waiting for you at this entrance, welcome and
hospitality. I feel at every leaf the pressure of your hand, which I return.
And thus throughout upon the journey, linked together we go.[12]

This quality of direct communication was almost perfectly described by John Burroughs, and the statement probably reflects
Whitman's own hopes and ideals as well, for he assisted with the
preparation of the book in which the statement appeared.

The dominant impression was of the living presence and voice. He
would have no curtains, he said, not the finest, between himself and
his reader; and in thus bringing me face to face with his subject I perceived he did not only escape conventional art, but I perceived an enlarged, enfranchised art in this very abnegation of art. "When half-
gods go, whole gods arrive." It was obvious to me that the new style
gained more than it lost, and that in this fullest operatic launching
forth of the voice, though it sounded strangely at first, and required the
ear to get used to it, there might be quite as much science, and a good
deal more power, than in the tuneful but constricted measures we were
accustomed to.[13]

Of course, just as in the opera house the music was inspiring but
incomplete as voiced by the artist until the abstract tone was translated by the sensitive listener into meanings and truth, so was it to
be important for the reader of Whitman's poetry to be creative.
The poet but launched the creative act, Whitman thought; the
reader must complete it. "Indeed, I have not done the work and
cannot do it," he said. "But you must do the work to really make

what is within the following song."[14] The poet but calls attention to natural phenomena; the reader must suddenly realize the meaning and significance, if the poem is successful.

Such—and from where it lurks, indeed within yourself, for every apparition in this world is but to rout the real object up from sleeping in yourself, that something, to remind you, may appear, before your very feet or under them—that fuses past and present and to-come in One, and never doubts them more.

A little lowly thing, yet shining brighter then the sun, perfuming strange the hour that bathes you, the spot you stand on, and every drop of blood that courses through your veins. Belief implicit, comprehending all,—may prove our journey's gift.[15]

The kind of creative reading of his poems which Whitman hoped for is perfectly revealed in a frank account of how the poems affected her by Mrs. Anne Gilchrist, who later came to be one of the poet's most devoted friends and admirers. The account was written before she knew what Whitman wanted in his readers, except as she sensed it in the poems themselves. It is easy to see why he came to regard her as his ideal reader. The passage follows:

I had not dreamed that words could cease to be words, and become electric streams like these. I do assure you that, strong as I am, I feel sometimes as if I had not bodily strength to read many of these poems. In . . . the poem beginning "Tears, Tears," etc., there is such a weight of emotion, such a tension of the heart, that mine refuses to beat under it,—stands quite still,—and I am obliged to lay the book down for a while. Or again . . . I am as one hurried through stormy seas, over high mountains, dazed with sunlight, stunned with a crowd and tumult of faces and voices, till I am breathless, bewildered, half dead . . . Living impulses flow out of these [poems].[16]

How curiously like Whitman's own response to music these words are.

It is necessary to turn to the poems themselves to discover the application of Whitman's theory that poetry, like opera, must be inspirational and suggestive, arousing in the reader a strong response through establishing a bond of communication directly with him. There are some lines, first of all, which reproduce the operatic situation in which such inspiration occurs, such as those in "A Passage to India,"[17] in which the impressive hero, Columbus, is suggested:

> As the chief histrion,
> Down to the footlights walks in some great scena,
> Dominating the rest I see the Admiral himself,
> (History's type of courage, action, faith,) . . .[18]

But this is only a reference to the opera stage. In the opening
sections of "Starting from Paumanok,"[19] there are lines more exactly suggesting the poet to be a performer appealing to an audience.

> See, projected through time,
> For me an audience interminable.

> With firm and regular step they wend, they never stop,
> Successions of men, Americanos, a hundred millions. . . .
> . . . .
> With faces turn'd sideways or backward towards me to
>   listen,
> With eyes retrospective towards me.

Then follow immediately some lines which in their very terminology could have come straight from the poet's experience in the
opera house.

> Americanos! conquerors! marches humanitarian!
> Foremost! century marches! Libertad! masses!
> For you a programme of chants.

> Chants of the prairies,
> Chants of the long-running Mississippi, and down to the
>   Mexican sea,
> . . . .
> Shooting in pulses of fire ceaseless to vivify all.[20]

Here, in other words, is an address to the audience, a presentation of
a "programme," and, most important, a description of the emotional experience hoped for. Elsewhere the poet again refers to the
"pulses of fire" which he aims at in his poems. In "Song at Sunset"[21]
we find the lines:

> I praise with electric voice,
> For I do not see one imperfection in the universe,
> And I do not see one cause or result lamentable at last in
>   the universe.[22]

A passage in "Song of Myself"[23] describes the performer-audience
situation almost exactly and suggests vividly how the poet en-
visioned himself in the performer's role.

> A call in the midst of the crowd,
> My own voice, orotund sweeping and final.
>
> Come my children,
> Come my boys and girls, my women, household and
> intimates,
> Now the performer launches his nerve, he has pass'd his
> prelude on the reeds within.
>
> Easily written loose-finger'd chords—I feel the thrum of
> your climax and close.[24]

It is important to notice how the poet, as inspiration begins to seize him, lapses into musical terms to describe his composition. The last line quoted, as a matter of fact, is not an inexact definition of the music in *Leaves of Grass*.

As has been suggested, the conception of his poems as involving both himself and his audience is reflected in various ways in Whitman. All have in common, however, the electrifying current of communication between artist and beholder. That was what was important to him. One evidence of this, certainly, is the realistic, and to readers of his own day, vulgar, intimacy with which he often approached his reader as an individual.

> But each man and each woman of you I lead upon a knoll,
> My left hand hooking you round the waist,
> My right hand pointing to landscapes of continents and
> the public road.[25]
>
> Shoulder your duds dear son, and I will mine, and let us
> hasten forth,
> Wonderful cities and free nations we shall fetch as we go.[26]

It must be noticed how the intimacies exist always for the possibility of stimulation. The poet walks close to the reader but only so that vast "landscapes of continents," as well as the significance of "the public road" close by, may be suggested.

What he hoped would be the result of this kind of uninhibited intimacy is suggested at the close of "Starting from Paumanok":

> O camerado close! O you and me at last, and us two only.
> O a word to clear one's path ahead endlessly!
> O something ecstatic and undemonstrable! O music wild!
> O now I triumph—and you shall also;

> O hand in hand—O wholesome pleasure—O one more
>   desirer and lover!
> O to haste firm holding—to haste, haste on with me.[27]

These lines show eloquently the significance Whitman attached to this mystic communion of two souls. Placed at the climax of a poem outlining his ambitions and hopes for his work, the communion is made to symbolize his ultimate artistic success. In other words, he has established contact with the one who is to respond to his art. They understand each other; together they may share the mystic revelations which are his to communicate. The communion is itself almost indescribable, and its products too subtle and thrilling to be analyzed. Once more the poet can only resort to music to suggest the ecstasy of artistic creation:

> O something ecstatic and undemonstrable!
> O music wild!

Often the relationship between "you" and "I" is pushed to the extraordinary intimacy of assuming that they are essentially one and the same. In this way Whitman conveyed his mystical sense of being the representative of all, different from "you" only in that he was a spokesman, with a poet's message to reveal. Instances of this usage are numerous, perhaps the most famous being the opening of "Song of Myself":

> I celebrate myself, and sing myself,
> And what I shall assume you shall assume,
> For every atom belonging to me as good belongs to you.[28]

And again from the close of the same poem:

> You will hardly know who I am or what I mean,
> But I shall be good health to you nevertheless,
> And filter and fibre your blood.[29]

"By Blue Ontario's Shore"[30] explains that the America which is to be the subject of great poems and chants is really only an extension of "you" and "I."

> O I see flashing that this America is only you and me,
> Its power, weapons, testimony, are you and me,
> Its crimes, lies, thefts, defections, are you and me,

> Its Congress is you and me, the officers, capitols, armies,
>   ships, are you and me,
> Its endless gestations of new States are you and me . . .[31]

Similar ideas are made the subject of one complete poem, "To You."[32] Here "you" is made to represent and idealize all men, and thus becomes the most appropriate subject for poetry. Though addressed to an ideal, the poem never loses its direct personal quality. A few lines isolated from the context may serve to show the closeness of the poet to his idealized audience:

> Whoever you are, now I place my hand upon you, that
>   you may be my poem,
> I whisper with my lips close to your ear,
> I have loved many women and men, but I love none
>   better than you.
>
> O I have been dilatory and dumb,
> I should have made my way straight to you long ago,
> I should have blabb'd nothing but you, I should have
>   chanted nothing but you.
> . . . .
> There is no endowment in man or woman that is not
>   tallied in you,
> There is no virtue, no beauty in man or woman, but as
>   good is in you,
> No pluck, no endurance in others, but as good is in you,
> No pleasure waiting for others, but an equal pleasure
>   waits for you.
>
> As for me, I give nothing to anyone except I give the like
>   carefully to you,
> I sing the songs of the glory of none, not God, sooner
>   than I sing the songs of the glory of you.[33]

Scores of poems might be cited further to exemplify Whitman's fondness for approaching his reader on terms of what once seemed daring intimacy in order to be sure of eliciting the kind of "response" he wanted, but two serve better than most. The first is "Crossing Brooklyn Ferry."[34] This is essentially an attempt to suggest that in the relentless flow of time, the elements of personality are not destroyed. The poet himself is the central symbol. Today he watches the river; generations hence, others will watch it, but he will be with them. In presenting the idea the poet draws especially close to the reader.

> I am with you, you men and women of a generation, or
>   ever so many generations hence,
> Just as you feel when you look on the river and sky, so I
>   felt,
> Just as any of you is one of a living crowd, I was one of a
>   crowd.[35]

Later come the lines:

> Closer yet I approach you,
> What thought you have of me now, I had as much of
>   you—I laid in my stores in advance,
> I consider'd long and seriously of you before you were
>   born.
>
> Who was to know what should come home to me?
> Who knows but I am enjoying this?
> Who knows, for all the distance, but I am as good as
>   looking at you now, for all you cannot see me?[36]

Closely related to these lines are those at the close of "So
Long!"[37] particularly important, for Whitman always used them to
close *Leaves of Grass* after the poem's first appearance in 1860.
The lines were to serve as his official farewell to his readers.

> My songs cease, I abandon them,
> From behind the screen where I hid I advance personally
>   solely to you.
> Camerado, this is no book,
> Who touches this touches a man,
> (Is it night? are we here together alone?)
> It is I you hold and who holds you,
> I spring from the pages into your arms—decease calls me
>   forth.
> . . . .
> An unknown sphere more real than I dream'd, more direct,
>   darts awakening rays about me, *So long!*
> Remember my words, I may again return,
> I love you, I depart from materials,
> I am as one disembodied, triumphant, dead.[38]

Here we have an unusually literal comment on the poet's relation to his work and the kind of "performance-response" relationship he hoped for with his reader. Imagining the prospect of death,
he is impelled to explain that his work is a representation and a
symbol of himself; "this is no book, who touches this touches a

man." The man is, furthermore, alive and physical and enjoys all physical sensations. Thus the poet through his work may caress and charm the reader and be charmed in return. An indissoluble bond is created between them. Once the comrade understands the mystic identity of the poet and the poem, though the poet die and "depart from materials," he is not dead, for the incarnate poem remains. Here the remarkable intimacy serves its highest purpose, of allowing the reader, whoever and whenever, to feel linked closely to the poet and to feel his "pulses of fire." Anyone who has had the eerie experience of hearing a recorded version of the quoted lines spoken in Whitman's own Camden residence at shadowy dusk can testify to his almost incredible success in identifying himself with his lines. The great mystic seems very near as we hear the words, "I may again return."

It is not only in the poems addressed specifically to the reader, however, that Whitman's reliance on his belief that the most artistic processes involve both performance and response can be detected. It forms the basis of his two finest creations: "Out of the Cradle"[39] and "When Lilacs Last in the Dooryard Bloom'd."[40] In both, the pivotal circumstance is the mystically beautiful bird song. In neither case, however, is the carol an end in itself. Its value lies in the fact that it awakens a meaningful response in the soul of the listener. In the former, a youth is inspired to poetry; in the latter, a poet comprehends the meaning of death. The phrases Whitman used to indicate the response of the listener are revealing. From the former poem:

> For I, that was a child, my tongue's use sleeping, now I
>   have heard you,
> Now in a moment I know what I am for, I awake. . . .[41]

In the Lincoln poem there are even more literal comments on the nature of the response:

> O liquid and free and tender!
> O wild and loose to my soul. . . .[42]
> And the charm of the carol rapt me,
> As I held as if by their hands my comrades in the night,
> And the voice of my spirit tallied the song of the bird.[43]
> To the tally of my soul,
> Loud and strong kept up the gray-brown bird. . . .[44]

Such lines show clearly how directly Whitman's conception of art as performance and response was derived from opera, for the bird song was always the symbol for operatic singing to him.

The net result to the body of his work of this aesthetic conviction of Whitman's was to place a great responsibility upon the reader. What he wanted all of his poems to do was to arouse a "tallying chant" in the reader, and an echo after he was gone. As he put it in "So Long":

> So I pass, a little time vocal, visible, contrary,
> Afterward a melodious echo, passionately bent for, (death
> making me really undying,)
> The best of me then when no longer visible, for toward
> that I have been incessantly preparing.[45]

He had commented on the reader's function in "Song of the Answerer":[46]

> The words of the true poems give you more than poems,
> They give you to form for yourself poems, religions, poli-
> tics, war, peace, behavior, histories, essays, daily life,
> and every thing else,
> They balance ranks, colors, races, creeds, and the sexes,
> They do not seek beauty, they are sought,
> Forever touching them or close upon them follows beauty,
> longing, fain, love-sick.[47]

He could give hints of truth only, he said. No idea could ever be positively and finally stated, for it would always give rise to other ideas in ever-expanding circles like the ripples from a pebble dropped in water. Thus no poem was ever finished; the reader would always have his part. Notice the presentation of this conviction in "Who Learns My Lesson Complete":

> Who learns my lesson complete?
> Boss, journeyman, apprentice, churchman and atheist,
> The stupid and the wise thinker, parents and offspring,
> merchant, clerk, porter and customer,
> Editor, author, artist, and schoolboy—draw nigh and com-
> mence;
> It is no lesson—it lets down the bars to a good lesson,
> And that to another, and every one to another still.[48]

The measure to which readers have been willing to accept the responsibility Whitman put upon them has always influenced their critical evaluation of the poet. He understood that this would be the case, and when he came to discuss his poems late in his life, in "A Backward Glance,"[49] he explained his artistic intentions, as if to ask not to be held accountable for what he had not tried to do.

The word I myself put primarily for the description of them as they stand at last, is the word Suggestiveness. I round and finish little, if anything; and could not, consistently with my scheme. The reader will always have his or her part to do, just as much as I have had mine. I seek less to state or display any theme or thought, and more to bring you, reader, into the atmosphere of the theme or thought—there to pursue your own flight.[50]

Thus understanding his intentions, we can perhaps be patient even with the catalogues of impressions and lists of poetic materials in "Song of Myself." We are to complete the poems ourselves. If we are unable to do so, the fault is our own. He gave us an example of a suitable method in Section 6,[51] where he composed an impressive reflection on "What is the Grass?" The simplest possible object, he implied, has untold poetic possibilities. We have only to consider it poetically.

All of Whitman's poetry, however, was designed to be suggestive, as indeed all good poetry is. That he always thought of himself as a "performer," and deliberately relied more strongly on the "response" of his readers than most other poets is in large part the result of his devotion to opera in the days when he was forming his artistic creed. He could hope for no greater satisfaction for his audience than the response he had given to operatic music. He appealed for the same kind of a response to his poems, for they were, as he once said, "spiritual—good, not from the direct but indirect meanings—to be perceived with the same perception that enjoys music. . . ."[52]

NOTES—CHAPTER III

1. Inclusive Edition, p. 179.
2. Ibid., p. 183.
3. This would indicate that Whitman was able to overlook acting of the same sort, probably even more "inflated," in operatic performances.
4. "November Boughs," Prose, III, 194.
5. Ibid., III, 190.
6. Ibid., III, 193.
7. Workshop, p. 131.

8. *Ibid.*, p. 127.
9. *A Child's Reminiscence*, p. 20.
10. *Prose*, II, 202.
11. *Workshop*, p. 187.
12. *Ibid.*, p. 173.
13. Burroughs, *op. cit.*, p. 194.
14. *Workshop*, p. 132.
15. *Ibid.*, p. 173.
16. *Letters of Anne Gilchrist and Walt Whitman*, p. 4. The quoted passage is from Mrs. Gilchrist's essay, "A Woman's Estimate of Walt Whitman," reprinted in this volume.
17. Inclusive Edition, p. 343.
18. *Ibid.*, p. 348.
19. *Ibid.*, p. 12.
20. *Ibid.*, p. 13.
21. *Ibid.*, p. 410.
22. *Ibid.*, p. 411.
23. *Ibid.*, p. 24.
24. *Ibid.*, p. 64.
25. *Ibid.*, p. 70.
26. *Ibid.*, p. 71.
27. *Ibid.*, p. 23.
28. *Ibid.*, p. 24.
29. *Ibid.*, p. 76.
30. *Ibid.*, p. 286.
31. *Ibid.*, p. 297.
32. *Ibid.*, p. 197.
33. *Ibid.*, p. 198.
34. *Ibid.*, p. 134.
35. *Ibid.*, p. 135.
36. *Ibid.*, p. 137.
37. *Ibid.*, p. 416.
38. *Ibid.*, p. 418.
39. *Ibid.*, p. 210.
40. *Ibid.*, p. 276.
41. *Ibid.*, p. 214.
42. *Ibid.*, p. 280.
43. *Ibid.*, p. 281.
44. *Ibid.*, p. 282.
45. *Ibid.*, p. 418.
46. *Ibid.*, p. 140.
47. *Ibid.*, p. 143.
48. *Ibid.*, p. 329.
49. *Ibid.*, p. 522.
50. *Ibid.*, p. 531.
51. *Ibid.*, p. 28.
52. *Prose*, VI, 8.

CHAPTER IV

Overture

IT WAS BELIEVED by many of Whitman's early critics, and it is still held in some circles, that his poetry is seriously deficient in form. This was in spite of the fact that the poet himself protested that his form and method were derived from the Italian opera and that his poetry should be approached and appreciated as if it were music. Undoubtedly one aspect of operatic construction which contributed its share to the poet's special kind of form was the operatic overture. It is perhaps not surprising that the casual among the poet's readers would not have sensed the musical form in his longer poems, for it is deliberately irregular and fluid. But the form is there, none the less, and if the poems are examined in the light of the large, cyclic rhythms of operatic overtures, it can be clearly detected.

One of the first writers to recognize this particular kind of structure, though he did not suggest its origin, was the poet's friend William Sloane Kennedy. He wrote:

With Whitman poetry has now become an instrument breathing a music in so vast a key that even the stately wheelings and solemn pomp of Milton's verse seem rather formal and mechanical. Whitman's dithyrambic chants, with their long, winding fiords of sound, require—like summer thunder or organ music—perspective of the ear, if the phrase will be allowed: they must be considered in the vocal mass, and not in parts; and when so considered, it will be found that nearly every page is held in solution by a deep running undertone of majestic rhythm.[1]

Kennedy also wrote: "His [Whitman's] poetic art is profoundly consonant with the laws of nature and symphonic music."[2]

Though Kennedy did not pursue the point, he might have proceeded to show that in the poet's work there is a relation between the two. Whitman was always aware of the powerful but irregular rhythms to be encountered in the natural world, and to some degree his attraction to the overture was the result of its use of the

142

same kind of flowing rhythms which he had responded to in nature. To some extent, of course, these natural rhythms affected his poetry directly. For example, in "Had I the Choice,"[3] he enumerated the gifts of some of the great bards of the past and then proceeded to say:

> These, these, O sea, all these I'd gladly barter,
> Would you the undulation of one wave, its trick to me
>   transfer,
> Or breathe one breath of yours upon my verse,
> And leave its odor there.

Not only the ocean but such things as the spiraling movements of the hawk flight and the strong surges of trees in the wind contributed to his conception of suitable rhythms for poetry.

In the operatic overture he encountered large rhythms very much like those of nature, but used for purposes of the artistic organization of material. In the overture he heard large, swelling undulations, the ebb and flow of melody and volume. In it were effects of appearance and reappearance, spiraling patterns which he could easily detect and whose structural values were easily apparent. Melodies of strongly contrasting character and tempo were so intertwined as to create a veritable fabric of rhythm.

It was probably the device of weaving the melodies together which accounted fundamentally for Whitman's interest in the form of the overtures, just as it was this device which gave them their characteristically broad rhythms. The device must have seemed ideal to him for the construction of his songs. His method of composing was to allow his poems to grow by accretion. Ideas and inspirations of the moment were jotted down on scraps of paper, and later, groups of such fragments would be gathered together. Of course he realized that all art must have form of some kind, though he was convinced that form should never be an end in itself and that it should never get in the way of the growth of an idea. Particularly in his longer poems there would have to be some sort of binding construction. What could have suited his purposes better than the weaving together of themes as in the overture? It would accommodate his individual method of composing; it would give the inspirational effect of music; and, what is not unimportant, it would give something of the effect of the great undulating swells of the ocean.

There are a good many evidences of Whitman's consciousness of this constructive device in the poems themselves, as well as elsewhere. For example, in *Democratic Vistas* we come upon the sentence: "Then still the thought returns (like the thread passage in overtures) giving the key and echo to these pages."[4] Similarly in many passages in the poems he showed himself to be particularly aware of the "theme" or "thread" or "strain," appearing and reappearing in a woven fabric. In "Starting from Paumanok":[5]

> O such themes. . . .
> Strains musical flowing through ages, now reaching hither,
> I take to your reckless and composite chords, add to them,
> and cheerfully pass them forward.[6]

And later in the same poem:

> And I will thread a thread through my poems that time
> and events are compact. . . .[7]

In "Songs of Myself"[8] the same structural idea appears. Following a list of possible poetic ingredients comes this line:

> And of these one and all I weave the song of myself.[9]

In "Song of the Banner at Daybreak,"[10] some lines early in the poem, spoken by the poet, one of several characters in the work, call attention graphically to the device of weaving themes together.

> I'll weave the chord and twine in,
> Man's desire and babe's desire, I'll twine them in . . .

Much the same idea recurs in "Song at Sunset,"[11] in words almost identical to those in the passage from "Starting from Paumanok":

> O strain musical flowing through ages and continents, now
> reaching me and America!
> I take your strong chords, intersperse them, and cheerfully
> pass them forward.[12]

It should be noticed, of course, that in most of such passages the references are to the materials of music, suggesting quite clearly that the original impulse toward the weaving device came from music.

The lines which best summarize the poet's feeling for the significance of the device, as well as the origin of his use of it, are to be found in the important short poem, "That Music Always Round Me,"[13] which closes:

> The triumphant tutti, the funeral wailings with sweet
>   flutes and violins, all these I fill myself with,
> I hear not the volumes of sound merely, I am moved by
>   the exquisite meanings,
> I listen to the different voices winding in and out, striving,
>   contending with fiery vehemence to excel each other
>   in emotion;
> I do not think the performers know themselves—but now
>   I think I begin to know them.[14]

From the very beginning of Leaves of Grass Whitman seems to have utilized the form of the overture with its waves of melody and interweaving of themes as a constructive device. An examination of the first edition of the work leads to such a conclusion. The book is dominated by a long poem, untitled, and divided only by breaks in the spacing of the lines. To its early readers it seemed almost wholly without form and nearly without meaning. It underwent considerable revision before it reached the version we know as "Song of Myself," and our reactions to it have similarly changed. Today we look at it as a kind of fundamental key to all of Whitman's work, and, as the place where all new readers may well begin. Recently a scholar has even taken pains to discover in it a logical arrangement of ideas.[15]

But if one studies the original version he is convinced at once that Whitman did not intend it to be logical. It had a different kind of form which he was well aware of, if readers could not detect it. For those who demanded some sort of visible plan he later numbered the sections, but even these do not highlight a logical construction so much as a musical one, which he had probably hoped originally would not need such a mechanical arrangement. With all of its revisions, however, the poem remains what it was at first, a fabric of themes woven and interwoven. They are not labeled and tagged, of course; they are simply ideas which the poet presents, temporarily abandons for other ideas, and returns to for development. Thus an idea is not exhaustively treated upon its first appearance; this would be the logical method of presentation. It was Whitman's plan to give the reader a sense of the growth of an idea, its organic expansion, by allowing it to develop beside and in the midst of other ideas. Each time it reappears it has taken on new meanings and significance. As all the ideas are woven together and blended, all seem to grow, and, in the mind of a sensitive reader, do grow. Occasionally the theme will be clearly stated, only, at its next appearance, to be exemplified and not stated at all. Every reader can recall most of these motifs or themes: the joy of physical sensations, the mystical significance of the physical aspects of nature, the meaning of death, the importance of the body and sex, the nature of the poet, personality and 'self,' and universal sympathy, to name a few. Sometimes it is a similarity of form in short passages like the series of 'parables,' including "What is the Grass?" (Section 6)[16] and "The Twenty-ninth Bather" (Section 11),[17] which is used like a recurring theme.

Today, understanding Whitman's method and his desire for organic structure, readers can detect these themes and derive pleasure from the way they are combined. Perhaps, however, even for today's readers, the poem might have been improved if the themes had not been blended quite so completely, if there were more contrast between them, for example. Certainly the poem would have been more intelligible to its early readers if this had been the case.

Another poem in the first edition, now known as "The Sleepers,"[18] reveals exactly the same kind of musical progression, as the poet moves among the sleepers, discovering the characteristics of each and their needs, and ministering to them. He recalls episodes that at first seem unrelated to the progress of the poem: the brave swimmer dashed on the rocks, Washington saying farewell to his army, the beautiful red squaw, the tragic shipwreck. But at last, like the bringing together of melodies in the finale of an overture, these are merged in the peace and blissful rest of night and death.

> Elements merge in the night. . . .
> I swear they are all averaged now—one is no better than
>   the other,
> The night and sleep have liken'd them and restored them.[19]

In the second edition of *Leaves* came another work, "Broad-Axe Poem" (now called "Song of the Broad-Axe"),[20] which is equally interesting in its thematic development. First comes an introductory section, preparing for the later material. The axe is presented as an emblem for America, which inevitably, as an emblem, brings a "long, varied train" of associations: people, occupations, spectacles, meanings. These, implies the introductory section, will be presented like "dabs of music, Fingers of the organist skipping staccato over the keys of the great organ."

Section 2 is a short-lined song of welcome and praise for all productive lands, whatever their products, climaxed with "lands of iron—lands of the make of the axe."[21] Section 3 is a contrasting long-lined presentation of the great variety of scenes where the axe is a key instrument, especially those of pioneer days when hardy, independent Americans used the axe to build their homes and establish their communities, but also scenes of later city life with its tragic fires and need for the axe as a tool of rescue.

Section 4 returns to the short, terse lines to state briefly the conviction that 'things' and cities perish. Only greatness in human nature survives and endures. 'Things' are only emblems, in other words. The close of the section gives the key to the following section: "A great city is that which has the greatest men and women."[22] Section 5 greatly elaborates this sentiment, analyzing in detail the qualities which make a city great. Section 6 takes its cue from Section 5. If great people make a great city, 'greatness' in people, greatness of soul may be considered for a moment.

But the poet has strayed from his central strain, and with Section 7 he returns to it. Here he contemplates the axe, its origin in unpromising looking, sterile lands, the ore fields, and makes up a catalogue of its significant uses down through history. Section 8 selects one of these uses, an evil one in which the axe became the instrument by which the tyrant imposed his will on his subjects, only to glory in the passing of this evil use and to celebrate the emergence of the axe as a symbol or emblem for a free America.

Now, in Sections 9, 10, and 11, the reader discovers why the axe is so highly appropriate a symbol. Lists of its varied wood products are enumerated, lists of its users detailed, lists of institutions depending upon it are catalogued, lists happy as well as tragic, all arising from a consideration of the axe as an emblem. At last in Section 12, with the poem returning once more to the short terse lines, Democracy itself emerges as the result and climax of all the considerations.

An examination of the crude notes Whitman made for this poem will show how significant was his structural planning in the finished product. He indicated first merely the "Broadaxe," and followed with these notes. "First as coming in the rough ore out of the earth— Then as being smelted and made into usable shape for working—then into some of the earlier weapons of the axe kind—battle-axe—headsman's axe—carpenter's broadaxe—(process of making, tempering and finishing the axe,) inquire fully."[23] There is also a long list of uses of the broadaxe, as well as a notation about "procession of portraits of the different users of the axe," ending with the pioneer. Here, too, the axe is noted as the suitable American emblem, rather than the eagle.

Another set of notes is labeled "Full Picture," and contains many jottings about possible scenes of activity involving the axe.[24] In all the notes there is nothing to suggest the subtle thematic arrangement the materials were to be given in the final version of the poem, with its little overture, suggesting (actually naming) the themes to follow, and even indicating the method of construction. It is important to notice that this indication (dabs of music, the organist at the organ) may be taken almost literally. While there are various themes in the poem (the axe and the various trains of thought inspired by it) and while they are presented so that they lead climactically to a glorification of Democracy, they also suggest the organ improvisation. Throughout the poem, one train of thought seems to inspire the next, and though, as in improvisation, the poet seems to wander from the starting point, being led from one idea to another, his sense of unity inevitably brings him back to the axe as an emblem and to what it stands for. Considered as music, not as logically planned construction, "Song of the Broad-Axe" becomes an extremely interesting example of subtle form.

Another structurally interesting poem appeared in the same edition of Leaves of Grass, called "Poem of Many in One" (later "By

Blue Ontario's Shore").[26] Here the poet was faced with binding together into an artistic unit a mass of convictions about himself as poet, and his mission and function in that role, much of which he had published as prose in the preface of 1855. Once again the solution is to group the ideas into themes and weave these into a pattern. A more obvious structural device was added in 1867 and further revised in 1871.[26] It is the fiction of having the poet hear a dramatic charge, announced by a gigantic phantom by Ontario's shore, to chant poems, especially of America, not neglecting Democracy and the hardships and trials it imposes. In 1867 the phantom was added only in the first section and at the poem's close in Section 19. In 1871, apparently feeling the need to introduce this unifying device into the heart of the poem, Whitman referred to the phantom in a line added to Section 9. Thus the meditations of the poem are given a reason for being; they are an answer to the phantom's charge. Again, as in the numbering of sections in "Song of Myself," perhaps this inclusion of an obvious device of form shows the poet's attempts to achieve a less subtle kind of organization than the musical one, a kind that his readers would understand.

He did not alter the presentation of the ideas, however, which are handled thematically. If we outline the poem by sections, we can see at once the interplay of subjects, which of course are not in any sense tagged; we must sense the meaning from the whole section not from any topic sentence. (Whitman said his meaning was always "not direct but indirect . . . to be perceived with the same perception that enjoys music, flowers and the beauty of men and women, free and luxuriant.")[27]

Section 1 The Phantom (Introduction—The Phantom's Charge)
Section 2 Self (Self as an ultimate end)
Section 3 Self (Self as deity)
Section 4 The Poet (Poet as stimulator)
Section 5 America (Like self, independent and ultimate)
Section 6 The Poet (Poet as representative of America)
Section 7 America (New dignity following preservation of Union)
Section 8 The Poet (Celebrates a forward-looking America)
Section 9 The Phantom (Demands bards native and grand)
Section 10 The Poet (Ideal poet defined)
Section 11 The Poet (Poet's mission includes treatment of war)

Section 12 American Poet (Requirements defined)

Section 13 America (Response to poet)

Section 14 Whitman (Qualifications as spokesman for America)

Section 15 America (A compact of individuals)

Section 16 Self (Individual responsible to himself)

Section 17 America (Composed of "you" and "me," individuals)

Section 18 Whitman (Absorbs all into himself)

Section 19 The Phantom (Mystic inspiration comes to Whitman)

Section 20 Finale (Calls for great bards of the future to continue the song)

The outline reveals that there are roughly five different themes which appear and reappear. (Of course they could be called by other titles.) The reader's feeling for the poem's unity and direction is increased, for example, when upon reading Section 16, he recalls the earlier treatments of the same theme of self and its importance. The blending of the themes is interesting to observe also, as, for example, those of America, the poet, and Whitman, the last coming finally to embrace the first two.

Another device in "By Blue Ontario's Shore" which contributes to the impression that the poem has a musical structure is the repeated introduction of parenthetical material, all sounding the same strain, as Allen has pointed out in his *Handbook*.[28] The theme is the dark one of danger to Mother-Democracy and Sister-States; it is announced in the first section like a small figure in a minor key, followed immediately by the first development of it.

> And sing me before you go the song of the throes of
>   Democracy.
>
> (Democracy, the destin'd conqueror yet treacherous lip-
>   smiles everywhere,
> And death and infidelity at every step.)[29]

The theme reappears a number of times, as for example:

> (Soul of love and tongue of fire!
> Eye to pierce the deepest deeps and sweep the world!
> Ah mother, prolific and full in all besides, yet how long
>   barren, barren?)[30]

In its last two appearances the theme modulates to a major key, with the introduction of a strongly optimistic note:

> (Mother, bend down, bend close to me your face,
> I know not what these plots and wars and deferments are
>   for,
> I know not fruition's success, but I know that through
>   war and crime your work goes on, and must yet go
>   on.)[31]

A shorter poem which appeared first in the edition of 1860 and of which our appreciation is increased if we approach it as a musical composition is "As I Ebb'd with the Ocean of Life."[32] It opens with a section devoted to the poet at the seashore, watching the windrows of drift material cast up by the ocean. Its keynote is sounded in the second line: "As I wended the shores I know."[32] Section 2, in effect, repeats the theme in a different key and mode: "As I wend to the shores I know not."[32] Now the poet faces the ocean of life and feels himself a part of the cast up drift, and doubts his ability to understand himself or the world. Section 3 introduces a slightly contrasting part in which the poet attempts by identifying himself with the island of Paumanok to find meanings. But meanings are not forthcoming, and in Section 4 the poet returns to a combination of themes one and two, resigning himself gloomily to his conception of himself as a fragment capriciously tossed upon the shore of life. The central image of the sea and its flotsam, used literally and figuratively and appearing throughout the poem, serves thematically to unify the poem in a remarkable way.

Drum-Taps, Whitman's next volume of poems, provides an especially notable example of his use of the overture for his own purposes. When he came to prepare his poems of the Civil War, interpreting the martial atmosphere of a nation at arms and utilizing the various themes of heroism and tragedy which always grow out of war, he doubtless felt that a kind of poetic introduction, transporting the reader from the great peaceful America he had been glorifying to a country geared to war, would be not only appropriate but necessary. The result was "First O Songs for a Prelude."[33] The change in the nation is symbolized by the changes in Manhattan; with dramatic suddenness the great city is transformed from a spectacular pageant of carefree living to a training ground for young soldiers of deadly earnestness and a depot where supplies and equipment for war are collected and stored. Opera music gives way to drum and fife. Avenue strollers are replaced by marching regiments. The transformation is sudden and complete.

Possibly for this reason the poem is relatively short, so short in fact, that there is small opportunity in it for a display of the variety of themes most overtures employed. There are to be noticed, however, some of the overture devices. The poem opens with a snare-drum roll, exactly like the distinctive overture to La Gazza Ladra which Whitman knew well.

> Lightly strike on the stretch'd tympanum pride and joy
>   in my city. . . .[33]

This is followed by a kind of exposition glorifying Manhattan and justifying its choice as a symbol. Next comes a terse statement of the sudden shock of war news, received in the night, and Manhattan's vigorous and determined response. Now follows the longest division of the prelude, picturing the varied activity that was the immediate result of the news of war. Professional men and workers leave their tasks and train for service. Scenes of hurried drilling, gathering supplies, preparation of equipment, sad farewells, all add up to a stern realization of war with all its implications. In this section the lines are much longer than in the others, and their free, uncontrolled and turbulent rhythms suggest the frantic activity described. The passage rises to a splendid climax in the two lines, each opened with a vigorous, crashing chord:

> War! an arm'd race is advancing! the welcome for battle,
>   no turning away;
> War! be it weeks, months, or years, an arm'd race is advancing to welcome it.[34]

At once the theme changes and the poem returns to the opening 'tune' of Manhattan as a symbol of wartime America and the ambition to celebrate both adequately in poetry. Again the lines are short, firm in rhythm, slow moving and deeply serious in effect, as the poet observes the new dignity, calm and confident, which war has brought to his city and nation. This will be the material of

poems to follow, and, as the poet says, "O to sing it well!"[35] Canby
has called attention to the use of the word "Arm'd" in this poem
which he feels is used as a thematic word, emphasizing the idea of
the work like a recurring drum-beat, and having some of the qualities
of Wagner's leit-motif, though he does not recognize the poem's
relationship to the operatic overture.[36]

Easy as it is to detect Whitman's consciousness of the technique
of the overture in such a poem, with its deliberate transportation of
the reader from one world to another, its "anticipating the strains"
of poems to follow, and its structural divisions, it is in the longer
poems such as we have noted and are to note, that his reliance on
the device is most significant.

"Proud Music of the Storm,"[37] which appeared first in 1868,
provides in its construction an excellent example of the interplay
of themes in an undulating rhythm. Allen says of it, "Nowhere else
did he [Whitman] use his characteristic symphonic structure with
greater unity of effect . . . It is his only poem which is literally a
symphony of sound, like Lanier's deliberate musical experiments."[38]
This is perhaps an overstatement of the case, for Whitman does
not manipulate words for their sound alone as Lanier often does,
but it is suggestive.

The introduction, Section 1, is addressed to the music of the
storm which is really a vast rhythm pervading all nature and human
activity and which speaks irresistibly to the poet in his chamber at
night. It is compounded of the "strong hum of the forest tree-tops,"
"the roar of pouring cataracts" and the like, but includes as well
"the sounds of distant guns" and "all the different bugle calls."
Section 2 is a translation of the music into its different aspects, as
it is perceived by the poet's soul or creative imagination, toward
which it is principally addressed. In a succession of short contrasting passages, which themselves suggest the changing melodies in
an overture, varieties of music are suggested: a marriage festival
song, the loud and tragic music of war, the unsophisticated ballads
of medieval times, and the inspirational tones of the great organ.
This last brings us back to

> . . . earth's own diapason,
> Of winds and woods and mighty ocean waves . . .

and suggests the importance of reconciling and fusing nature and art in "a new composite orchestra":

> And man and art with Nature fused again.[39]

Section 3 is in effect a history of the poet's developing musical appreciation with its climax in Italian opera and the singing of Marietta Alboni. Section 4 returns to the manner of Section 2 with its evocation of widely differing varieties of music, each in a short characteristic passage. Section 5 continues the manner, emphasizing European religious choral music, reaching its climax in the cry of the poet:

> Give me to hold all sounds, (I madly struggling cry,)
> Fill me with all the voices of the universe,
> Endow me with their throbbings, Nature's also,
> The tempests, waters, winds, operas and chants, marches
>   and dances,
> Utter, pour in, for I would take them all![40]

Section 6 brings the poem to a close by returning to the structural device of the poet in his chamber, waking from a dream in which the music of nature and man had been heard. He recalls the strong and varied effects and at length goes forth refreshed, realizing that the inspiration of the music had not only given him a new "rhythmus," or rhythmic pattern in which to express his ideas, but had given him the ideas as well by making him articulate. Thus the poem is at once a comment upon nature and music as sources of technique and, particularly in its passing from one kind of music to another, an example of form based essentially on the structure of the overture.

The most perfect example of musical structure in Whitman has been reserved till last. It is his masterpiece, "When Lilacs Last in the Dooryard Bloom'd."[41] At least one poem from each edition of Leaves of Grass and from Drum-Taps has been discussed previously to show that he was consistently employing and perfecting the subtle type of structure which he had heard in opera overtures. In this great poem, composed at the height of his power, he displays a control over the material of his work and a skill in construction that are in large part the secret of the poem's greatness. It is the climax of his work in every sense, certainly in that of formal accomplishment. It was not at all unprepared for, as his earlier efforts show. And at least one other great example of formal skill followed it. But it was never to be equaled again.

The lyric can be shown to follow with surprising closeness the sonata form upon which most classical symphonies are based. It is impossible to say with finality whether Whitman was closely aware of this special pattern for weaving musical themes together or not. Certainly he had opportunities to hear it, not only in the symphonies which he must have heard at orchestral concerts but also in certain operatic overtures, notably that to Von Weber's *Der Freischütz* which follows the sonata pattern closely. On the other hand, nowhere does he refer to the sonata or suggest that he was familiar with its special intricacies. Furthermore, he never referred to a specific symphony.

Whether he was closely aware of the details of the form or not, it is of great interest to observe the parallels between the poem and the sonata, if only to emphasize the intricate skill with which he wove together the various 'strains' in the poem, approximating, perhaps subconsciously, the formal skill of the great composers of music.

First, the sonata form itself may be briefly summarized. This can be done most clearly in outline fashion.

Introduction
    An optional section, usually slow, setting the mood for music to follow, often suggesting, but rarely stating, the themes to follow.
First Part: Exposition
   1. First theme
     A subject or tune of indeterminate length but of strongly characterized melody and rhythm, usually vigorous and strong.
   2. Bridge Passage
     A linking section, sometimes introducing new melodies, however.
   3. Second theme
     A subject chosen to contrast strongly with the opening theme in mood and rhythm and stated in a different key.
   4. Closing passage
     A concluding subject, sometimes new, sometimes a modification of the first theme.
Second Part: Development
    This section is without established design, but offers the in-

genious composer an opportunity to employ all themes previously introduced in modified statement, in combination, in dramatic contrast, and in all varieties of free treatment.

Third Part: Recapitulation

1. First theme

A return of the original first theme in its original form and key.

2. Bridge passage

A short linking section.

3. Second theme

The original second theme, now stated in the same key as the first theme.

4. Closing passage

A short section in the same key.

Coda

A more or less elaborate finale, often making prominent use of the first theme, to give the effect of conclusion through 'return' to the opening material, or of completing a cycle.[42]

Placed beside this simplified outline, an analysis of "When Lilacs Last in the Dooryard Bloom'd" will reveal many parallels. Section 1 is the Introduction, suggesting with brevity the mood of grief, the spring season, and at its close hinting at the three symbols which are to be treated as musical themes. Sections 2 through 4 comprise the Exposition. Section 2 states the first theme, the star, symbol for the murdered President Lincoln. Appropriately, its tone is dark and its rhythm slow (achieved by reducing the unaccented syllables to the barest minimum), but it is presented with surging power and masses of tone to suggest the inconsolable and overwhelming grief which the death of the President has occasioned.

Section 3 introduces the second theme, the lilac, or the poet's tribute to Lincoln. (It will be observed that the Bridge passage is omitted.) Here a strongly contrasting rhythm is encountered, lighter in tone and much more rapid. The lines are nearly twice as long and contain hardly as many accents as those in Section 2. The section is closed with a short, emphatic line suggesting the interpretation of the symbolism.

Section 4 presents the Closing Passage, here used to introduce a new or third theme, probably the most important of all, the bird song, which becomes the symbol for a realization of the ultimate significance and meaning of death, as opposed to superficial grief at the passing of an individual person, however important or imposing he may be. It should be noted in passing that the three themes are not in any way related as they are presented in the Exposition part of the poem. Many beginning readers of Whitman find this an evidence of irresponsible incoherence on the part of the poet, not realizing that the coherence must be looked for in the construction of the whole, not between parts.

The Development section of the poem comprises Sections 5 through 14, and demonstrates a virtuosity in manipulating the three major themes as great as that of the greatest composer. Sections 5, 6, and 7 utilize Theme II fundamentally but enlarged to include not only the tribute, the sprig of lilac, but the coffin to which it is to be given. The lilac becomes a part of the season which produces it, and contrasts are introduced in the incongruities of dirges and tolling bells as the coffin passes through the luxuriant and vital spring. Section 7, as a kind of parenthetical interlude, suggests the expanded symbolism for Theme II, a song not alone for Lincoln but for Death itself. Section 8 returns to Theme I but in a different key. Now the star evokes not powerful, overflowing grief, but contemplation of possible meanings and recollections of the star before its disappearance. Sections 9, 10, and 11 deal with Theme III, but in combination with the other themes. The bird song sounds in the night, but the star and the lilac overpower it. (The poet wishes to contemplate death in the abstract, but his poignant grief at the "fact" of Lincoln's death or the passing of Lincoln, and his consideration of appropriate songs of tribute, prevent him.)

Section 12 leads into Section 13 by suggesting some of the materials that go into the bird song, for example the wonderful appropriateness and beauty of enveloping night which follows the splendid day. Then in Section 13 the bird sings on (Theme III almost in its original form) while Themes I and II sound more and more faintly and are soon to be overpowered.

Section 14 provides the great climax for the Development part of the poem. With modulating and tremulous chords (gradual shifting away from personal grief to contemplation of nature and its processes) the reader is prepared to hear the soaring lyric of the bird's song, so melodious, so touching, so inevitable that the other themes are completely overshadowed and overwhelmed. (Death is beautiful, natural, and right, not to be feared but praised, not a destroyer but a deliveress.)

Section 15 corresponds roughly to a brief Recapitulation, detailing a response to the magnificent lyric, though not reintroducing Themes I and II. The final section, 16, may be regarded as the Coda, in which with consummate skill all the implications of the previous sections are combined into a finale, reaching its compact and eloquent conclusion in the last nine lines:

> Yet each to keep and all, retrievements out of the night,
> The song, the wondrous chant of the gray-brown bird,
> And the tallying chant, the echo arous'd in my soul,
> With the lustrous and drooping star with the countenance
>   full of woe,
> With the holders holding my hand nearing the call of the
>   bird,
> Comrades mine and I in the midst, and their memory
>   ever to keep, for the dead I loved so well,
> For the sweetest, wisest soul of all my days and lands—
>   and this for his dear sake,
> Lilac and star and bird twined with the chant of my soul,
> There in the fragrant pines and the cedars dusk and dim.[43]

It is not necessary to insist that Whitman composed his poem in terms of Exposition, Development, Recapitulation, and Coda. It is unlikely that he was familiar with the words; at least he never used them as they apply to the sonata. It is of extreme importance, however, to observe how, having heard themes of independent identity woven together and combined and developed toward a climax, producing a musical structure of satisfying beauty, Whitman could take three symbols and with instinctive judgment and taste similarly fashion them into a verbal fabric of richness and beauty. In the last analysis the sonata is a form built upon the logical exposition and development of a group of related ideas. Perhaps Whitman, at the peak of his inspiration and skill, faced with the necessity and desire to achieve such a form, evolved one quite independent of its musical counterpart, though certainly derived basically from his familiarity with opera overtures.

It has been claimed that "When Lilacs Last in the Dooryard Bloom'd" is exactly similar to a Rondo in form.[44] This is certainly not the case. The Rondo is a musical pattern of any number of themes, but gives great emphasis to the one introduced first. Using Roman numerals to identify themes, the Rondo pattern would be somewhat as follows: I, II, I, III, I, IV, I.[45] The distinctive characteristic is that theme I appears after each new subject. Themes appear and reappear in "When Lilacs Last in the Dooryard Bloom'd," but not in such a pattern.

The list of poems which might be shown to be built on a musical pattern has by no means been exhausted. Unquestionably, in all of the larger poems something like this type of structure was in the back of Whitman's mind. He did not always achieve the triumph of the Lincoln poem, by any means. Too often he seems to have been led away from considerations of structure to the sweep of ideas, as one suggested another. As his poems stand, however, there can be discovered in them a structure which gives them system without restraint and a form, derived from music, which is organic rather than mechanical or logical.

It was not only the form of the overture which impressed and influenced Whitman, however. He was always keenly aware of the artistic justification for placing this instrumental piece at the beginning of an operatic production, and in his own work he often attempted to fill the same need with overture-like poems.

First of all, he recognized the need for something to bridge the gap from a workaday world to the world of the imagination, whether on the operatic stage or on the printed page. Something more than the mere drawing of a curtain in the theatre or the opening of the covers of a book was necessary to permit the gradual withdrawal from the real and entry into the unreal. He made himself explicit in his essay on the opera:

The orchestra is full, being composed of nearly forty performers; and at the signal of the leader they begin. Now if you have any music in you, you will experience a new and heavenly pleasure. Every man in that band is a master of his instrument. The Opera-house, with the gas-lights—the rich and novel spectacle—the beautiful women—vanish from your eyes and thoughts at the first beat of the drum . . . With the rise of the curtain you are transported afar—such power has music.[46]

In his poem, "The Mystic Trumpeter,"[47] the same effect of being transported from one realm to another is described:

Blow trumpeter free and clear, I follow thee,
While at thy liquid prelude, glad, serene,
The fretting world, the streets, the noisy hours of day
    withdraw,
A holy calm descends like dew upon me,
I walk in cool refreshing night the walks of Paradise. . . .[48]

On one occasion Whitman even used the overture in a figure describing the inspirational effect he wanted in all his poems. In "From Pent-up Aching Rivers,"[49] are the lines:

Singing the true song of the soul fitful at random . . .
The overture lightly sounding, the strain anticipating. . . .[50]

This is really, of course, only another version of his often voiced conception of his art as something which is merely an emotional and imaginative stimulus to activity on the reader's part. The poem is the "overture"; the response will be the "strain."

That Whitman appreciated thoroughly the artistic purpose of the overture (or that which it was designed to serve) is shown by his own preoccupation with prefaces and prologue-poems as *Leaves of Grass* took shape. He was wholly aware of what would seem strange in his work to most of his readers, and he felt the need of something like an overture to assist the reader into the proper frame of mind for appreciating the work and its nature. The introductory material usually employed one of two methods; either it was a commentary on the themes to follow and a summary of them, or it attempted to evoke the mood which was to prevail in the following selections.

The first instance of Whitman's 'overture' is, of course, the Preface to the first edition of *Leaves of Grass*, 1855.[51] Several circumstances point to the fact that this was to be more than a routine explanation of the poems. In its long paragraphs and almost equally long sentences, broken into parts by groups of dots, apparently to emphasize the rhythm more than the meaning, it is obvious that the prose was to be regarded not as ordinary prose but as rhythmical utterance only slightly less poetic than the poems themselves, and in decidedly the same general rhythmical tradition. The progress of the ideas is flowing and rhythmical, not logical, just as the great nameless poem[52] which followed (later "Song of Myself") is not logical.

In other words, its ideas were not explanations but initial suggestions of the themes to follow, exactly as in the overture. In form and material this was an overture; its form comparable to, but less intense and regular than, that of the poems to follow, and its material not so much analysis as ideas which having been contemplated themselves would make the ideas of the following poems meaningful and inspiring.

In the second edition of the book, 1856, the famous letter to Emerson, though printed in an appendix,[53] in a sense removed the need for a preface, though the "Poem of Walt Whitman, An American"[54] (later "Song of Myself") was placed first and in a way served as an introduction (as it always has to Whitman's work). With the appearance of the third edition, 1860, an almost operatic structure in the volume may be observed, with its opening poem "Proto-Leaf"[55] (later "Starting from Paumanok") serving as a poetic overture, and "So Long"[56] standing as a finale, as it was to do throughout all subsequent editions. In the former poem, which may show that the poet now believed that the purposes of the overture could best be served by actual poetry rather than by poetic prose, he not only summarized his poetic program and announced his themes, but clarified his role as poet-seer. The latter work expresses movingly and with something of a flourish, as finales should, what he hoped his poems had accomplished.

Within the volume, other uses of the prologue-poem can be discovered. One such work stands as an introduction to a collection of sixteen poems new to this edition called "Chants Democratic." The poem, called "Apostroph,"[57] was later discarded, but as it stands in its original version it is perfectly overture-like in its announcement of themes, often word for word, to be used in the poems to follow. An example is the following passage which prepares for the poem known now as "Song of the Broad-Axe."

> O a wan and terrible emblem, by me adopted!
> O shapes arising! shapes of the future centuries!
> O muscle and pluck forever for me!
> O workmen and workwomen forever for me!
> O farmers and sailors! O drivers of horses forever for me!
> O I will make the new bardic list of trades and tools!
> O you coarse and willful! I love you![58]

With the appearance of Drum-Taps in 1865, an overture was especially needed, for the material and tone of the poems had been radically altered by the shattering experiences of the war. "First O Songs for a Prelude"[59] served the purpose.

The 1867 edition of Leaves of Grass, notable for the many revisions of all the poems and their rearrangement in the volume, opened with "Inscription"[60] (later "One's-Self I Sing"), which was from this time on to be the opening poem in all editions. Though a poem, not a traditional preface, "Inscription" states the themes of the poems to follow and even suggests their order. The themes as given are: (1) One's-self, (2) Man's physiology, (3) "the word of the modern . . . En-Masse," (4) "my days . . . the Lands . . . hapless war," (5) an appeal to the reader as audience. Here was an overture which provided almost a table of contents for the volume which was taking shape.

In the 1871-72 edition the "Inscription" had been lengthened from a poem to a section of poems, all of which the poet probably felt further clarified his purposes and increased his reader's understanding.[61] He maintained the section of Inscriptions in his final arrangement of the volume, and it is helpful now to think of them as serving the purposes of the overture in the opera house. They show Whitman's deep indebtedness to operatic overtures in matters of literary purpose, just as so many of his poems do in matters of literary form.

NOTES—CHAPTER IV

1. William Sloane Kennedy, Reminiscences of Walt Whitman (London, 1896), p. 164.
2. Ibid., p. 162.
3. Inclusive Edition, p. 425.
4. Prose, II, 89.
5. Inclusive Edition, p. 12.
6. Ibid., p. 17.
7. Ibid., p. 18.
8. Ibid., p. 24.
9. Ibid., p. 37.
10. Ibid., p. 241.
11. Ibid., p. 410.
12. Ibid., p. 411.
13. Ibid., p. 374.

14. *Ibid.*, p. 374.
15. Carl F. Strauch, "Structure of Walt Whitman's Song of Myself," *English Journal*, XXVII, 597-607 (September, 1938).
16. Inclusive Edition, p. 28.
17. *Ibid.*, p. 32.
18. *Ibid.*, p. 355.
19. *Ibid.*, p. 360.
20. *Ibid.*, p. 156.
21. *Ibid.*, p. 157.
22. *Ibid.*, p. 160.
23. *Ibid.*, p. 612.
24. *Ibid.*, p. 613.
25. *Ibid.*, p. 286.
26. See Variorum Readings, *Ibid.*, pp. 656-66.
27. Prose, VI, 8.
28. Allen, *Handbook*, p. 183.
29. Inclusive Edition, p. 286.
30. *Ibid.*, p. 291.
31. *Ibid.*, p. 298.
32. *Ibid.*, p. 216.
33. *Ibid.*, p. 237.
34. *Ibid.*, p. 238.
35. *Ibid.*, p. 239.
36. Canby, *op. cit.*, p. 323.
37. Inclusive Edition, p. 337.
38. Allen, *Handbook*, p. 199.
39. Inclusive Edition, p. 338.
40. *Ibid.*, p. 341.
41. *Ibid.*, p. 276.
42. Lawrence Abbott, *Approach to Music* (New York: Farrar and Rinehart, 1940), pp. 111-13.
43. Inclusive Edition, p. 283.
44. Emory Holloway, "Review of Hugh I'Anson Fausset: 'Walt Whitman, Poet of Democracy,'" *American Literature*, XIV, 319 (November, 1942).
45. Abbott, *op. cit.*, p. 109.
46. *New York Dissected*, p. 20.
47. Inclusive Edition, p. 389.
48. *Ibid.*, p. 390.
49. *Ibid.*, p. 77.
50. *Ibid.*, p. 78.
51. *Leaves of Grass* (Brooklyn, New York, 1855), pp. iii-xii.
52. *Ibid.*, p. 13.
53. *Leaves of Grass* (Brooklyn, New York, 1856), p. 345.
54. *Ibid.*, pp. 5-100.
55. *Leaves of Grass* (Boston: Thayer and Eldridge, 1860-61), pp. 5-22.
56. *Ibid.*, p. 451.

57. *Ibid.*, p. 105.
58. *Ibid.*, p. 106.
59. *Walt Whitman's Drum-Taps* (New York, 1865), p. 5.
60. *Leaves of Grass* (New York, 1867), p. 5.
61. *Leaves of Grass* (Washington, D.C., 1872), pp. 7-96.

CHAPTER V

Recitative and Aria

THE FORM of the Italian operas Whitman knew is most obviously distinguished by two strikingly different styles of vocal writing: recitative and aria. Each served its own purpose in helping to unfold the drama of the opera, and each was so highly conventionalized and differentiated from the other that even the most uncultivated opera-goer could recognize the most important characteristics of the two styles.

Recitative was employed for conversational material for those passages which merely advanced the action of the plot, whatever the intensity of the situation might be. It was written in declamatory style, with rhythms closely approximating those of actual speech. The style varied from almost monotonous recitation, with the lines chanted on one note, to highly impassioned declamations voiced in the widest variations of pitch and rhythm. There was never any melodic pattern of progress and return; the movement was simply that of actual talk, intensified by being uttered in musical tones on pitch. The style was made non-lyrical also by treating phrases as predominantly unaccompanied units, followed by dramatic chords in the accompaniment, usually rolled when played by a single instrument like the harpsichord, and in their harmonic structure bringing the declaimed phrases to a conclusion. (The non-melodic vocal line did not permit such a concluding effect.) A tradition in the performance of recitatives was that though in the score accompanying chords might be indicated to concur with the last note or two of a vocal phrase, they were not sounded until the voice had become silent. This gave a very distinctive effect, like instrumental punctuation for the voiced phrases. These were the chords Whitman was doubtless referring to when he wrote, after a declamatory passage:

Easily written, loose-finger'd chords—I feel the thrum of your climax and close.[1]

(The line points directly to the fact that as he composed his recitatives he was actually conscious of a kind of instrumental accompaniment, which he could indicate only by punctuation and the spacing of the lines, but which none the less helped him feel a kind of structure in his chanted proclamations.)

At the emotional peaks of the lyric dramas, such moments as those when the hero declares his love or the heroine gives way to an expression of violent grief, it was of course necessary to write melodic song of sustained and flowing character, song which might serve to interpret the sentiments the characters were voicing. This kind of song, the aria, was the real justification for opera, blending music and language to achieve communicative heights impossible to either alone, and was the crowning glory of the Italian operas Whitman knew. The arias employed legato phrases of incredible length, designed to display the rich color of the great Italian voices of the time. Often the long phrases were embellished by florid runs and trills, sometimes planned by the composer to increase the musical effectiveness of the flowing vocal line, but too often, one fears, merely to display the bravura art of the singer, whose incredibly relaxed method of vocal production, bel canto, enabled him or her to encompass the fearful difficulties without sacrificing volume or color of tone. Such operas as Norma, La Favorita, and La Cenerentola are rarely performed today for there are now few singers with the requisite capabilities to cope with their demands. We are told that Marietta Alboni, Whitman's idol, was the last of the great contraltos who could sing with great volume, great flexibility, and great range without sacrificing the natural richness of her wonderful voice.[2] Of necessity Whitman would have become so familiar with these two styles of composition during his "singing years" that they would have seemed second nature to him. No one could hear such flamboyant declamation and such flowing airs, learning both sufficiently well to sing and hum passages of them on occasion, without absorbing almost instinctively the tricks of the style. It is logical to suppose that as he experimented with getting his ideas into verse, finding the conventional stanza forms and lines a strait-jacket to his imagination, almost without realizing it, he should have begun to cast his words into the musical patterns which were always in his mind. His ideas needed to be chanted, he felt; he was a bard, opening great vistas to the imagination of his countrymen. He needed the large freedom of opera, not the confinements of stanza and lines. It was the most logical thing in the world that the long, unnamed poem opening the first edition of *Leaves of Grass* should not be in blank verse or Spenserian stanzas, but a long recitative, rising at times to the emotional and lyrical heights of the aria.

Whitman did not attempt to disguise the sources of his structural method. From the beginning of his poetic composition in the manner of the *Leaves* he alternated the terms *recitative* and *chant* and *song* in describing his work. Seventy-nine times in the poems alone he spoke of his chants and on eight occasions he identified his work as *recitative*. Presumably he used the terms somewhat interchangeably, *chant* being the least technical and most widely understood word, with *recitative* the technical term, exactly describing his method. No other poet before Whitman had used the term to describe his poems. It was not a loose usage with Whitman; he used it because it applied.

Throughout his work Whitman reveals the special effects of the operatic recitative. Edward Carpenter, in his reminiscences about Whitman, was one of the first writers to point this out. He wrote, "Often the music is that of the 'recitative'—sonorous, bold, free, not returning into itself like a melody, but moving forward with suggestions of things to follow."[3] Practically any passage will bear out the truth of his observation. It is not hard to find the irregular but controlled rhythm closely approximating the rhythm of speech, the consistent employment of the devices of parallelism and reiteration, the bardic proclamations and the declamatory rhetoric, and the movement of a passage always by independent lines or phrases, between which it would be no surprise to hear one or two chords of accompaniment.

The poems almost everywhere provide lines as examples; for instance, the ringing declaration:

> I am the poet of the Body and I am the poet of the Soul,
> The pleasures of heaven are with me and the pains of hell
>   are with me,
> The first I graft and increase upon myself, the latter I
>   translate into a new tongue.[4]

The repetitions and balances of the lines suggest at once a rapid chanting delivery. Or notice other lines from the same poem:

> Have you outstript the rest? are you the President?
> It is a trifle, they will more than arrive there every one,
>   and still pass on.

The first of the lines is the rhetorical question of the orator, of course, but it is also the semi-shouted, declamatory cry of the recitative singer, slowed down and strengthened by a relatively great number of accents. The line is followed by the contrasting chant of only a few accents.

The famous and much discussed catalogue passages are characteristic recitative. Sometimes these are in sentence form:

> The pure contralto sings in the organ loft,
> The carpenter dresses his plank, the tongue of his fore-
>   plane whistles its wild ascending lisp. . . .[5]

Sometimes they are mere lists of phrases:

> By the city's quadrangular houses—in log huts, camping
>   with lumbermen,
> Along the ruts of the turnpike, along the dry gulch and
>   rivulet bed. . . .[6]

But operatic recitative has not only the straight-line, unvaried pitch, chanting effects of these lines. Some passages are very dramatic, and so devised as to emphasize certain words or moods by causing some notes to be held and speeding up others, and by arranging the tone pattern so as to emphasize certain notes by giving them climactic positions high or low in the scale. A short passage of recitative from *Ernani* will illustrate the point.[7] In its opening phrase emphasis is secured through both timing and climax. Notice how the following phrases repeat single notes, varying the regular rhythm only to suggest the accents of speech. In the final phrases again emphasis is secured for "dishonor" and "treachery" by both time and climax.

Allegro

Oh, dread a - maze-ment! Here in my dwell-ing's

most__ se - cure re - cess - es, must I

find that the af-fi-anced bride of Sil-va par-leys with two vile se-

duc-ers! What ho! Ap-pear my squires and faith-ful

sol-diers! One and all be ye wit-ness that dis-

hon - or, and treach-er-y, hath this day be-fall'n your mas - ter.

In Section 37 of "Song of Myself,"[8] the similarity is at once apparent.

> You laggards there on guard! look to your arms!
> In at the conquer'd doors they crowd! I am possess'd!

But the passage continues with chant rather than dramatic and high-pitched declamation.

> Embody all presences outlaw'd or suffering,
> See myself in prison shaped like another man,
> And feel the dull unintermitted pain,
> For me the keepers of convicts shoulder their carbines
>   and keep watch,
> It is I let out in the morning and barr'd at night.

The opening of Section 38 returns to the staccato shout, the short, violent cry which the recitative often involved, then proceeds to longer phrases or lines, but maintaining the same violence of emotion:

> Enough! enough! enough!
> Somehow I have been stunn'd. Stand back!
> . . . .
>
> That I could forget the mockers and insults!
> That I could forget the trickling tears and the blows of
>   the bludgeons and hammers!
> That I could look with a separate look on my own cruci-
>   fixion and bloody crowning![9]

The reader can almost hear a strong baritone voice proclaiming these words, his ringing tones punctuated by heavy, crashing chords in the orchestra. Far more common in Whitman, however, is the less dramatic utterance which was noted at first, the quiet, thoughtful lines which seem to chant themselves on a single repeated note, falling slightly in pitch at the close of the line to indicate the completion of the phrase, and only occasionally, as in the third line below, the evenly flowing rhythm interrupted by rhythmic pauses for emphasis:

> I have said that the soul is not more than the body,
> And I have said that the body is not more than the soul,
> And nothing, not God, is greater to one than one's self
>   is. . . .[10]

There is obviously no place to stop in citing examples of Whitman's work as recitative. He called it all recitative, and he was almost literally correct. Certainly the first edition of *Leaves of Grass* can be appreciated structurally in no other light. Its largest organization was thematic like the overture. Its smaller parts were put together like the parts of the chanted recitative, the only kind of construction sufficiently free to serve the poet's purposes.

Just as the opera composer occasionally felt the need of interrupting the chanted flow of his drama to provide his singer full opportunity to express the emotion of the moment in lofty, lyrical music, so Whitman often interrupted his chants with their rhythms of speech to compose a lyrical passage conveying particularly deep emotion, a passage which corresponds exactly to the aria in opera. "Words are mean before the language of music,"[11] he once said, and for his most intense moments music was what he provided.

A good example of such an interruption is the famous Section 21 of "Song of Myself."[12] The section identifies the poet as embracing both physical and spiritual qualities in his temperament as well as in his projected work, and shows him able to respond in a mystical way to natural beauty. The latter fact is presented in lines beginning:

> I am he that walks with the tender and growing night,
> I call to the earth and sea half-held by the night.

The words of the "call" follow and constitute one of the greatest lyrical passages in all of Whitman. Here he did not wish to talk "about" the emotion he felt for earth; he wished to convey the mystic rapture directly to the reader. The solution was to compose an aria of sustained and powerful beauty like those which he had heard so often and which had touched him so deeply.

> Smile O voluptuous cool-breath'd earth!
> Earth of the slumbering and liquid trees!
> Earth of departed sunset—earth of the mountains misty-
>   topt!
> Earth of the vitreous pour of the full moon just tinged
>   with blue!
> Earth of shine and dark mottling the tide of the river!
> Earth of the limpid gray of clouds brighter and clearer
>   for my sake!
> Far-swooping elbow'd earth—rich apple-blossom'd earth!
> Smile, for your lover comes.

A few lines later in Section 22 a shorter aria addressed to the sea has similar flowing beauty.

The obvious difference between Whitman's arias and recitatives is that the material of the former is relatively more emotional and more compactly presented. The aria is less wordy, less diffuse than the recitative. Its movement is not rapid and chanting but melodious, with a restrained, relatively slow progression, one of the poet's notable heritages from Italian opera. The effect is achieved by the fact that the relative number of stresses in the line is increased. It could be shown, too, that the aria passages are more regularly metrical than the recitative sections. But this characteristic was undoubtedly not deliberately cultivated by Whitman. It was rather a natural result of his musical intentions. He rarely wrote in a consistently regular meter, but he had no objections to it if the singing-style of a given passage fell naturally into it. He told his friend Traubel once, "What I am after is the content not the music of words. Perhaps the music happens—it does no harm: I do not go in search for it."[13] They had been talking of what he called "the poetic lilt" or meter.

In the quoted aria it will be noted that the two lines introducing it are a transition between the two methods, and show the characteristics of both. But the first three lines of the aria proper are perfect examples of their kind. If they are read as they should be, to sound all their music and to achieve all their emphasis, every word save two prepositions will contain an accent. By the time the reader comes upon the passage he will have built up in himself a feeling for the regularity of recurring stresses, with usually an equal amount of time between them. Here suddenly is a series of stresses; the reader has no recourse but to slow down, to sound the stressed syllables as long as need be to fulfill the time requirement. With the tone sustained in this fashion, the voice may, indeed must, take on added richness of color, and the effect of song not speech, aria not recitative, is the result. With fewer stresses and more syllables than typical recitative lines, the lines of the arias are usually much shorter. Notice that the first three lines of the quoted aria are divided by dashes, the caesura in effect slowing the reader down still more. Though the parts of lines might be allowed to stand alone as complete phrases, the poet probably wished them to be read together on one breath, hence spaced them as single lines.

Whitman clearly thought of his early poems as long recitatives with the kind of undulating or cyclic construction that has already been spoken of. In these, the arias were not part of the construction so much as necessary vehicles for the presentation of especially lyrical material. (They occur prominently only in the initial poem, now known as "Song of Myself.") That he did not abandon this type of poem, however, is shown by the later "Song of the Exposition,"[14] originally recited by the author under the title "After All, Not to Create Only." In this poem, following an analysis of our heritage from the past and the responsibility of the present to build its own peculiar greatness on a foundation of the past, the poet reaches his climax in his song to America, with parts beginning:

> And thou America,
> Thy offspring towering e'er so high, yet higher Thee above
>   all towering . . .
> Thee, ever thee, I sing.
>
> Behold, the sea itself,
> And on its limitless, heaving breast, the ships . . .
>
> All thine, O sacred Union! . . .
> We dedicate, dread Mother, all to thee![15]

In these arias, not pure types, there are lines somewhat like those of recitative, but the passages are prevailingly songlike.

In the poems so far mentioned the aria is treated merely as a kind of interruption to the recitative. There is evidence, however, that in other poems Whitman worked out a kind of structure utilizing the aria as an integral part of it. The two styles seem to be combined into an operatic scena, or in fact a miniature opera. An example is "On the Beach at Night."[16] The poem opens with a description of the beach scene and places the two characters, the weeping child and its father, against the menacing background.

> From the beach the child holding the hand of her father,
> Those burial clouds that lower victorious soon to devour
>   all,
> Watching, silently weeps.

So concludes the recitative section. At once the father (or the poet) speaks and his words are a sustained lyric:

> Weep not, child,
> Weep not, my darling . . .
> The ravening clouds shall not long be victorious . . .
> Something there is more immortal even than the stars. . . .

Here again the aria is not so pure in type as we find elsewhere in Whitman, but the effect of the division of the poem into the two different styles is unmistakable.

In two of his greatest poems, technically perhaps the most perfect of all, "Out of the Cradle Endlessly Rocking"[17] and "When Lilacs Last in the Dooryard Bloom'd,"[18] Whitman employed the recitative-aria structure with consummate skill. In these poems perhaps more than in any others, even the non-musical reader can clearly detect Whitman's own distinction between the styles. The first of the two, which was the occasion for the author's comment that all of his poems were constructed in the manner of the Italian opera, was once described by him, anonymously, as a "curious warble." He went on to say, "The purport of this wild and plaintive song, well-enveloped, and eluding definition, is positive and unquestionable, like the effect of music. The piece will bear reading many times—perhaps, indeed, only comes forth, as from recesses, by many repetitions."[19]

In the poem a boy, whom the poet identifies as himself, wanders to the seashore on a romantic night and hears a remarkable bird song. He absorbs it and *translates* it, the translation becoming a central part of the poem. To distinguish it from the descriptive and narrative introduction, it is cast in the form of an aria, and this time, so that there can be no confusing the two styles, it is printed in italics.

All of the aria's characteristics which have previously been noted are exemplified in the bird song in perfect form. Look at the opening lines:

> *Shine! shine! shine!*
> *Pour down your warmth great sun!*
> *While we bask, we two together,*
>
> *Two together!*[20]

The first line here is especially impressive. Here are three identical sounds, and nothing more, making up a line. The voice must add beauty and richness to them. An opera composer, Bellini, for example, would have been able to put down in notes exactly what he wanted the voice to do by way of enriching the sounds, as he did in the opening phrases of the great aria, "Casta Diva."[21] Whitman trusted to the instincts of his reader not to hurry the line, to enhance it as only the sound of the human voice could do. It is of more than a little interest to discover in this connection that the line, and all the others exactly like it in form throughout the aria, consisted of only two syllables when the work originally appeared in 1859.[22] In 1867 the poet added the third repetition of the word, partly to bring it closer to the actual phrase of the bird and probably also as a concession to the fact that most hasty readers failed to prolong the tone sufficiently for the effect he wanted. Furthermore, the addition of another word permits a more interesting tonal pattern for the phrase. With two words, the reader has few possibilities for pitch variation; he may rise on the first and descend on the second, or rise on both or descend on both. With the addition of the third word the possibilities are numerous, the most logical being sustained notes, low on the first, high on the second, and intermediate on the third. This reading gives a rise and fall pattern of charm and variety. The fact of these alterations shows unquestionably that Whitman was by no means a careless, insensitive workman, but rather a craftsman with the same kind of interest in his work that a musician must have.

As the boy in the poem returns to the seashore he hears the love song of the bird change to a song first of waiting, then of overwhelming sorrow, as one of the birds fails to return. The tragic aria is longer than the initial one, but except for the minor key and the material of grief it is constructed exactly like the former; it is still the translation of the bird's song. Again the aria is introduced:

> Listen'd to keep, to sing, now translating the notes,
> Following you my brother.[23]

Again there is the three-note phrase woven through it like the opening subject in an opera aria:

> Soothe! soothe! soothe!
> Loud! loud! loud!

But there is an artistic variation in the third occurrence:

> Land! land! O land![24]

And in the last occurrence a still greater variation occurs:

> O past! O happy life! O songs of joy![25]

Incidentally this line originally read simply "O past! O joy!" The present version, except for the word "happy," added in 1881, was prepared in 1867.[26] The addition of the third exclamation shows that the poet thought of the line as a part of the repeated pattern, giving pleasure in its repetitions like subjects in a melody. What is really only a further variation of the same device of the reiterated note occurs in the last line of the aria but two, when the word *loved* is repeated not three but five times. Here is the final paroxysm of grief, the final and ultimate cry of despair.

Whitman may have found a hint as to the effectiveness of this repeated note in the operas of Rossini and Verdi, for as the latter's biographer, Toye, pointed out, one of Verdi's favorite methods for expressing strong emotion was the repetition of a single note, a trick which he copied from Rossini's opera *Aureliano in Palmira*.[27] He may also have got the idea from Tennyson, of whom he once wrote: "To me, Tennyson shows more than any poet I know (perhaps has been a warning to me) how much is in the finest verbalism. There is such a latent charm in mere words, cunning collections, and in the voice ringing them, which he has caught and brought out, beyond all others—as in the line,

> And hollow, hollow, hollow, all delight."[28]

Tennyson's lyric "Break, Break, Break" had been published in 1842, seventeen years before "Out of the Cradle."

Reiteration of a different sort is also to be found in the aria, achieving effects appropriate to poetry but possibly derived from music. For example, at the ends of sections of the aria, phrases are repeated:

> But my love soothes not me, not me . . .
>
> It is lagging—O think it is heavy with love, with love . . .
>
> O madly the sea pushes upon the land,
> With love, with love . . .
>
> Surely you must know who is here, is here. . . .[29]

The repetitions, added in 1867 when Whitman apparently studied anew the musical qualities of the aria, have the effect of echo or antiphon, and give a wailing, haunting quality to the lines. The repetitions also serve to tie together the passages which they close, of course. The two arias, one joyfully caroling love and the other intoning tragedy, are also bound together, though separated by many lines of recitative, by the repetition of a phrase just as passages of music are bound together by the repetition of a figure or theme. Closing the first aria:

> While we two keep together.[30]

Closing the second:

> We two together no more.[31]

If there were any doubt in the reader's mind as to the poet's artistic intentions in this poem, it is dispelled by the short line at the close of the lyric:

> The aria sinking. . . .[32]

The poem goes on to a close with a recitative explaining the significance of the aria to Whitman, a passage of great importance in understanding his work.

So, in a sense, does "Out of the Cradle" emerge as a kind of 'opera without music,' composed of recitatives and arias in the Italian style, and, like the operas it was fashioned after, telling its tragic story of love, separation, and death.

The second of the two great poems, "When Lilacs Last in the Dooryard Bloom'd," is closer to the symphony than the opera in construction, as already pointed out, and it contains more recitative than aria. However, in this poem, too, the aria is used with perfect artistry, and the work cannot be appreciated unless approached with a feeling for operatic style. One of the three symbols of which the poem is compounded, the most significant and climactic one, in fact, is the song of a bird, again cast into aria form. The song clarifies for the poet his vague and unresolved thoughts on the subject of death and is expressed not in lines of reflective or analytical poetry but in an aria, that musical form fully capable of conveying meanings denied to words, as Whitman had so often proved in the opera house. The death aria goes far to make the poem in which it appears one of the great threnodies in the language. The death of Lincoln is the point of departure toward it. The universal greatness of the poem lies in the song, a profoundly optimistic, even jubilant, interpretation of the meaning of death in the whole scheme of things.

In the death aria, as in the others, there are accent-weighted lines, with beautiful, low vowel sounds prolonged perforce. The movement is one of amazing fluidity, secured by the avoiding of gutturals and stopped consonants and a heavy reliance on liquid consonants and participial verb forms:

> For the sure-enwinding arms of cool-enfolding death.
>
> Laved in the flood of thy bliss O death.[33]

It is extremely important, as the verbal melody and beauty of such passages are praised, and they can be praised almost without reservation, to remember that the lyric was no mere exercise in capturing lovely sounds. Verbal beauties and melodious sounds were never an end in themselves to Whitman. Here he was attempting to state his convictions about death. They are stated musically, but the ideas are still the important consideration.

Before leaving these two poems, we need to make a distinction in their use of the aria. In "Out of the Cradle" the only aria passages are those in italics, the bird's songs. In the Lincoln poem there is an italicized aria of course, but there are also other arias, partly to help set apart and identify the different themes of the poem and thus contribute to its thematic organization, but largely to provide an appropriately heightened emotional expression to the great surges of grief that sweep over the poet. These arias are not italicized and are thus not to be regarded so climactically as the death aria, but they are none the less emotional moments for which the aria technique would be appropriate. The first of these is Section 2, the apostrophe which introduces the first symbol, the star. Sections 9 and 13, the preliminary responses to the bird's song, preparatory to the great aria itself, are also best appreciated as arias. Occasionally here, as in other poems, however, Whitman does not sharply differentiate between the aria and the recitative; rather, he combines qualities of both in a single section. Section 7 is such a passage.

In operatic form similar to the two poems just discussed, though much less successful, is "Song of the Redwood Tree,"[34] first published in 1874, considerably later than the others. Here a five-line recitative introduces "a giant voice . . . of a mighty dying tree in

the redwood forest dense." There follows a similarly short introductory aria, printed in italics as in the other poems.

Farewell my brethren,
Farewell O earth and sky, farewell ye neighboring waters,
My time has ended, my term has come.

The poet then returns to recitative for an elaboration of the
setting for the song in both sight and sound, the ocean's surge
providing "base and accompaniment low and hoarse" for the death
chant of the tree. Next comes the aria itself, in which the tree sings
of its antiquity, its pride, and its acceptance of death, yielding
place to a "superber race," "predicted long." The aria is interrupted:

Then to a loftier strain,
Still prouder, more ecstatic rose the chant. . . .[35]

Now the tree sings of a new race, not of Asia or Europe but of
Nature, which like the giant trees may flourish in the New World.

For man of you, your characteristic race,
Here may he hardy, sweet, gigantic grow, here tower pro-
  portionate to Nature,
Here climb the vast pure spaces unconfined, uncheck'd by
  wall or roof,
Here laugh with storm or sun, here joy, here patiently
  inure,
Here heed himself, unfold himself, (not others' formulas
  heed,) here fill his time,
To duly fall, to aid, unreck'd at last,
To disappear, to serve.[36]

The poem is not improved by three concluding sections of recitative, in which the poet in somewhat diffuse language reëchoes
the burden of the aria, the hope for the development of a great
race in the new world. Nowhere in the poem is there the effectiveness of phrase, rhythm, or word that was achieved in the earlier
poems, though it is interesting to observe the precise form attempted again.

In one other poem, probably written early in the Civil War,
Whitman attempted to give a poem an operatic structure, "Song
of the Banner at Daybreak."[37] The form here was apparently ex-

perimental and it was not attempted again. In reality it is a combination of the kind of thematic form Whitman discovered in
opera overtures and a purely operatic structure. The material concerns the poet and three symbols; the poet who is considering
what the nature of his work shall be; the child, symbol of the sensitive and responsive but unsophisticated audience of readers; the
father, symbol of selfish, cautious, practical commercialism; and
the banner, symbol of the Union of States, threatened by war, with
the pennant, symbol of war.

Instead of treating the symbols as musical themes and weaving
them together as he had sometimes done, here he personified
them and treated them exactly like characters in an opera, each
with passages of recitative and aria. The poet opens with a recitative foreshadowing the ideas of the poem and suggesting the meaning of the symbols. The pennant then sings a short aria, highly reiterative in structure and with meaning in character for the symbol.

> Come up here, bard, bard,
> Come up here, soul, soul,
> Come up here, dear little child,
> To fly in the clouds and winds with me, and play with the
>   measureless light.[38]

The child follows in a responding recitative and is similarly answered by the father. Next the poet sings a flowing aria glorying
in the beauties of nature and identifying himself. The child then
ventures beyond its tentative opening recitative and launches into
a rapturous aria describing the vision of the banner it beholds in
the sky. The earth-bound father answers in recitative, quieting the
inspired child; the father is given no aria in the entire poem, appropriately enough. So the poem progresses until the poet, having
observed the inspiration of the child and the selfish limitations of
the father, accepts the challenge of the banner and the pennant
and resolves to celebrate the Union, for better or worse including
the terrors of war, forgetting the themes of selfish thrift which
placed profit above Union and failed to recognize the fact that if
the Union were lost all would be lost. The enduring Union is

> Out of reach, an idea only, yet furiously fought for, risking
>   bloody death, loved by me,

So loved—O you banner leading the day with stars brought
    from the night! . . .
I see but you, O warlike pennant! O banner so broad, with
    stripes, I sing you only,
Flapping up there in the wind.[39]

The poem is of great interest for its experimentation in structure.
It cannot be claimed as one of the completely successful works of
its author, however, for its ideas are somewhat confused and its
wording not so memorable as that in other poems.

So far poems in which the recitative and aria were combined by
Whitman for purposes of structure, contrast, and the appropriate
presentation of material have been considered. There is another
usage of the aria, however. Occasionally the entire material for a
poem seemed so essentially lyrical to the poet that he cast it into
an aria without accompanying recitative. These short lyrics are
best appreciated if approached as arias, too, not simply as lyrics. For
they have the form of the operatic aria. This form has not been explained till now, for it is best exemplified in Whitman in his short,
isolated arias. In the Italian operas, the aria, as a set piece of composition, was usually given a structure or formal design, both to
increase its beauty and to distinguish it from the non-melodic
recitative. Reduced to its simplest terms this form consisted of an
opening figure or tune, followed by a contrasting figure usually involving a greater amount of embellishment, followed again by a
return to the original tune, often changed ever so slightly.[40] It
required no great amount of musical cultivation to detect these
themes or parts of an aria. The two popular romanzas for tenor in
La Favorita, "Spirto Gentil"[41] and "Una Vergine,"[42] both special
favorites of Whitman, show the three part arias in their most
recognizable form. Anyone who can hum a tune can hear in them
the theme, contrasting section and return to the original theme.

A perfect example of such construction is the short lyric
"Tears."[43] The theme here is the repeated word "Tears," given
three times. (This is the same device of the repeated note which
was observed in "Out of the Cradle," a fact which in itself relates
this aria to the other. "Tears" appeared first in the edition of 1867,
the edition in which the former aria was revised to make use of the
repeated note pattern. Such facts seem to indicate that Whitman

regarded this lyric as a composition similar to the bird song in "Out of the Cradle.") The theme is followed by a development in lines of increasing length and mounting intensity, to be followed in turn by a return to the original theme. One critic has pointed out that the poem falls into three free verse stanzas, on the basis of its accentual patterns;[44] the three stanzas correspond roughly with the three divisions of the aria.

Undeniably this kind of progress and return, or "envelope" structure, as it has been called in Whitman,[45] is common in literature and in all kinds of art. But since other aspects of such a poem as "Tears" suggest the aria, and since Whitman unquestionably knew scores of such aria tunes and hummed them to himself, it seems a fair guess that the form was derived, if only subconsciously, from opera.

Another excellent example of his use of the form, showing that it was far from accidental with him, is "By the Bivouac's Fitful Flame."[46] Here, however, the opening figure consists strictly of two lines rather than one, and at the conclusion the sense of return is remarkably achieved by reversing the order of the two lines so that the reader seems to be retraveling the road he took, to end at the spot where he began.

The same device is employed in "One Hour to Madness and Joy."[47] In its declamatory, not to say exclamatory, style, this poem suggests the recitative rather than the aria, yet a closer examination indicates that the poet aimed at the effect of unrestrained singing, not rhythmic chanting. He is singing at the very top of his voice, uninhibited, torrential song flowing from him as physical raptures for once drive him to reckless disregard for his own pleasures. And yet, even here, where Whitman is glorying in freedom, it is possible to detect his sense of musical form welding the apparently wild cries together into an aria.

An interesting example of how this feeling for musical form, perhaps not wholly conscious, sometimes operated to enable Whitman to build his diffuse and incoherent ideas into a solid structure is to be found in a comparative examination of the different versions of the elaborate "Inscription" for Leaves of Grass published by Clifton J. Furness in Walt Whitman's Workshop.[48] Though all the ideas in the Inscriptions found their way into various poems, the Inscriptions themselves, in the form in which Furness reproduced them, were never published by Whitman. Indeed for many years they were lost and came to light only after Whitman's death. But though the poet never used them and was apparently never quite satisfied with their expression, they are important documents, for they concern the ideas at the very heart of his work and they attempt to give clear, memorable, and inspiring expression to those ideas.

When the first version, in a kind of mannered, rhythmic prose is compared with the last, a somewhat unusually constructed poem, it seems clear that the poet was working toward some sort of musical form. The first version is merely a rambling "Letter to the Reader." In discursive paragraphs the poet discusses the intimate relationship which must exist between him and the reader and enumerates and explains the various themes of the poetry to follow; individuality, suggestiveness, physiology, the New World, belief. He also explains that he is proposing to inspire the reader and that the reader make much or little of the work, as he will. The important fact is, however, that there is not the slightest evidence of structure. The ideas are jumbled together in the most haphazard way, and the reader completes the Inscription with the feeling that he has been wallowing in a mass of fluid thought.

The fifth revision of the work is greatly different. It is only a little more than half as long. Ideas have been crystallized and more compactly expressed. The long wordy paragraphs have become something like the long line which is associated with Whitman, though here the line, sometimes including more than one sentence, is closer to a verse paragraph or stanza. Most important, however, is the fact that it is now not a rambling letter but an announcement, organized and clear. It begins:

Small is the theme of the following chant, yet the greatest—namely, One's-self, a simple, separate person. That for the use of the New World, I sing.[49]

Following this thematic statement, its various implications are developed. First, all the aspects of personality are presented, physical and spiritual. Then the role of personality in the New World, or Democracy, is suggested. Finally, the method of "singing" is explained and the responsibilities of both poet and reader outlined as the poet assumes them. At last there is a return to the theme stated at the outset, of course varied slightly in presentation:

Indeed this is no book but more a man, within whose breast the common heart is throbbing so much. No printed leaves but human lips, O friend, for your sake freely speaking.

The Epos of a life;—the road you tread today,—the workman's shop, or a farmer's field, the city's hum, or woods or trackless wild—O'er river lake or sea—(with shows I knew of crimson war)—along the single thread, so interspersed Him of the Lands (perhaps yourself) identical, I sing.[50]

In other words, though this poem is not in any sense to be regarded as an aria, it does display an application and extension of the aria structure to ideas which had apparently been very hard to get suitably organized and which were very important to their author. It shows quite clearly the statement of theme, development, and recapitulation method by which many musical compositions are built and is an indication of Whitman's awareness of this method.

Two still further revised versions of the Inscription finally found their way into Leaves of Grass. One now stands as the very first poem, "One's-Self I Sing,"[51] and it is interesting to notice that it is really a drastically condensed rendering of the original, and more important, it retains clearly the progress and return structure. The other poem, "Small the Theme of My Chant,"[52] which consists of sections of the original rather than revisions of it, does not display the musical form and suffers as a result. It reads like a fragment, in other words.

To return to materials closer to the actual aria, however, occasionally Whitman conceived a poem which is related to the aria more in the general effect than from any technical qualities. Such a poem is "Prayer of Columbus,"[53] which, as Canby has pointed out, "reads like the last aria of the tenor in a tragic opera."[54] Whitman would doubtless have been more pleased with that comment than with one which follows to the effect that the Prayer's music is Tennysonian. Whitman respected to the full Tennyson's ability to utilize the musical possibilities of words, but he felt that Tennyson was usually overconcerned with the matter.

Perfectly befitting a prayer, the mood of this poem is quiet, humble, imploring, remarkably so for Whitman, and, though purporting to deal with Columbus, is so deeply personal in tone that it must be taken to be autobiographical. The poet is reconciled to death and affirms his unshaken faith in God. In the slowly moving, carefully wrought phrases, the note of profound sincerity reaches out and touches the reader exactly as music had touched the poet in the opera house. The poem is filled with beautiful and memorable lines, whose controlled rhythm and planned sound permit the ideas to affect the reader in the most personal way.

> I am too full of woe! . . .
>
> Breathe, bathe myself once more in thee, commune with thee. . . .
>
> The urge, the ardor, the unconquerable will. . . .[55]
>
> Old, poor, and paralyzed, I thank thee. . . .[56]

Such lines and many others are irresistibly affecting music, and show, like others we have looked at, how much Whitman was influenced in style by the music which, as he said, was always round him.

NOTES—CHAPTER V

1. Inclusive Edition, p. 65.
2. Brockway, Weinstock, op. cit., p. 142.
3. Edward Carpenter, Days with Walt Whitman (London, 1906), p. 119.
4. Inclusive Edition, p. 41.
5. Ibid., p. 34.
6. Ibid., p. 51.
7. Giuseppe Verdi, Ernani, ed. Berthold Tours (London: Novello, Ewer and Co., Undated), p. 52.
8. Inclusive Edition, p. 60.
9. Ibid., p. 61.
10. Ibid., p. 73.
11. Uncollected Poetry and Prose, II, 98.
12. Inclusive Edition, p. 41.
13. Traubel, op. cit., I, 163.
14. Inclusive Edition, p. 176.
15. Ibid., p. 172.
16. Ibid., p. 220.
17. Ibid., p. 210.
18. Ibid., p. 276.

19. A Child's Reminiscence, p. 10.
20. Inclusive Edition, p. 211.
21. Vincenzo Bellini, Norma (Paris: Maurice Schlesinger, Undated), p. 56.
22. Inclusive Edition, p. 636.
23. Ibid., p. 212.
24. Ibid., p. 213.
25. Ibid., p. 214.
26. Ibid., p. 637.
27. Francis Toye, Giuseppe Verdi, His Life and Works (London: William Heinemann, Ltd., 1931), p. 44.
28. "A word about Tennyson," Prose, III, 146.
29. Inclusive Edition, p. 212.
30. Ibid., p. 211.
31. Ibid., p. 214.
32. Ibid., p. 214.
33. Ibid., p. 281.
34. Ibid., p. 175.
35. Ibid., p. 176.
36. Ibid., p. 177.
37. Ibid., p. 241.
38. Ibid., p. 242.
39. Ibid., p. 246.
40. Abbott, op. cit., p. 140.
41. Gaetano Donizetti, La Favorita, edd. Arthur Sullivan, J. Pittman (London, Undated), p. 252.
42. Ibid., p. 11.
43. Inclusive Edition, p. 218.
44. Sculley Bradley, "The Fundamental Metrical Principle in Whitman's Poetry," American Literature, X, 449 (January, 1939).
45. Allen, Handbook, p. 399.
46. Inclusive Edition, p. 255.
47. Ibid., p. 90.
48. Workshop, pp. 167-74.
49. Ibid., p. 173.
50. Ibid., p. 174.
51. Inclusive Edition, p. 1.
52. Ibid., p. 434.
53. Ibid., p. 352.
54. Canby, op. cit., p. 286.
55. Inclusive Edition, p. 352.
56. Ibid., p. 353.

Chapter VI

Phrase and Measure

IT MUST ALWAYS be remembered that in the days when Whitman sat again and again in the opera house, inspired and uplifted by the floods of golden sound he heard there, he was also at work on *Leaves of Grass* evolving its technique and struggling with its details. Opera had taught him that for the ideas he wanted to express the techniques of conventional poetry would not serve and that he would have to devise a freer method. He had decided that the ultimate effect he wanted in his poems was exactly that of operatic music, and opera had given him ideas about the larger aspects of a new structure. What could be more natural than that he should turn to opera for suggestions about the smaller technical details which would give his lines the freedom he wanted? Some of opera's more detailed lessons, like the larger ones, he probably absorbed subconsciously, for he was constantly in the midst of "that music," but many of them he must have learned deliberately.

In devising a suitable poetic manner, one of the problems he would have had to solve would have been the creation of a properly flexible line as a poetic unit. Certainly the conventional line with its established number of accents was too restricted. Whether its meaning came to a full stop at the end of the line or was carried over into the following one, the fact that there was a regular number of stresses and that the words were so spaced on the page as to call attention to the regularity would be bound to give a pendulum-swinging monotony which would be death to the surging, free music Whitman wanted. "The poetic quality is not marshal'd in rhyme and uniformity," he wrote in his preface in 1855.[1] And in an unpublished note he wrote, "America needs her own poems in her own body and spirit and different from all hitherto—freer—more muscular, comprehending more and unspeakably grander."[2]

What was the unit of expression on the operatic stage which gave the impression of freedom rather than regularity and restraint? A

moment's listening would give the answer: the phrase, the musical
phrase, molded in opera by the singer's voice and limited by his

breath. The meaning of the text could be accommodated and, just as important, shades of emotion could be suggested by the contour of the phrase. It could be leisurely and rambling, or short and exclamatory, serene and happy or choked with emotion, legato or staccato. Though it had perceptible shape in its rise and fall, its progress and return, its crescendo and diminuendo, its form was a variable and adaptable thing, not an unyielding mold into which material must be forced or for which ideas must be trimmed to fit. Furthermore, the operatic phrase was inseparably related to the performer's voice; it permitted the inflections natural to the expression of emotion as well as meaning. In short, here was a perfect unit of expression, with form, which is requisite to all art, and at the same time freedom, so necessary to Whitman's expansive material.

As illustrations of the varieties in phrasing which suggest fluid movement rather than regularity, two vocal passages from operatic scenes which Whitman knew well may be examined. The first, already noted in another connection, is from *Ernani* by Verdi, and portrays the emotions of Don Ruy Gomez de Silva when he discovers the infidelity of Elvira, his affianced bride. The phrases and accents are indicated in the usual fashion.[3]

Another scene is that in *Norma* by Bellini in which the Druid priestess prays to the Moon Goddess as the worshipers kneel about her.[4]

One can see easily how the contrasting moods of the two quotations are reflected in their phrasing. In the first, with its initial anger changing to heart-breaking anguish, the phrases begin with rapid movement and many syllables, changing into short, sobbing cries in the slower section. In the second, a noble and eloquent prayer, the phrases contain few syllables but these are sustained as long as possible with imploring effect, and are so decorated musically as to evoke all the possible beauty from a rich soprano voice (and incidentally make the aria so difficult that only one or two sopranos in a musical generation ever attempt to sing it).

It must be understood, of course, that a 'phrase' or line of poetry may contain many more syllables than a phrase of vocal music, for the reason that individual syllables are usually sustained longer when sung than when spoken. On the other hand, if the poet thinks of his line as a musical phrase, it may contain very few syllables, the poet depending on the voice of the reader to translate the accented syllables into prolonged sound, increasing emphasis and heightening meaning, both by decreasing the tempo and by enriching the color of the sound.

For these reasons Whitman could write in "Song of Myself," Section 3,[5] two lines very different in length, but each a phrase with its own qualities of time, color, and contour.

> I have heard what the talkers were talking, the talk of the
>   beginning and the end,
>
> Urge and urge and urge. . . .

The first, with its six accents and twenty syllables, suggests what to the poet was meaningless chatter and babble. The second, with three accents and five syllables, conveys the slow, deep, eternal desires which make "endings" impossible. Properly read, both lines disclose the fact that they are based on a single breath and that they can be molded into a perceptible contour.

Again, in Section 21[6] of the same poem, there are the lines:

> The pleasures of heaven are with me and the pains of hell
>   are with me,
>
> Smile O voluptuous cool-breath'd earth!
> Smile for your lover comes.

Each of the lines is an individual phrase and easily recognizable as such. Though greatly different in length, each has an obviously perceptible rise and fall, which gives it a unity and identity of its own, appropriate to its meaning.

Examples might be compiled endlessly; two more may suffice here. From "Out of the Cradle Endlessly Rocking":

> Over the sterile sands and the fields beyond, where the child leaving his bed wander'd alone, bareheaded, barefoot,[7]
>
> Shine! shine! shine![8]

The first line is an appropriate phrase for the moving, narrative quality of the material. The second begins a passionate song. In lines of the first type, syllables may be piled up as long as there is breath; in the second, the breath must be used for rich, colorful tone. Both are complete 'phrases' in the musical sense, however.

It is the quality of the emotion which invariably determines the shape of phrases used to convey it. This is true, as everyone will agree, in all spoken utterances, and skillful dramatists have always recognized it. It is most noticeable in opera, however, where composers have taken advantage of this psychological fact to increase the evidence of emotion and identify its quality by giving characters phrases carefully shaped to express anger, ecstatic happiness, and the like. In opera, more obviously and literally than in drama, every varying tonal inflection of the phrase is planned and controlled by musical notation. In Whitman's two great operatic poems, "Out of the Cradle"[9] and "When Lilacs Last in the Dooryard Bloom'd,"[10] we can discover easily that he, too, has recognized the necessity of phrasing for emotion, phrasing so that the voice, the greatest possible vehicle for conveying emotion, may have perfect opportunity to do so, and to identify the proper character of the emotion.

In the former poem, the first lyric sings of the ecstatic joy of love: "We two together." Such joy naturally overflows in exclamations of rapture, like the opening: "Shine! shine! shine!" The phrases are short and impulsive:

> Two together!
> Winds blow south, or winds blow north,
> Day come white, or night come black. . . .[11]

The following lyric in the same poem is very different, singing not joy in union but sorrow in separation. The songs are alike in one respect, however. In the second, the uncontrolled and wild despair also results in short exclamatory phrases. But here the movement of the song is halted by an abundance of punctuation, largely exclamation points. The phrases are now broken and choking.

> O throat! O trembling throat!
> Sound clearer through the atmosphere!
>
> O darkness! O in vain!
> O I am very sick and sorrowful!
>
> O throat! O throbbing heart![12]

How different is the death lyric of "When Lilacs Last in the Dooryard Bloom'd." Only in one line are exclamation points to be found, and these are followed by one of the most completely liquid lines in the song. The phrases are *cantabile* in the extreme, with even the breaks at the ends of lines less emphatic than usual. Every care seems to have been taken to preserve the continuity of the melody. The reason is not hard to find. This is a song of serenity and confidence. Out of grief and doubt has come understanding of one of life's great mysteries. The song conveying that understanding must be calm and untroubled, its phrases unhurried and placid.

> The night in silence under many a star,
> The ocean shore and the husky whispering wave whose
>   voice I know,
> And the soul turning to thee O vast and well-veil'd death,
> And the body gratefully nestling close to thee.[13]

If it is true that Whitman thought of the line as a musical phrase, a unit, capable of being related to other phrases but essentially complete in itself, it should follow that he would permit no enjambment in his work. If he allowed his meaning to overflow from one line to another, that fact would show that the line was not an independent unit in his mind. The circumstance is, of course, that there is virtually no enjambment at all in Whitman. One scholar who has taken the pains to count the lines insists that "in more than 10, 500 lines in *Leaves of Grass*, there are, by my count, only twenty run-on lines."[14] Of course some lines are more closely related than others, but a line without end-punctuation is practically nonexistent, and usually the line is a unit of meaning, even when it is not a sentence. For example, lines where the material is cast into the form of an independent clause, though not punctuated as a sentence, have an obviously independent effect:

> I think I could turn and live with animals, they're so placid
>   and self-contain'd,
> I stand and look at them long and long.[15]

Lines of which the material consists of dependent clauses are given an effect of independent identity by the exact repetition of phrasal form:

> Where the mocking-bird sounds his delicious gurgles,
>   cackles, screams, weeps,
> Where the hay-rick stands in the barn-yard, where the dry-
>   stalks are scatter'd, where the brood-cow waits in the
>   hovel. . . .[16]

Sometimes the lines are composed of mere phrases. These are given identity in the same way:

> Ever the hard unsunk ground,
> Ever the eaters and drinkers, ever the upward and down-
>   ward sun, ever the air and ceaseless tides. . . .[17]

Other lines, where the material is not formed into repeated syntactical forms, though this device is used with remarkable frequency, become independent units either by their construction as sentences or the natural independence of their meaning.

In the light of such reasoning about the line, it is easy to see why Whitman found conventional end-rhyme artificial and affected. To him the design of the phrase or line identified it as a unit; its ending did not need to be tagged. Furthermore, lines did not need to be joined together by repetition of end sounds. The relationship between lines of a section would have to come from the same overall design of the phrase itself which served to make the line a unit. For example, in "Out of the Cradle" a variety of devices used to relate the lines into patterns without end-rhyme are at once apparent, as indeed they are in nearly every poem.

First there is the repetition of the opening of the line, making the phrases almost identical in contour:

> Out of the cradle endlessly rocking,
> Out of the mocking-bird's throat, the musical shuttle,
> Out of the Ninth-month midnight. . . .

There is also the use of openings which are not identical, but strongly similar in syntax and meaning:

> Down from the shower'd halo,
> Up from the mystic play of shadows twining and twisting
>   as if they were alive,
> Out from the patches of briers and blackberries. . . .[18]

To mention only one more example, there is the similar 'fall' or close of lines:

> The aria sinking,
> All else continuing, the stars shining,
> The winds blowing, the notes of the bird continuous
>   echoing,
> With angry moans the fierce old mother incessantly
>   moaning. . . .[19]

In the case of this example, the use of the present participle suggests the fluid, continuing effect of the bird's song. The extreme variation of line length in a short space may also be noted, and the reasons for the variations. The first short line suggests the breathless pause at the moment of the song's end; then as its magic and that of the natural surroundings begin to work their spell, the lines increase in length and rapidity of tempo, rising to their greatest length and intensity as the mystical and emotional experience reaches its climax. This is a perfect example of Whitman's artistic use of varying contours for special effects, and he must have felt that conventional rhyme would have detracted from rather than added to the free movement of the passage. Certainly it would have distracted the reader's response from the whole phrases or lines by calling attention to repeated sounds at their closes.

One other aspect of Whitman's conception of the line or 'phrase' of poetry is his use of the caesura, which has been much discussed.[20] Particularly in the first edition of Leaves of Grass he seemed to be conscious of the importance of the various breaks in the lines, a fact which becomes apparent when his punctuation is examined. Certain tendencies are apparent here, though no settled policy can be discovered. In lines that are to give a particularly liquid and flowing effect, an unbroken musical strain, punctuation is reduced to the barest minimum if used at all. For example:

> Smile O voluptuous cool-breath'd earth,[21]

The same thing is true where the poet wanted a special unity of meaning:

> I find I incorporate gneiss and coal and long threaded
> moss and fruits and grains and esculent roots,[22]

Where the pauses resulting from ordinary punctuation will not harm the contour of a phrase (or where the contour is not especially important) punctuation is employed normally. Where special pauses are required within the line, pauses that will not break the phrase but heighten its effectiveness, a series of four periods is used. In what later became Section 26 of "Song of Myself" this usage is especially interesting, for it shows how the poet wished the reader to pause with him and, in effect, listen to certain sounds. It will be observed that the lines, even with the indicated pauses, are still units.

> I think I will do nothing for a long time but listen,
> And accrue what I hear into myself . . . . and let sounds
> contribute toward me.
>
> I hear bravuras of birds . . . . the bustle of growing wheat
> . . . . gossip of flames . . . . clack of sticks cooking my
> meals.
>
> I hear the sound of the human voice . . . . a sound I love,
> I hear all sounds as they are turned to their uses . . . .
> sounds of the city and sounds out of the city . . . .
> sounds of the day and night;
> Talkative young ones to those that like them . . . . the reci-
> tative of fish-pedlars and fruit-pedlars . . . . the loud
> laugh of workpeople at their meals,
> The angry base of disjointed friendship . . . . the faint
> tones of the sick. . . .[23]

Occasionally, in the first edition, groups of two and three, rather than the usual four, periods appear. At first glance this would seem to be an attempt to give a sort of time value to the pauses. Such an interpretation is hardly borne out by a close examination of the usages; the differences between the four- and two-period instances are negligible. (The inconsistencies could easily be errors in typesetting.)

In his final revisions punctuation was still important to Whitman. He was careful to use end punctuation invariably, usually the comma for lines within the paragraph groupings and a period at the end of such a group. There are exceptions, to be sure, but his consistency, regardless of preceding grammatical construction, shows his feeling that the line units were essentially equal or at least parallel. He abandoned the groups of periods and substituted commas, perhaps feeling that the periods created too great a visual break in the line unit, and used commas regardless of the grammatical construction of the line:

> I hear the chorus, it is a grand opera.

In the revised lines, in any case, it seems that Whitman was still careful to place caesuras where he wanted them for a variety of effects. The topic is of interest here only insofar as it is related to his musical conception of the line as a whole. At first glance one might think that the caesura breaks the phrase into parts and that the line can no longer be regarded as a unit, since a phrase in vocal music is not usually thought to extend through a rest or break. There are two explanations, however, to show that this is not the case. First, occasionally two or three small phrases in music, each in a sense independent, are clearly organized into a larger phrase, itself a genuine unit though made up of small parts. This is what Whitman does in such a line as:

> I hear the bravuras of birds, bustle of growing wheat,
>   gossip of flames, clack of sticks cooking my meals. . . .

The second explanation is that the caesura (whether indicated by comma or other mark) is, in effect, not so much a rest, bringing to a stop the sound of the voice, as it is a held note, or note of greater time value than others, prolonging the sound of the vowel just preceding it for a time, to secure richness of effect, emphasis, or merely to give the reader time to assimilate all the meaning from the phrase before progressing. Such a line is:

> I hear the sound I love, the sound of the human voice.[24]

More extreme breaks in the line which still do not destroy the phrasal unity are to be found in such lines as:

> Soothe! soothe! soothe![25]

Here the exclamation points do not indicate an exclamatory effect so much as a greatly prolonged sound.

A third important possibility is that Whitman wished to give his musical phrases or lines pauses which should have the effect of those in operatic recitative, when accompanying chords from the orchestra were sounded as a kind of emphatic punctuation to the vocal line.

To generalize, it is possible to believe that Whitman was highly conscious of breaks in his lines and of their various effects, as all poets must be, but that the breaks were always devices within a unit, never a major stop, or the end of a thought unit. His varied use of the caesura was a part of his feeling for the line as a musical phrase.

In conventional poetry the smaller unit of the metrical foot, with its established number of syllables and its regular arrangement of them, contributes quite as much to the impression of rigorous system as the regular line; at least so Whitman felt. Of course skillful metrists had been able to introduce remarkable variety into their uses of a regular metrical pattern, but the fact remained that it was an imposed form. It seemed to Whitman that the idea must always generate its own form, even in the small element of the verse foot. Could music be of assistance in designing a new, freer kind of poetic foot? What was the 'foot' of music, the unit of which phrases were compounded? It was the measure, of course, with its recurring accent which every listener can detect, whether marching to a band, whirling to the strains of a waltz, or listening to an operatic aria, where, as in most vocal music, the sense accent falls on the initial beat, thus calling attention to it. (The verbal phrase may, of course, begin anywhere in a measure, the syllables preceding the first accent being called the 'pick-up' notes, an effect like anacrusis in verse.)

In the measure of music the notes are not limited in number. In the waltz, there are not always just three notes, the first accented and the others unaccented; there may be any number of notes in the measure, and though the listener is always conscious of the first beat, the phrasal accent may fall on any beat in the measure. Translated into terms of poetry this would mean that a foot might have any number of syllables grouped with each accent, the determining principle being the demands of the phrase or line, its movement and meaning, not the fact that every accent in the line must be followed or preceded by an unaccented one—not some preëstablished pattern, in short.

Again, some measures of operatic song which Whitman loved should be examined. A possible example is a melody often sung by his favorite, Alboni, in the opera *La Favorita*. It occurs when the king's mistress debates with herself whether or not she can allow herself to marry her real lover without confessing her past.[26]

What a variety of phrasing results from varying the number of notes in individual measures, from eleven to two, thus controlling the flow and the emotional significance of the phrase. In the opening measures Leonora is torn by indecision and doubt; in the later phrases she has reached her decision and sings calmly and richly of her great love.

It is easy to see that Whitman treated the poetic foot as exactly such a flexible unit, the measure of music. Though for years it was overlooked, it has now been established that he was perfectly conscious of the recurring accents in his lines.[27] What obscured the fact for so long was the fact that he did not feel responsible for maintaining a fixed number of syllables to accompany each accent. He was aware of the poetic foot, but to him it was the servant of the line or phrase, which in turn served the impulse or idea. There could be no cramping or syllable counting; the foot must permit any number of syllables just as the measure permitted any number of notes or rests.

Some representative lines of Whitman should now be noted as examples of his conception of the foot as a flexible unit, for instance one from "Out of the Cradle":

> Over the sterile sands and the fields beyond, where the
>   child leaving his bed wander'd alone, bareheaded,
>   barefoot. . . .[28]

Translated into metrical feet, this will look as follows:

$$\cup\ \cup\ \cup\ \cup\ \diagup\ \big|\ \cup\ \cup\ \cup\ \diagup\ \big\|\ \cup\ \cup\ \diagup\ \big|\ \times\ \diagup\ \big|\ \cup\ \cup\ \diagup\ \big|\ \times\ \diagup\ \big|\ \cup\ \cup\ \diagup\ \big\|\ \times\ \diagup\ \big|\ \cup\ \cup\ \diagup\ \big|\ \cup$$

The line suggests movement and action primarily, though toward its close the emotion of loneliness is suggested. Appropriately the opening feet are full and rapid while the closing ones are shorter, forcing the reader to prolong the sounds to give each foot an equivalent amount of time. The sensitive reader does this automatically, feeling that the accents should be sounded with regularity. This is what T. S. Omond calls the "isochronous period" in his A Study of Metre, insisting that there is always a regular period of time between stresses in poetry, no matter how many syllables there may be.[29] In music, of course, the element of chance and the taste of a sensitive performer do not enter into the timing to so great an extent; performers are forced to observe the composer's wishes by the time values assigned to notes and rests.

Another line of poetry, another one from "Out of the Cradle," shows a very different effect. This time the line is slow and dark with emotion:

> Low hangs the moon, it rose late. . . .[30]

Translated into metrical feet, this will look as follows:

$$\text{´} \mid \text{´} \mid \text{ᴗ} \quad \text{´} \parallel \text{ᴗ ´} \mid \text{´}$$

Contrast the number of syllables in each foot here with those in the line above. Whitman has insured the prolonged sound of his dark vowels by reducing the unaccented syllables; it is as if he were making the first word in the line a whole note in a measure, not depriving it of time by introducing other notes to be sounded within the time limits of the measure.[31]

Thus by treating the poetic foot as a flexible unit capable of reflecting the subtlest and most delicate variations in movement and rhythm, Whitman made easily available to himself devices which composers of music have always had at their disposal. In strictly conventional poetry it had been difficult to manage subtle shifts in rhythm to suggest shades of meaning and feeling without changing the prevailing meter of the poem. Such a change would have usually seemed too abrupt and obvious. The relatively great freedom of the composer in varying numbers of notes, their patterns and their accents, within the regular framework of the measure gave music a rhythmic fluidity which Whitman wanted in his songs.

Perhaps one more example right here will further clarify this point. Sections 2 and 3 of that most musical of all Whitman's poem's, "When Lilacs Last in the Dooryard Bloom'd," with accents indicated, provide a startling contrast:

2

O pówerful wéstern fállen stár!

O shádes of níght—O móody, téarful níght!

O gréat stár disappéar'd—O the black múrk that hídes the
stár

O cruel hands that hold me powerless—O helpless soul
   of me!

O harsh surrounding cloud that will not free my soul.

3

In the dooryard fronting an old farm-house near the whitewash'd palings,

Stands the lilac-bush tall-growing with heart-shaped leaves

of rich green,

With many a pointed blossom rising delicate, with the perfume strong I love,

With every leaf a miracle—and from this bush in the
   dooryard,

With delicate-color'd blossoms and heart-shaped leaves of

rich green,

A sprig with its flower I break.[32]

It can be seen at once that by varying the content and form of
the foot the poet changed the movement and mood of the passages
completely. In this poem, as in many others, he wished to suggest
rising and falling emotion, great surges of feeling alternating with
somewhat more casual connecting passages. He was able to do this
in part by his musical use of the foot as a unit. In Section 2, the
drooping star, symbol of Lincoln's death, momentarily overwhelms
the poet. In Section 3, he recovers and is able to proceed with the
task of preparing his tribute. The effects of the two passages had to
be strikingly different, as different as the effects of rage and sorrow
in the *Ernani* music quoted above. Whitman's conception of the

foot as a flexible unit made this possible here and throughout his poetry.

It should be noted in passing that Whitman's usage in what are normally spoken of as rising and falling meters was also irregular. Within one poem, often in lines side by side, examples of both rhythms may be discovered. English poetry is of course prevailingly rising in rhythm, that is, iambic and anapestic rather than trochaic and dactyllic, probably because speech in English falls naturally into such rhythms. The greater percentage of Whitman's lines are traditional in this respect, but he often changes the rhythm, particularly in the more notably rhythmic and musical passages. It would seem that in lines where he felt himself closest to music he instinctively shifted to an exact duplication of musical rhythm, with its beat on the first element of the measure. Examples of such lines might be the opening ones from "Whispers of Heavenly Death:"

Whispers of | heavenly | death | murmur'd I | hear

Labial | gossip of | night, || sibilant | chorals

Footsteps | gently as|cending, || mystical | breezes | wafted |

soft and | low[33]

It has been pointed out that Whitman's rhythm and the wide variety of feet he used constantly were not new in English poetry, that the greatest poets in English have always permitted themselves variety in meter and, except in necclassical periods, have rarely limited themselves to counting syllables. In other words, it has been held that when Whitman scorned syllable counting, he was associating himself with a great tradition of English poetry which began in Old English times. This is of course true, but Whitman was not aware of it. He thought of himself as revolting from tradition in verse, from conventions in technique which seemed restricting to him, though the restrictions have always been more apparent than real. It is likely that he was first inspired to this revolt, then assisted in it by the technique of opera.

It is of course incidental, but it should perhaps be pointed out that Whitman's musical conception of the line and foot is one of the qualities which have attracted so many composers to his work as verbal text for their musical composition. His work has been set to music more often than that of any other American poet. What composers find in Whitman is the phrase already molded; it is not necessary to go forward and backward in the lines, repeating words and groups of words to effect a suitable text for a musical phrase. (Even the composers of the operas Whitman loved had to treat their librettos in this way, and for that reason he was likely not influenced at all in his own poems by the librettos he studied. The lines of the libretto do not correspond to the vocal phrase, which is what he knew and remembered.)

In setting Whitman to music the composer finds the phrases already fashioned, and the reiteration necessary to hold the phrases together already provided for. The composer needs only to add the notes.

NOTES—CHAPTER VI

1. Inclusive Edition, p. 493.
2. Workshop, p. 67.
3. Giuseppe Verdi, Ernani, ed. Berthold Tours (London: Novello, Ewer and Co., Undated), p. 52.
4. Vincenzo Bellini, Norma (Paris: Maurice Schlesinger, Undated), p. 56.
5. Inclusive Edition, p. 25.
6. Ibid., p. 41.
7. Ibid., p. 210
8. Ibid., p. 211.
9. Ibid., p. 270.
10. Ibid., p. 276.
11. Ibid., p. 211.
12. Ibid., p. 213.
13. Ibid., p. 282.
14. Autrey Nell Wiley, "Reiterative Devices in Leaves of Grass," American Literature, I, 161 (May, 1929).
15. Inclusive Edition, p. 50.
16. Ibid., p. 53.
17. Ibid., p. 65.
18. Ibid., p. 210.
19. Ibid., p. 214.
20. Allen, Handbook, pp. 415-17.
21. Leaves of Grass (Brooklyn, New York, 1855), p. 27.

22. *Ibid.*, p. 34. Some lines which were broken in the first edition were later united without punctuation for unity of effect. For example,

> I am the poet of the body,
> And I am the poet of the soul.

became in later editions:

> I am the poet of the body and I am the poet of the soul. . . .

23. *Ibid.*, p. 31.

24. Inclusive Edition, p. 47.

25. *Ibid.*, p. 212.

26. Donizetti, *La Favorita*, p. 163.

27. Bradley, *op. cit.*, pp. 437-59.

28. Inclusive Edition, p. 210.

29. T. S. Omond, *A Study of Metre* (London, 1920), Chapter 1.

30. Inclusive Edition, p. 212.

31. In 1880, long after Whitman had evolved his technique, Sidney Lanier published his *The Science of English Verse*, in which he studied exhaustively the relations between the rhythms of music and verse. Lanier's work is in no sense intended as a defense of the type of foot or measure employed by Whitman, though indirectly it serves to explain the latter's method. Lanier attempted to show that all standard English verse, as read sensitively, can be "scanned" adequately only in terms of musical notation, and he demonstrated that even conventional verse, so "scanned," is highly irregular. It was his belief that the regular verse patterns provided sufficient opportunity for variation, through the imposition of the rhythms of speech, to make them interesting and effective. It was Whitman's purpose to dispose of regular syllabic patterns altogether, and to treat the foot wholly as a measure in music.—Sidney Lanier, *The Science of English Verse*, ed. Paull Franklin Baum (Centennial Edition, II, Baltimore: The Johns Hopkins Press, 1945).

32. Inclusive Edition, p. 276.

33. *Ibid.*, p. 369.

Melody

D ESPITE HIS great interest in opera, Whitman never claimed for his poetry what he called "verbal melody." In "A Backward Glance," for example, he wrote, "I know well enough, too, that . . . especially in verbal melody and all the conventional technique of poetry not only the divine works that today stand ahead in the world's reading, but dozens more, transcend (some of them immeasurably transcend) all I have done or could do."[1]

He by no means meant to imply that this was a serious weakness in his work. Indeed he had observed that a preoccupation with such matters sometimes developed into a flaw in the work of such otherwise impressive poets as Poe and Lanier. Speaking of the latter to his friend Horace Traubel on one occasion, Whitman said, "This extreme sense of the melodic, a virtue in itself, when carried into the art of the writer becomes a fault. Why? Why, because it tends to place the first emphasis on tone, sound—on the lilt . . . Study Lanier's choice of words—they are too often fit rather for sound than sense."[2]

Such comment was related to Whitman's deep conviction that all aspects of form in poetry which restricted the organic development of the idea into its own form were inartistic. It seemed to him that constant care to achieve lush richness of sound through what the prosodist calls alliteration, assonance, phonetic syzygy and the like, could end only in forcing the idea into a preformed mold. However appropriate the sound might be to the idea, the idea must grow naturally, without the restraints of such detailed considerations.

There is more to melody than richness of tone, however. In fact, melody is only incidentally tone; it is primarily pattern, of both sound and rhythm. Lanier and Poe could have shown, of course, that the tone of their verse, their "verbal melody," was compounded from patterns of sound, patterns of great delicacy and subtlety. But it was the subtlety and delicacy which Whitman found restraining; it was not the pattern. In fact, whenever pattern seemed not to restrain the growth of an idea Whitman employed it in giving his poems structure. The pattern could never be a preformed mold, however, like alliteration and rhyme or the sonnet and stanza. It must be completely flexible and yielding.

Like anyone, cultivated or uncultivated, who had listened to great amounts of music, especially opera, Whitman must have realized that in musical composition melody is based upon repetition. The listener hears endless repetitions of phrases and figures, patterns of rhythm and tone varying in length from two or three notes to several measures, and his delight lies chiefly in the pleasurable recognition of these patterns as they recur. The reader has only to hum to himself the tune of "Ol' Man River" to discover the importance of repetition in this popular tune. The opening four-note rhythmic figure occurs eighteen times during the melody, while a contrasting pattern, "You an' me," is heard five times.[3] It is the absence of such repetitions of up and down patterns of tone and pulsations in rhythm that make so much of so-called 'modern' music distasteful to the casual listener. On the other hand, the well-known 'dit dit dit dah' pattern of tone and accent in the first movement of Beethoven's Fifth Symphony, repeated skillfully as it is two hundred and forty-two times in that eight-minute composition, is what has given the movement its strong character.[3] In the great opera tunes which Whitman hummed to himself there was much repetition. It was chiefly repetition of phrase which he could have detected, of course, and instances of it may be seen in the opera melodies already quoted.

Melodically, the tunes Whitman knew left their mark on his poetic style, and it is an injustice to say that his poetry has no melody, for few other poets have ever used repetition with an effect so closely paralleling that of melodic form. One must understand, of course, that it is the movement of melody, perhaps we should say the structure, in which Whitman was interested, rather than in prevailing tonal quality at any given moment.

One of Whitman's biographers, De Selincourt, in fact the only one of recent times who has given much attention to the importance of music in the poet's developing art, has some interesting observations on this point. He explains first that as we proceed through a melody in music, we carry the sense of past effects along with us. Each phrase depends upon preceding phrases and effects for its charm, though through its slight variation, its contrast, its harmonic background, it must add its contribution to the general flow of musical ideas. De Selincourt finds the progression of Whitman's poetry comparable and adds, "Not only is the method of progression similar: the means of progression have also much in common. The chief difference between musical and verbal expression, as a rule, is that words, carrying each their modicum of meaning, have done their part when they have delivered it, while notes, being meaningless except in combination, develop new meanings by presenting a single combination in varying contexts or with varying accompaniment. In fact, repetition, which the artist in language scrupulously avoids, is the foundation and substance of musical expression. Now Whitman, for reasons we have touched on, uses words and phrases more as if they were notes than any other writer. ... It was to him part of the virtue and essence of life that its forms and processes were endlessly reduplicated; and poetry, which was delight in life, must somehow, he thought, mirror this elemental abundance."[4] The writer goes on to explain that Whitman thus repeats himself endlessly, as nature hammers away at our perceptions till we respond fully. It is important that in Whitman this repetition is usually managed as it is in music, and we can appreciate it best if we think of it in these terms rather than as rhetoric, as it has usually been considered. Once the reader develops a feeling for these musical patterns he will find most of Whitman's repetitions not tiresome but attractive in their own way.

Any page of *Leaves of Grass* will yield many examples of repetition, for it is Whitman's most often used device. An examination of some of the passages will disclose at once that in some of them the repetition is rhetorical, like that of the orator, who to emphasize a point pounds the rostrum and shouts his phrase over and over again. Whitman falls naturally into this manner when he speaks of oratory:

> O the orator's joys!
> To inflate the chest, to roll the thunder of the voice out
>   from the ribs and throat,

> To make the people rage, weep, hate, desire, with yourself,
> To lead America—to quell America with a great tongue.[5]

And the repeated rhetorical question, an orator's trick, is easy to discover.

> What do you suppose creation is?
> What do you suppose will satisfy the soul, except to walk
>   free and own no superior?
> What do you suppose I would intimate to you in a hun-
>   dred ways, but that man or woman is as good as God?[6]

Usually, however, the impulse behind the passages with repetitions is too clearly non-oratorical for us to accept the device as merely that of the orator. For example, it is to be discovered in what have been called the arias. Here, certainly, it serves a melodic purpose of its own. Glance once more at the arias previously quoted and at the lines from "Song of Myself":

> Sea of stretch'd ground-swells,
> Sea breathing broad and convulsive breaths,
> Sea of the brine of life and of unshovell'd yet always-ready
>   graves. . . .[7]

In such lines it is not pulpit-pounding emphasis which is sought; it is rather a recurring word, which, as a short pattern of notes makes a melody distinctive and memorable, will help to hold the song-like lines together. Emotional intensity is the natural result of such repetition, just as the repetition of the opening phrase of the quoted aria from La Favorita intensifies that emotional music.

In the examples just referred to, and, indeed, in most of the examples of repetition and parallel structure of lines quoted in previous chapters, it will be observed that the repeated elements stand first in the lines. This circumstance is to be found throughout Whitman's poetry. It has been estimated that forty-one percent of the more than 10,500 lines of Leaves of Grass contain such initial reiteration, a fact which shows a remarkable tendency.[8] One possible explanation for this stylistic idiosyncrasy is a musical one. In nearly all musical repetitions, and as has been said, melodic structure is based on repeated patterns, the similarities are discovered at the beginnings of figures and subjects. Whether long or short, the melodic elements being repeated begin alike. When a repeated figure is to be varied, the variation is introduced at the close of the pattern.

Similarly, Whitman is preoccupied with the beginnings of lines, not so often with their endings. (This is perhaps one reason for his distaste for end-rhyme.) Again one may open *Leaves of Grass* anywhere to find examples of such initial reiteration. From "Song of Myself" some lines beginning with identical words may be chosen:

> In vain the speeding or shyness,
> In vain the plutonic rocks send their old heat against my
>   approach,
> In vain the mastodon retreats beneath its own powder'd
>   bones,
> In vain objects stand leagues off and assume manifold
>   shapes,
> In vain the ocean settling in hollows and the great mon-
>   sters lying low,
> In vain the buzzard houses herself with the sky,
> In vain the snake slides through the creepers and logs. . . .[9]

A passage of similar repetitions but with differing grammatical construction may be noticed in "By Blue Ontario's Shore":

> I will confront these shows of the day and night,
> I will know if I am to be less than they,
> I will see if I am not as majestic as they,
> I will see if I am not as subtle and real as they,
> I will see if I am to be less generous than they. . . .[10]

It is recitative sections such as these which most clearly exemplify the special convictions of De Selincourt about the melodic movement of Whitman's lines. Over and over again the poems unfold, constructing themselves, as Whitman believed they should, one line building on another, with words repeated for the reader as if they were notes without meaning, with only sound, but with each line adding its new material to the whole poetic conception. When the reader learns to chant the words for their contribution to pattern, such passages lose what might be thought their monotony and become pleasurable.

A less obvious, and as a result a more artistic, example of initial reiteration is to be found in "Crossing Brooklyn Ferry." Here the repetitions are not prolonged. Rather they are used with subtlety to keep the structure of the passage flexible and to suggest not only the patterns of music but in this case the actual growth and unfolding of the idea. Section 3 of the poem follows.

It *avails not*, time nor place—distance *avails not*,
I am with *you*, *you* men and women of a *generation*, or
    ever so many *generations* hence,
Just as you feel when you look on the river and the sky,
    so *I felt*,
Just as any of you is one of a living *crowd*, *I was* one of a
    crowd,
Just as you are refreshed by the gladness of the river and
    the bright flow, *I was refreshed*,
Just as you stand and lean on the rail, yet *hurry* with the
    swift current, *I stood* yet *was hurried*,
Just as you look on the numberless masts of ships and the
    thick-stemm'd pipes of steamboats, *I look'd*.

I too many and many a time cross'd the river of old,
Watched the Twelfth-month sea-gulls, *saw* them high in
    the air floating with motionless wings, oscillating their
    bodies,
Saw how the glistening yellow lit up parts of their bodies
    and left the rest in strong shadow,
Saw the slow-wheeling circles and the gradual edging
    toward the south,
Saw the reflection of the summer sky in the water,
Had my eyes dazzled by the shimmering track of beams,
Look'd at the fine centrifugal spokes of light round the
    shape of my head in the sunlit water,
Look'd on the haze on the hills southward and south-west-
    ward,
Look'd on the vapor as it flew in fleeces tinged with violet,
Look'd toward the lower bay to notice the vessels arriving,
Saw their approach, *saw* aboard those that were near me,
Saw the white sails of schooners and sloops, *saw* the ships
    at anchor. . . .[11]

To show how words, phrases, and grammatical constructions have been repeated and woven through the context of the passage, they have been here italicized. Unquestionably the parallel line construction of the first division suggests the balanced rhetoric of the orator. Here Whitman is not being oratorical, however, and though the passage may owe something to his interest in and knowledge of oratory, it seems just as likely that in such quiet, reflective lines as these, he is repeating as the composer does, to build up mood and intensify emotion. It is particularly worth noticing how in the second part of the section while repeating a grammatical construction, he introduces sub-groups of reiterations by changing the verbs. Several important effects are thus achieved. One is the suggestion of calm, unhurried gazing, watching for a time one set of effects, then shifting slightly to perceive another kind of impressions. The sub-group of repetitions seem to hold the reader and force him to gaze with the poet at the varied types of visual impressions. Another effect is that an over-all impression of the situation gradually unfolds or grows on the reader's consciousness. Here the initial reiteration of melody is handled with great artistry.

But repetition to secure the pleasurable effects of melodic reiteration is found not only in initial usages, as the opening lines in the quoted passage show. The short poem "I Hear America Singing" will reveal at once that Whitman was conscious of the special pleasure of reëncountering a word or phrase within a line. In this poem the word "singing," or its variant "song," is the key word or melodic figure, and appears in every line but one. The result is not only an intensification of the meaning of the poem, but as well a kind of "singing" melody throughout.

> I hear America singing, the varied carols I hear,
> Those of mechanics, each one singing his as it should be
>   blithe and strong,
> The carpenter singing his as he measures his plank or
>   beam,
> The mason singing his as he makes ready for work, or
>   leaves off work,
> The boatman singing what belongs to him in his boat, the
>   deck-hand singing on the steamboat deck,
> The shoemaker singing as he sits on his bench, the hatter
>   singing as he stands. . . .[12]

A similar effect with a similar word is to be noticed in "Out of the Cradle":

> *Shake out carols!*
> *Solitary here, the night's carols!*
> *Carols of lonesome love! death's carols!*

> Carols under that lagging, yellow, waning moon!
> O under that moon where she droops almost down into
>   the sea!
> O reckless despairing carols.[13]

Such repetitions are best appreciated if we think of them as melodic inventions. Clearly something more than mere rhetorical emphasis is sought in such a passage as the last quoted.

This device of the repetition of a word, which came to Whitman from the operatic music he knew, often resulted in a great increase in the vocal syzygy of his lines, whether he deliberately sought the effect or not. For example, the opening lines from "Tears" show how his reiteration of the title word contributes to the linking patterns of t and d sounds, enriching the music of the lines notably.

> Tears! tears! tears!
> In the night, in solitude, tears,
> On the white shore dripping, dripping, suck'd in by the
>   sand,
> Tears, not a star shining, all dark and desolate,
> Moist tears from the eyes of a muffled head. . . .[14]

Such "verbal melody," in reality essential to all great poetry, was never shunned by Whitman, though he insisted that it should never become an end in itself and that poets should never wrench their ideas out of proper focus simply in order to achieve it.[15]

Another type of repetition within lines of which Whitman was fond is exactly comparable to similar repetitions in melodic lines by which some of music's most delightful effects are secured. This is a repetition of a pattern, not a word, within a line. In music, the pattern is stated; then without pause it is restated, perhaps varied slightly in its falling contour, in its volume requirement, or in its pitch. The effect is something like echo or antiphon, and gives the phrase involved an inescapable charm.

Many of Whitman's best-known lines come to mind at once as examples of such a practice.

> I hear America singing, the varied carols I hear. . . .[16]

> I celebrate myself, and sing myself,
> And what I assume you shall assume. . . .[17]

> I am the poet of the Body and I am the poet of the Soul,

> The pleasures of heaven are with me and the pains of hell
> are with me. . . .[18]
>
> I ascend from the moon, I ascend from the night. . . .[19]
>
> Loud O my throat, and clear O soul! . . .[20]
>
> Beat! beat! drums!—blow! bugles! blow! . . .
> So fierce you whirr and pound you drums—so shrill you
> bugles blow.[21]

The examples need no comment except to call attention to the
interesting ways in which the poet secures variety in the repetition.
Most of the variations are comparable to those of music, variations
in pitch, volume, or falling contour of phrase.

One of the subtlest of all Whitman's poems from the standpoint
of melodic repetition is "Vigil Strange I Kept on the Field One
Night." Nearly all of the different ways of repeating for effect are
to be observed here, and one may even say that the great charm of
the poem is based on its remarkable use of reiteration. The entire
poem is here quoted and all the repetitions of words or phrases, or
variants, italicized so that the quite unusual amount of such reiteration may be at once apparent.

> Vigil strange I kept on the field one night;
> When you my son and my comrade dropt at my side that
> day,
> One look I but gave which your dear eyes return'd with a
> look I shall never forget,
> One touch of your hand to mine O boy, reach'd up as you
> lay on the ground,
> Then onward I sped in the battle, the even-contested
> battle,
> Till late in the night reliev'd to the place at last again I
> made my way,
> Found you in death so cold dear comrade, found your body
> son of responding kisses, (never again on earth
> responding,)
> Bared your face in the starlight, curious the scene, cool
> blew the moderate night-wind,
> Long there and then in vigil I stood, dimly around me the
> battlefield spreading,
> Vigil wondrous and vigil sweet there in the fragrant silent
> night,

But not a tear fell, not even a long-drawn sigh, *long, long*
     I gazed,
Then on the earth partially reclining sat by your side lean-
     ing my chin in my hands,
Passing *sweet hours, immortal and mystic hours* with you
     dearest comrade—*not a tear, not a word,*
Vigil of silence, love and death, *vigil for you* my son and
     my soldier,
As *onward* silently stars aloft, *eastward* new ones upward
     stole,
Vigil final for you brave boy, (I could not save you, swift
     was your death,
I faithfully loved you and cared for you living, I think we
     shall surely meet again,)
Till at latest lingering of the night, indeed just as the dawn
     appear'd,
My comrade I wrapt in his blanket, *envelop'd* well his
     form,
Folded the blanket well, tucking it *carefully* overhead and
     carefully under feet,
And *there and then* and bathed by the rising sun, *my son*
     in his grave, in his rude-dug *grave I deposited,*
Ending *my vigil strange* with that, *vigil of night* and battle-
     field dim,
Vigil for boy of responding kisses, (never again on earth
     responding,)
Vigil for comrade swiftly slain, *vigil I never forget,* how as
     day brighten'd,
I rose from the chill ground and *folded my soldier well* in
     his *blanket,*
And buried him where he fell.[22]

Selecting only one of the figures, one may enumerate its occur-
rences: vigil strange (1.1); in vigil I stood (1.9); vigil wondrous
(1.10); vigil sweet (1.10); vigil of silence (1.14); vigil for you (1.14);
vigil final (1.16); vigil strange (1.22); vigil of night (1.22); vigil for
boy (1.23); vigil for comrade (1.24); vigil I never forget (1.24). It
will be observed that all the variations follow rather than precede
the repeated word; it is the beginnings which must usually be similar. Here are twelve uses of the same term in a twenty-six line poem.
Every sensitive reader will admit, however, that with each recurrence the word is given added significance and that the mystical
quality of the occasion presented in the poem is intensified with

each return of the word, just as each recurrence of the primary figure of a deeply sad melody makes it more touching. In this poem, however, it is important to notice the amazing fabric of repetitions, not in lists, but in woven patterns giving the poem a richness of tone and effect altogether remarkable.

It is important to note also that percentage studies have shown that all types of repetition in Whitman became a significant device only after 1855 with the first *Leaves of Grass*. In his scattered early poems initial repetition is to be found in only two or three lines, for example, and, while epanalepsis is found in ten per cent of the early lines, it occurs in forty-one per cent of the lines after 1855.[23] It seems likely that the kinds of repetition which have been the subject of this chapter were evolved as a part of a style based largely on operatic music.

NOTES—CHAPTER VII

1. Inclusive Edition, p. 527.
2. Traubel, *op. cit.*, I, 170.
3. Abbott, *op. cit.*, p. 47.
4. De Selincourt, *op. cit.*, p. 108.
5. Inclusive Edition, p. 152.
6. *Ibid.*, p. 324.
7. *Ibid.*, p. 42.
8. Wiley, *op. cit.*, p. 161.
9. Inclusive Edition, p. 50.
10. *Ibid.*, p. 298.
11. *Ibid.*, p. 135.
12. *Ibid.*, p. 10.
13. *Ibid.*, p. 213.
14. *Ibid.*, p. 218.
15. For other poetic conventions, see Lois Ware, "Poetic Conventions in *Leaves of Grass*," *Studies in Philology*, XXVI, 47-57 (January, 1929).
16. Inclusive Edition, p. 10.
17. *Ibid.*, p. 24.
18. *Ibid.*, p. 41.
19. *Ibid.*, p. 74.
20. *Ibid.*, p. 304.
21. *Ibid.*, p. 240.
22. *Ibid.*, p. 257.
23. Wiley, *op. cit.*, p. 169.

Dynamics

ONE ASPECT of operatic music which Whitman undoubtedly found greatly to his taste was its wide range in dynamics. The Italian voices, with their full-throated power always in reserve for strong climaxes and their velvety richness in tender, lyrical moments, were a source of never-ending delight to him. His joy in the opera orchestra's rousing *fortissimos* was almost childlike. Describing such a moment, he once wrote, "And now, a long, tumultuous, crowded finale ending with a grand crash of all the instruments together, every one, it would seem, making as much noise as it possibly can—an effect which we perceive you don't like at all, but which we privately confess in your ear is one of the greatest treats we obtain from a visit to the opera."[1]

We are inclined today to think of the Italian operas as collections of tunes, rather than as symphonies of sound in the Wagnerian or Verdian sense. They are primarily tuneful, of course, but they are not lacking in exhilarating volumes of tone. Anyone who has heard the overture to *William Tell* by Rossini will recall the storm section with its mounting waves of sound and stirring climax. Rossini was fond of 'storm' passages, and he included them in at least a half dozen of his operas. Storms of course provided him with an opportunity for stimulating his audiences with loud music, but he never became cheaply theatrical in his use of them and never merely imitative. He invariably translated them into purely musical terms in keeping with the exigencies of his plots.[2] Perhaps the best examples are in *La Cenerentola* and in *The Barber of Seville*, where the orchestral interludes depicting the storms heighten the tensions of the dramatic action.

But storms were not Rossini's only device for introducing great volumes of sound into his scores. Another was a trick which has become famous as the "Rossini Crescendo." Perhaps the best-known example is the aria "La Colunnia" from *The Barber of Seville*. In this number Don Basilio explains a plan by which the spreading of malicious gossip can be used to destroy a victim. Skillfully handled, he says, calumny begins with a whisper, then swells to a zephyr, and finally rises to a torrent that destroys the victim. Rossini presents this gradually intensifying tornado by a long crescendo in the orchestra, a single six-note phrase being repeated over and over again, beginning softly and ending with a tremendous *fortissimo*.[3]

The Verdi operas of Whitman's day were notable for their rousing choral effects. Best known today probably is the ringing "Anvil Chorus" from *Il Trovatore*, but other operas of this composer did not fail to introduce some spectacular ensemble singing, well calculated to stir the audience. One of these passages Whitman himself described, the opening chorus of *Ernani*:

It is the stormy music of Giuseppe Verdi. It is the noble opera of Ernani. With the rise of the curtain you are transported afar—such power has music. You behold the mountains of Aragon and the bandits in their secure retreat, feasting, drinking, gaming, and singing. And such singing, and such an instrumental accompaniment! Their wild, rollicking spirits pour themselves out in that opening chorus.[4]

As the quotation shows, such devices for quickening the pulses of listeners were by no means lost on Whitman, and when he came to compose poems which he hoped would stir his readers in a similar way he also wrote *fortissimo*. His predominant mood is joyful and optimistic, and he deliberately cultivated a jubilant ring in his bardic rhapsodies. Such poems as "Song of the Open Road," "A Song of Joys," "Song of the Broad-Axe," many parts of "Song of Myself," and parts of many other poems rarely drop below *forte* in their dynamics. Naturally, as he grew older and undertook the presentation of more somber material the music softened somewhat, but throughout his poetic career Whitman revealed a fondness for effects as big in sound as they were in significance.

It is by no means true, however, that Whitman's poems are 'loud' invariably. He could easily have learned at the opera that loud music is most stirring when it is heard in contrast to softer passages. Many of his poems show that he learned well the value of contrasts. For example, "A Broadway Pageant" opens with a quiet four-line description of a procession through New York of Japanese envoys who are "leaning back in their open barouches, bareheaded, impassive."[5] In four succeeding lines the poet increases the volume of sound as he considers his own reaction to the Broadway pageant, ending with the line:

> But I will sing you a song of what I behold Libertad.

His own song unstops a torrent of sound, packed with words which are not only loud in their pronunciation but suggest tremendous masses of sound, all of course in an attempt to convey to the reader the phenomenal richness and variety of the activity in the beloved city.

> When million-footed Manhattan unpent descends to her pavements,
> When the thunder-cracking guns arouse me with the proud roar I love,
> When the round-mouth'd guns out of the smoke and smell I love spit their salutes,
> When the fire-flashing guns have fully alerted me, and heaven-clouds canopy my city with a delicate thin haze,
> When gorgeous the countless straight stems, the forests at the wharves, thicken with colors. . . .

Following this outburst of sound, the poem becomes relatively quiet and reflective as the poet contrasts his own country, so exciting and new, with "venerable Asia," and states his conviction that the proud, young nation now takes its place with the great of the world and becomes in effect the center of world activity.

The same subject matter, the exhilarating noises of the city, led Whitman to a similar contrast in dynamics in "Give Me the Splendid Silent Sun."[6] Following his lines of yearning for the silence and solitude of nature, the realization comes that these are unsatisfactory and insufficient. It is the city, Broadway, that he really longs for, Broadway with its "turbulent, musical chorus," which he re-creates with appropriate volume.

> Give me Broadway, with the soldiers marching—give me the sound of the trumpets and drums!
> . . . .
> The dense brigade bound for the war, with high piled military wagons following;

> People, endless, streaming, with strong voices, passions,
>   pageants,
> Manhattan streets with their powerful throbs, with beat-
>   ing drums as now,
> The endless and noisy chorus, the rustle and clank of
>   muskets, (even the sight of the wounded,)
> Manhattan crowds, with their turbulent musical chorus!
> Manhattan faces and eyes forever for me.[7]

The poem cited above, and there are many more, shows strong contrasts in dynamics, loud passages placed against softer ones. A more musical usage of the principles of dynamics is the crescendo, that controlled and gradually increasing volume of sound which is almost unaccountably exciting to the listener. A splendidly artistic example of such a usage may be discovered in the lyric, "Tears."

> Tears! tears! tears!
> In the night, in solitude, tears,
> On the white shore dripping, dripping, suck'd in by the
>   sand,
> Tears, not a star shining, all dark and desolate,
> Moist tears from the eyes of a muffled head;
> O who is that ghost? that form in the dark, with tears?
> What shapeless lump is that, bent, crouch'd there on the
>   sand?
> Streaming tears, sobbing tears, throes, choked with wild
>   cries;
> O storm, embodied, rising, careering with swift steps along
>   the beach!
> O wild and dismal night storm, with wind—O belching
>   and desperate!
> O shade so sedate and decorous by day, with calm coun-
>   tenance and regulated pace,
> But away at night as you fly, none looking—O then the
>   unloosen'd ocean,
> Of tears! tears! tears![8]

First of all the quiet and subdued opening with its slow and sustained measures suggesting almost silent grief should be noted. Alone on the beach at night the sorrowful one gives way to his sorrow, and, as the tears flow, the passion is intensified until it breaks with the fury of an uncontrollable night storm. In music the crescendo is almost invariably accompanied by quickening tempo, which in turn permits phrases of longer length. So in "Tears" the initial *adagio* becomes in the space of a few lines a frantic *prestissimo*, and quiet words like *solitude, night,* and *tears,* give way to the violence of *sobbing, choked, wild cries, storm, careering, belching,* and *desperate.* As the effects of speed and volume increase, the lines become progressivly longer, from three stresses to eight at the climax. All of the devices combine to suggest with tremendous impact the experience of silent grief escaping its confinements and rising unchecked to a virtual paroxysm. The poem, artistically, does not end at the climax. It is followed by a *diminuendo,* naturally much more rapid than the *crescendo,* since it is not the primary reason for being of the poem. The reader needs to be returned to the quiet with which the poem opened, to a sense of grief once more under control. In this way the re-created emotion becomes much more convincing and the artistic need for 'return,' for the completion of the cycle, is satisfied. The *diminuendo* must be brief, for it is the shattering experience of grief getting out of hand which the poet is presenting, not the control of grief. So in three lines the poem becomes quiet, slows down, and ends with the very words, on the same low level of dynamics, with which it began.

The effect of a musical crescendo without actually increasing the volume of the lines through the use of words which seem loud, may be observed in "Song of the Broad-Axe." The axe is developed in the poem as the emblem of America, and at the conclusion the poet wishes to suggest the development of which America is capable. He does this symbolically by suggesting the expansiveness of the emblem itself, or more literally, the products which come from the axe and their importance throughout the range of American life. From a short literal exclamation, we are led through longer lines and with increasing tempo to a symbolic climax. The effect is the same as that of the *crescendo* in music.

> The axe leaps!
> The solid forest gives fluid utterances,
> They tumble forth, they rise and form,
> Hut, tent, landing, survey,
> Flail, plough, pick, crowbar, spade,
> Shingle, rail, prop, wainscot, jamb, lath, panel, gable,
> Citadel, ceiling, saloon, academy, organ, exhibition-house,
>   library, . . .

Capitols of States, and capitol of the nation of States,
Long stately rows in avenues, hospitals for orphans or for
    the poor or sick,
Manhattan steamboats and clippers taking the measure of
    all seas.[9]

For the remainder of the poem the development of America is
suggested in a series of sections beginning alike and each dupli-
cating the passage just quoted in an effect of crescendo. Again the
symbolic terms of the products of the axe, aspects of American life
of increasing significance, are enumerated and celebrated. At last
the final climax is reached in a passage which shows Democracy
as a world force to be the result and fulfilment of all the elements
previously chanted. Each of the seven sections beginning, "The
shapes arise!"[9] suggests the onward movement of developing America by the increasingly rapid tempo. Each section, furthermore,
progresses relentlessly toward the climax, the shape of Democracy
itself. The artistic effect here is that of the musical composition
which mounts higher and higher in volume and intensity as it
sweeps toward its close, and of which the finale is at last stated in
chords so massive and solid that the listener is left breathless for a
moment.

The shapes arise!
The shape measur'd, saw'd, jack'd, join'd, stain'd,
The coffin-shape for the dead to lie within in his shroud,
The shape got out in posts, in the bedstead posts, in the
    posts of the bride's bed,
The shape of the little trough, the shape of the rockers
    beneath, the shape of the babe's cradle,
The shape of the floor-planks, the floor-planks for dancer's
    feet,
The shape of the planks of the family home, the home of
    the friendly parents and children,
The shape of the roof of the home of the happy young
    man and woman, the roof over the well married young
    man and woman,
The roof over the supper joyously cook'd by the chaste
    wife, and joyously eaten by the chaste husband, con-
    tent after his day's work.[10]
. . . .
The shapes arise!
Shapes of doors giving many exits and entrances,

The door passing the dissever'd friend flush'd and in haste,
The door that admits good news and bad news,
The door whence the son left home confident and puff'd
    up,
The door he enter'd again from a long and scandalous
    absence, diseas'd, broken down, without innocence,
    without means.[11]
. . . .

The main shapes arise!
Shapes of Democracy total, result of centuries,
Shapes ever projecting other shapes,
Shapes of turbulent manly cities,
Shapes of the friends and home-givers of the whole earth,
Shapes bracing the earth and braced with the whole earth.[11]

Occasionally Whitman permitted himself what was probably a luxury, in the light of his temperament and fondness for big effects: the poem which begins *fortissimo* and never moderates. A characteristic and well-known example of such a poetic manner is "Beat! Beat! Drums!" Here the poet is sounding the call to war, suggesting symbolically, with drums and bugles drowning out every sound of peaceful activity, how all efforts needed to be directed to the prosecution of the war. In a sense the entire poem is a technical *tour de force*, the poet's idea being to suggest loud, irresistible sound, swallowing up all lesser sound. Actually the loud sound is confined to the opening and closing lines of each section, the intervening lines being given to the sound that is overwhelmed. This device keeps the poem from being merely blatant and at the same time does not lessen the fundamental effect. The complete effect of the work is one of breadth and volume which never abate, and which are intensified by the repetition of the opening lines of sections and the repetition with slight variations of the closing lines. The final section well represents the others.

Beat! beat! drums!—blow! bugles! blow!
Make no parley—stop for no expostulation,
Mind not the timid—mind not the weeper or prayer,
Mind not the old man beseeching the young man,
Let not the child's voice be heard, nor the mother's
    entreaties,

> Make even the trestles to shake the dead where they lie
>   awaiting the hearses,
> So strong you thump O terrible drums—so loud you
>   bugles blow.[12]

Whitman was attracted to 'bigness' wherever he found it. The ocean was naturally one of his favorite topics, and whatever was expansive and illimitable fascinated him. It is thus not surprising that he should have found storms, nature's uncontrollable spasms, exciting and stimulating. Storms and their magnificent sounds were to him an almost mystical experience. In *Specimen Days*, for example, he listed three of "life's rare and blessed hours" which he treasured: "the wild sea storm I once saw one winter day off Fire Island—the elder Booth in Richard, that famous night nearly forty years ago in the Old Bowery—or Alboni in the children's scene in Norma."[13]

In the light of his interest in storms and the fact that he had often heard them interpreted artistically in music, it is not surprising that Whitman should have attempted to make use of them in his poems. How he utilized the storm for imagery in the lyric "Tears"[14] has already been pointed out. Usually, as in "Tears," the storm is not re-created for its own sake, but to intensify the effect of other material. (It will be recalled that this is how Rossini used storm material also.) The most extended and noteworthy example of such a usage is "Proud Music of the Storm," which is among other things a remarkable study in dynamics. Here the "hidden orchestras," "choruses," and "vast chords" of the storm bring to the dreaming poet wide varieties of music, which he finally discovers to be not "a dream of raging storm" but "poems bridging the way from Life to Death," which he was to compose. In short, aspects of the storm are the inspiration for poetry. It is the opening of the poem, however, which is impressive as a sonorous evocation of the storm itself, with its sweeping chords and strong tones.

> Proud music of the storm,
> Blast that careers so free, whistling across the prairies,
> Strong hum of forest tree-tops—wind of the mountains,
> Personified dim shapes—you hidden orchestras,
> You serenades of phantoms with instruments alert,
> Bending with Nature's rhythmus all the tongues of
>   nations;

You chords left as by vast composers—you choruses,
You formless, free, religious dances—you from the Orient,
You undertone of rivers, roar of pouring cataracts,
You sounds from distant guns with galloping cavalry,
Echoes of camps with all the different bugle calls,
Trooping tumultuous, filling the midnight late, bending
    me powerless,
Entering my lonesome slumber-chamber, why have you
    seiz'd me?[15]

In a shorter poem, "Rise O Days from Your Fathomless Deeps,"
the storm is used even more pervasively as background imagery,
and many of the lines disclose with brilliance Whitman's love for
the wildness of nature. In an opening section he recounts his experiences with storms:

. . . I sail'd out to sea,
I sail'd through the storm, I was refresh'd by the storm,
I watch'd with joy the threatening maws of the waves,
I mark'd the white combs where they career'd so high,
    curling over,
I heard the wind piping, I saw the black clouds,
Saw from below what arose and mounted, (O superb!
    O wild as my heart, and powerful!)
Heard the continuous thunder as it bellow'd after the
    lightening,
Noted the slender and jagged threads of lightning as sud-
    den and fast amid the din they chased each other
    across the sky. . . .[16]

There follows a section suggesting that the irresistible strides of
Democracy in establishing and maintaining itself, even with ruthless
war, are storm-like in their engulfing sweep.

What was that swell I saw on the ocean? behold what
    comes here,
How it climbs with daring feet and hands—how it dashes!
How the true thunder bellows after the lightning—how
    bright the flashes of lightning!
How Democracy with desperate vengeful port strides
    on, shown through the dark by those flashes of
    lightning!

Then, without abandoning the imagery of the storm, the poet implies that his passion for the untamed and unrestrained aspects of

nature which he had found exemplified in storms is now satisfied in beholding the emergence of the free man and a democratic America.

> Hungering, hungering, hungering, for primal energies and
> Nature's dauntlessness,
> I refresh'd myself with it only, I could relish it only,
> I waited the bursting forth of the pent fire—on the water
> and air I waited long;
> But now I no longer wait, I am fully satisfied, I am glutted,
> I have witness'd the true lightning, I have witness'd my
> cities electric,
> I have lived to behold man burst forth and warlike America
> rise,
> Hence I will seek no more the food of the northern solitary
> wilds,
> No more the mountains roam or sail the stormy sea.[17]

"To the Man-of-War-Bird," a shorter lyric of remarkable rhythmic regularity for Whitman (written more than ten years after "Rise O Days," 1876) once more displays his great love for the storm and his remarkable gift for re-creating its effects. This time he addresses the Man-of-War-Bird which has ridden out the tempest at sea, has pitted its strength against the elemental fury of the gale, and has emerged triumphant. Could the bird but have had his imagination, his soul, the poet cries, this would have been no instinctive struggle for survival, but an exhilarating contest with the elements of nature. Again, notice the loud music of the poem, especially in the storm lines.

> Thou who has slept all night upon the storm,
> Waking renew'd on thy prodigious pinions,
> (Burst the wild storm? above it thou ascended'st
> And rested on the sky, thy slave that cradled thee,)
> . . . .
> Thou born to match the gale, (thou art all wings,)
> To cope with heaven and earth and sea and hurricane,
> Thou ship of air that never furl'st thy sails,
> . . . .
> That sport'st amid the lightning-flash and thunder-cloud,
> In them, in thy experiences, had'st thou my soul,
> What joys! what joys were thine![18]

Occasionally the sounds of the storm are re-created seemingly for their own sake, much as a landscape painter would create a storm scene. Such a poem is "Patroling Barnegat." Many of the impressions are wholly of sound, even though the poet is in reality describing a scene. Whitman's response to nature was usually first to its sounds, and his joy in a storm was his joy in the storm's roaring and crashing music. Only the powerful chords of actual music or the husky music of the sea could similarly stimulate him.

> Wild, wild the storm, and the sea high running,
> Steady the roar of the gale, with incessant undertone muttering,
> Shouts of demoniac laughter fitfully piercing and pealing,
> Waves, air, midnight, their savagest trinity lashing,
> Out in the shadows there milk-white combs careering,
> On beachy slush and sand spirits of snow fierce slanting,
> Where through the murk the easterly death-wind breasting,
> Through cutting swirl and spray watchful and firm advancing,
> (That in the distance! is that a wreck? is the red signal flaring?)
> Slush and sand of the beach tireless till daylight wending,
> Steadily, slowly, through hoarse roar never remitting,
> Along the midnight edge by those milk-white combs careering,
> A group of dim weird forms, struggling, the night confronting,
> That savage trinity warily watching.[19]

The big-voiced singer finds it easier to sing loud than soft, though often he must discipline his voice and achieve effects of tenderness and quiet. It is greatly to Whitman's credit that he did not always sing at the top of his voice, to use his own phrase, however much his temperament may have led him in that direction. Many of the poems already quoted provide eloquent examples of his ability to write softly. One thinks at once of "Out of the Cradle Endlessly Rocking"[20] and "When Lilacs Last in the Dooryard Bloom'd,"[21] with their presentations of night and the quiet carols of birds. One thinks, too, of the hushed "Night on the Prairies,"[22] with its atmosphere of restfulness and calm after the toil-filled day, an atmosphere which leads the poet to suspect that death will bring a necessary complement to life as night to day. And there is also sustained *pianissimo* music in "By the Bivouac's Fitful Flame,"[23] solemn and slow in movement, with every phrase and word suggesting the silence of night.

In all likelihood it would be claiming too much to insist that all of Whitman's strong feeling for dynamics, his attention to volume and contrasts in volume, was the result of his opera-going. Much of it developed quite naturally, as it does in all good poets. When a poet writes of the night by a campfire, he instinctively seeks for effects of quietness. But it is certainly not too much to believe that when Whitman wrote "With music strong I come,"[24] he meant exactly what he said. From his own stimulation through music strong in the opera house, the storms and crescendos of Rossini, the great choral climaxes of Verdi, and the contrasting elements of the arias of Bellini and Donizetti, came a desire to create similarly moving poetry, and in achieving it to experiment with volume in verse.

NOTES—CHAPTER VIII

1. *Uncollected Poetry and Prose*, II, 97.
2. Toye, *op. cit.*, p. 252.
3. Newman, *op. cit.*, II, 219.
4. *New York Dissected*, p. 20.
5. Inclusive Edition, p. 206.
6. *Ibid.*, p. 264.
7. *Ibid.*, p. 265.
8. *Ibid.*, p. 218.
9. *Ibid.*, p. 163.
10. *Ibid.*, p. 164.
11. *Ibid.*, p. 165.
12. *Ibid.*, p. 240.
13. *Prose*, I, 292.
14. Inclusive Edition, p. 218.
15. *Ibid.*, p. 337.
16. *Ibid.*, p. 247.
17. *Ibid.*, p. 248.
18. *Ibid.*, p. 219.
19. *Ibid.*, p. 223.
20. *Ibid.*, p. 210.
21. *Ibid.*, p. 276.
22. *Ibid.*, p. 376.
23. *Ibid.*, p. 255.
24. *Ibid.*, p. 38.

CHAPTER IX

Conclusion

ONE BASIC FACT emerges from the foregoing comment
on Whitman and operatic music. It is that opera was a fundamental influence upon him, so fundamental, indeed, that a full
appreciation of his objectives and accomplishments in verse can
scarcely be attained without recognition of it.

Essential to such a recognition is an awareness of the intensity
of Whitman's devotion to this specialized art form. Opera to him
was not merely a device for occupying an idle hour. It was not
merely an easily available and favorite type of amusement, to be
indulged in casually, as we frequent the moving pictures today. It
was these, but it was much more. It was an art which had a peculiar
and powerful fascination for him. The attraction was increased
rather than diminished by his early denials of opera's charm. Lacking understanding of the conventions and objectives of this form,
he was at first mystified by it, then repelled by what seemed foreign
about it. It is a tribute both to the essential values of opera and to
Whitman's innate capacity to appreciate art that he overcame his
early prejudices and learned not only to understand opera but to
love it passionately.

The circumstance which brought opera and Whitman together
inevitably was his almost abnormal sensitivity to the sounds of the
human voice. No other writer has confessed so often a stimulation
by, and a love for, voices. With Whitman the topic was at times
almost a monomania. By good luck his journalistic days in Brooklyn
and New York coincided with one of the golden moments in the
history of opera in this country, a moment when the musical
fashion insisted upon a type of opera in which the voices of singers
were displayed as never before or since, and a moment when singers
of heroic stature had miraculously appeared to perform.

The great display vehicles of Rossini and Bellini sung by some of
the greatest voices the world has ever known, presented under cir-

cumstances that had come to be glamorous events, proved to be irresistible to the young journalist, for he was not only interested in voices and music, but loved drama and spectacle on both sides of the footlights. He loved people as human beings; at the opera he found them, artistically analyzed and heightened on the stage, and gathered for observation in interesting representations of all classes in the audience.

Inevitably Whitman haunted the opera house. Most of the time attendance cost him nothing, and the returns in satisfaction and inspiration were immeasurable. Certain operas he heard over and over, so that the smallest details of their plots were familiar to him. He sat in all parts of the house, absorbing the reactions of the different types of auditors. He studied the orchestra, its instrumentation, and its contribution to the magic of the occasion. He contrasted the relative effectiveness of the various singers in their parts. Night after night he returned to the theatre to hear the "peerless compositions."

Naturally certain singers, because of qualities of warmth and expressiveness in their voices and because of their personalities, became favorites. The most notable was Marietta Alboni, the Italian contralto whose career in this country was as short as it was brilliant. Some of the men were almost equally idolized: Bettini, the tenor, for the sweetness of his voice, and Badiali, the baritone, for his handsome and masculine appearance as well as his noble tones. But it was not singers alone who made an impression on Whitman. It was the institution of opera, compounded of great voices, great music, great drama, and a great occasion. Together they were sufficient to start a poet on his way.

It is most important to realize that Whitman's passion for opera was at its height, generally speaking, during the forties and fifties of his century. In the first of these decades his published comments on opera are varied, and though there is positive evidence of his attraction to operatic music, in these years he was learning to understand it and resolving some of the doubts in his mind about the suitability of the imported art for America. By 1851 all doubts had been put aside and he had become a most ardent devotee and champion.

We know that between 1850 and 1855, years about which

Whitman was always very secretive, he became a poet of great individuality. During these years he first thought of himself as a poet, dedicated to the accomplishment of a poet's mission. In these years he evolved a program of poetic activity for his entire career, developed a literary theory, complete and highly distinctive, and experimented with a technique which he believed to be revolutionary and especially appropriate for his poems. We also know that during these years he was in constant attendance at the opera, and that the season which brought the climax of his musical experience, the singing of Alboni, came midway in the period, the season of 1852-53. Whitman said that he heard Alboni every time she sang in New York. Records disclose that she appeared in ten different operas (presumably several times in each), gave twelve concerts of operatic music, and participated in a festival presentation of Rossini's exciting oratorio, *Stabat Mater*. The implication is inescapable that during his most important creative years Whitman was absorbed in opera to a degree almost incredible. No other influence during these years could possibly have had so great an effect upon him. Even had he tried he could scarcely have prevented opera from coloring his work.

His regular opera-going continued until the Civil War, during which he was in Washington, though even on brief visits to Brooklyn and New York he crowded in a few performances. Following the war, when he lived in Washington and later in Camden, partially crippled, he could no longer attend, but his recollections of his "singing years" never dimmed, and he professed indebtedness as long as he lived. Naturally, of course, the influence was most operative and most important in the early fifties when he was developing his characteristic style.

The powerful influence of operatic music expressed itself in two ways in Whitman's work. The first is the more general way of inspiration, the second, method. Whitman was a genuine mystic; that has long been established. But the mystical state is for many mystics not automatic or easily come by. Many are lifted to mystic perception of truth only with the aid of powerful external forces. For some the beauty of nature has served. Whitman also became peculiarly responsive to nature, but the force which alone was sufficiently inspirational to elevate him to genuine mystical heights was operatic music. The first account from his pen of a mystical experience was of one induced by music, and in the notebooks he kept while he was preparing the first *Leaves of Grass* he recorded an almost clinical account of such a moment. Later, in his great poem, "Out of the Cradle Endlessly Rocking," he confessed symbolically that through emotional experiences of shattering intensity, the music of the opera house awakened him to his poet's destiny.

Like all genuine mystical experiences, these were significant because of their revelations to the poet. In these moments of inexplicable rapture, truth was made plain to the poet. He came to perceive the meaning of life, and, more important to him, the meaning of death, and of all things bridging the gap from one to the other, as he said. The details of existence, monotonous, sordid, exhilarating and beautiful, all fell into their proper places, and he fell heir to a boundless optimism and confidence in ultimate good. He did not hear these things in the music; music opened his mind, or his soul, and the profound convictions flowed in unbidden.

A peculiar fact about such moments is that for Whitman, either in the experience or in the recollection, there was something essentially sexual in them. He never wrote of such an occasion except in terms of sexual excitement. We cannot be sure whether the moments were so experienced, as the result of his admittedly abnormal sexual nature, or whether in recording them he deliberately attempted to avoid what to him would have been the mistake of glorifying the soul at the expense of the body. At any rate the sexual imagery is always present. Perhaps the easiest explanation is that his response to the voice, so peculiarly strong, was in some special way a sexual one. Since it was vocal music which inspired him, perhaps the mystical experiences were never separable from physical ones in his recollections, and his poetic accounts were a release through art of emotional needs.

In any case, music made Whitman a kind of prophet. His perceptions, so profoundly believed in, must be expressed to the world and in such a manner that the world could not choose but hear. The world, or more particularly America, must be electrified. It must become a vast audience, and he must be the singer. He must chant his songs with pulses of fire, like the great bards of antiquity. He must utter with strong, imperious voice the truths which lay in the hearts of all men. He must be the voice of all the inarticulate souls who had not been awakened as he had been. He must "translate" his inspirations into poetry. Those overpowering moments in opera must become starting points for "translations" of his own, in which he and his readers might recapture the excitement of intimate artistic communication.

Only vocal music would serve as the vehicle of these vast chants, for only vocal music seemed sufficiently inspirational. Conventional poetry seemed wholly inadequate for the special task. In opera there was a larger, freer music, and it was this that he would need to capture. He would have to devise "songs" which should somehow preserve the sound of the voice and stimulate the reader or listener as opera could do. This would serve two purposes: it would provide the public with something like the ennobling art of opera, which, ideally, would itself have become widely available for the people. But his poetic chants would in some measure make up for the fact that opera could probably never surmount the obstacles to widespread American acceptance. Furthermore, if he could make his poems song-like, his own highest purposes would be served.

In some such way did opera first inspire Whitman to poetry and then color his conception of the kind of verse which would best serve his needs. Then, fired with ambition to compose, he was faced with the task of devising a suitable technique. If conventional methods would not serve, something must be found to take their place, for no poetry is formless. Inevitably he turned to opera, and, as he himself said, followed its methods strictly in the structure of his songs.

In spite of his protestations, readers should not look in Whitman's work for the kind of musical evidence we can find in that of a trained and practicing musician like Sidney Lanier. Whitman's technical knowledge of music was always elementary, and he seemed to prefer it that way. At least he never professed anything more than that. Opera to him was something whose spell was magic, and whose liquid and flowing sounds transported him. It was surely of small concern that Alboni sang Norma in a lower key than Grisi used. The important fact was that when Norma,

Alboni or Grisi, contemplated the murder of her children, the music moved him unspeakably.

To be sure, when he sought for the elements of a technique which would give his words the soaring, unrestrained freedom which he heard in opera he resorted to some of opera's technical devices. But they were the most obvious ones, and everyone who could hum an opera tune was aware of them. These devices are everywhere exemplified. It cannot be proved, of course, that he took them all from opera, and no one can say precisely where the influence operated subconsciously and where he studied opera deliberately. But this is scarcely important. What is important is that the analogies become apparent.

Proceeding from the most general to the most detailed aspect of this operatic method as he understood it, one may mention first "Suggestiveness." Whitman's entire conception of poetic art was in terms of music, as he had experienced it. The highest virtue of music was not that it brought beautiful sounds to his ear, pleasurable as that was. The great virtue of music was that it "started to life thousands of songs" in him; it aroused a "tallying chant" in his soul. It was the tallying chant which was significant. So his songs were to be like music in that they were to be starting points; they were to be the equivalent of musical sounds. They were to initiate trains of thought in their readers; they were to suggest meanings and to reveal the possibility of meanings in objects and circumstances which to the reader may have seemed wholly without promise. Whitman deliberately sought to awake a "tallying chant" in the soul of his reader, and he even counted on the magic of his reader's voice to color and enrich his lines, as the singer brings notes from a musical score to vibrant life.

To achieve this end, Whitman cultivated the manner of a performer communicating with an audience. To various critics this device has seemed egotistical, oratorical, ranting, vulgar. Fundamentally, it is none of these. It is the manifestation of a deeply held conviction that great art is a two-way process; that the beholder must have his part in the creation. Inevitably Whitman was not always successful in this "I-You" manner; at its best, however, it gives his work an intimacy and suggestiveness which make it appealing. Though it may not be obvious at once, quite certainly the manner was derived from the opera house.

Part of the thrill in opera came to Whitman from the magnificent volumes of sound that the choruses and orchestras were capable of achieving. The sweeping breadth of these *fortissimos* were violently exciting to him. Naturally, his poetry reveals similarly broad effects. "With music strong I come," he said, and he meant it. But he was also aware of the value of contrasts, which opera often relies upon. Some of his finest poems are quiet and still throughout their entire length. In other words, opera taught him valuable lessons in dynamics, of which he was very conscious.

In putting the material of his songs together Whitman found the method of the operatic overture exactly suitable. It was his conviction that poetic ideas must grow in the poems that express them. For that reason he could not bring himself to analyze an idea and parcel out its parts to various tightly restricted sections of a poem. Rather he found it congenial to treat his ideas like musical themes, to state them indirectly and incompletely, then proceed to others, only to return to the first. Letting each theme appear and reappear, confusing as it was to his early readers, gave his longer work the structure of large musical compositions, and it can be understood only in such terms. For him, the importance of the musical structure was that it permitted the idea to grow; each time the theme reappeared it had acquired added meaning and richness, for him and for the reader.

For the details of his structure, he found the two vocal styles of Italian opera, recitative and aria, appropriate for his poems. The recitative, highly rhythmic and emotional, punctuated by instrumental accompaniment with thrilling effect, and in its chanted delivery giving the impression of the rhythms of speech, he found well adapted to the bulk of his work, which he thought of as a sort of bardic chant. For variety and the expression of material naturally lyrical, the aria, with its highly melodic, flowing, sustained vocal line, became the model. Sometimes it was inserted into longer recitative passages as a kind of lyrical climax; sometimes it was composed independently.

These two musical styles almost wholly explain Whitman's manner. Without a knowledge of the traditional delivery of oper-

atic recitative, with its strong accents, its long phrases, its pauses
for accompanying chords, its chanted effect, Whitman's lines cannot be properly read. Nor can his arias be vocalized as he heard
them in his mind unless one has heard the sustained legato
phrases of "O mio Fernando" or "Casta Diva," with their vowel
sounds prolonged to incredible lengths. His lines are echoes of
such music, and they are most effective to us when we perceive the
relationship.

In still narrower detail music contributed to Whitman's method.
He found the musical phrase, a unit of great flexibility and adapta-
bility, far more suitable for his purposes than the lines of standard
poetry with their established numbers of accents or stresses. In music
he observed that the phrase served the idea behind it, in contour,
in length, and in general effect. For Whitman the line became a
phrase of vocal music, controlled by the reader's breath, related
to other phrases, but end-stopped and complete in itself. And to
it he gave the same great variety in contour and length which he
found in music. Furthermore, as in good music, variations in Whitman's phrases are not arbitrary or mechanical. If a phrase is short,
there is a reason for it; if it is long and lightly accented, there is
a reason for it also. In short, Whitman's craftsmanship in matters
of the line is best understood in terms of the phrase of music.

From music also Whitman presumably took his conception of the
poetic foot, for he used it precisely as if it were a measure of music.
In vocal music there is usually one sense accent in each measure,
with as many or as few other notes as the context or the musical
phrase may require. So in Whitman there are feet of six or eight
syllables and feet of one. The governing principle was not an established pattern of accented and unaccented syllables. The foot
existed to serve the idea it was helping to convey, and to do so it
needed to be completely variable.

The important fact in all these aspects of method is not that
they were revolutionary, for they were less so than Whitman
thought. It is that having conceived of his poetry as prophetic
utterance or bardic rhapsody, he proceeded with care and thought to
formulate a method which would permit the most eloquent possible
presentation of that distinctive poetry, a method based on operatic
music which should provide new freedoms and grandeur. When

these conscious attempts are understood, Whitman gains in stature as an artist. He was not merely an excited but bumbling and incoherent scribbler whose poetry was in general simply prose made fancy. He was a deliberate artist working toward goals which he understood perfectly. It cannot be denied that he often failed to reach them. When he did reach them, however, "When Lilacs Last in the Dooryard Bloom'd" was the result.

Poetry, even that of mystics and innovators like Whitman, is not created in a vacuum. And such poetry reveals its value most completely if readers understand its origins, its creator's objectives, and the sources of his methods. In the case of Walt Whitman one must understand all his enthusiasms, such as those for oratory and for nature, which have been examined in the past. But principally one must recognize his passion for opera. Then his poems open themselves, and their meanings and art "come forth, as from recesses."

Bibliography

I BIBLIOGRAPHY

Allen, Gay Wilson. *Twenty-Five Years of Walt Whitman Bibliography, 1918-1942.* Boston: The F. W. Faxon Company, rev. ed., 1943.

II THE WORKS OF WALT WHITMAN

Franklin Evans; Or the Inebriate. New York, 1842. Pamphlet.

Voices From the Press. A Collection of Essays, Sketches, and Poems. Edited by James J. Brenton. New York: Charles B. Norton, 1850. Contains "The Tomb Blossoms," reprinted from *The Democratic Review.*

Leaves of Grass. Brooklyn, New York, 1855. First Edition.

Leaves of Grass. Brooklyn, New York, 1856. Second Edition.

Leaves of Grass. Boston: Thayer and Eldridge, 1860-61. Third Edition.

Walt Whitman's Drum-Taps. New York, 1865.

Leaves of Grass. New York, 1867. Fourth Edition.

Leaves of Grass. Washington, D. C., 1871. Fifth Edition.

After All Not to Create Only. Recited by Walt Whitman on Invitation of Managers American Institute, On Opening Their 40th Annual Exhibition. New York, noon, September 7th, 1871. Boston: Roberts Brothers, 1871.

Memoranda of the War. Author's Publication. Camden, New Jersey, 1875-76.

Leaves of Grass. Boston: James R. Osgood and Company, 1881-82. Seventh Edition.

Prose Works. Philadelphia: David McKay, undated.

In Re Walt Whitman. Edited by his literary executors, Horace L. Traubel, Richard Maurice Bucke, Thomas B. Harned. Published by the editors through David McKay. Philadelphia, 1893.

Calamus. A Series of Letters Written during the Years 1868-1880. By Walt Whitman to a Young Friend (Peter Doyle). Edited with an introduction by Richard Maurice Bucke, M.D., one of Whitman's Literary Executors. Boston: Laurens Maynard, 1897.

The Wound Dresser. A Series of Letters Written from the Hospitals in Washington during the War of Rebellion. Edited by Richard Maurice Bucke, M.D., one of Whitman's literary executors. Boston: Small, Maynard and Company, 1898.

Notes and Fragments: Left by Walt Whitman and now edited by Dr. Richard Maurice Bucke, one of his Literary Executors. Printed for private distribution only, 1899.

Complete Prose Works. Specimen Days and Collect, November Boughs, and Good-Bye My Fancy. Boston: Small, Maynard and Company, 1901.

The Complete Writings of Walt Whitman. Issued under the editorial supervision of his Literary Executors, Richard Maurice Bucke, Thomas B.

Harned, and Horace L. Traubel. With additional bibliographical and critical material by Oscar Lovell Triggs, Ph.D. New York and London: G. P. Putnam's Sons, 1902. 10 vols.

Walt Whitman's Diary in Canada. With Extracts from other of his Diaries and Literary Note-Books. Edited by William Sloane Kennedy. Boston: Small, Maynard and Company, 1904.

An American Primer. With Facsimiles of the Original Manuscript. Edited by Horace Traubel. Boston: Small, Maynard and Company, 1904.

The Letters of Anne Gilchrist and Walt Whitman. Edited by Thomas B. Harned. New York: Doubleday, Doran and Company, 1918.

The Gathering of the Forces. Editorials, essays, literary and dramatic reviews and other material written by Walt Whitman as editor of the Brooklyn *Daily Eagle* in 1846 and 1847. Edited by Cleveland Rodgers and John Black. With a foreword and a sketch of Whitman's life and work during two unknown years. New York and London: G. P. Putnam's Sons, 1920. 2 vols.

The Uncollected Poetry and Prose of Walt Whitman. Much of which has been but recently discovered with various early manuscripts now first published. Collected and edited by Emory Holloway. New York: Doubleday, Doran and Company, 1921. 2 vols.

Pictures. An unpublished poem by Walt Whitman. With an introduction and notes by Emory Holloway. New York: The Pine House, 1927.

The Half Breed and Other Stories. Edited by Thomas Olive Mabbott. New York: Columbia University Press, 1927.

Walt Whitman's Workshop. Edited by Clifton Joseph Furness. Cambridge: Harvard University Press, 1928.

A Child's Reminiscence. Collected by Thomas O. Mabbott and Rollo G. Silver, with Introduction and Notes. Seattle: University of Washington Book Store, 1930. University of Washington Quartos, No. 1.

I Sit and Look Out. Editorials from the Brooklyn *Daily Times.* Selected and edited by Emory Holloway and Vernolian Schwartz. New York: Columbia University Press, 1932.

Walt Whitman and the Civil War. A Collection of original articles and manuscripts. Edited by Charles I. Glicksberg. Philadelphia: University of Pennsylvania Press, 1933.

New York Dissected. A sheaf of recently discovered newspaper articles by the author of *Leaves of Grass.* Introduction and Notes by Emory Holloway and Ralph Adimari. New York: Rufus Rockwell Wilson, Inc., 1936.

Letters Written by Walt Whitman to His Mother 1866-1872. Introduction by Rollo G. Silver. New York: A. F. Goldsmith, 1936.

Leaves of Grass. Inclusive Edition. From the text of the edition authorized and editorially supervised by his literary executors, Richard Maurice Bucke, Thomas B. Harned, and Horace L. Traubel. Garden City, New York: Doubleday and Company, Inc., 1946.

Faint Clews & Indirections: Manuscripts of Walt Whitman and His Family. Edited by Clarence Gohdes and Rollo G. Silver. Durham, North Carolina: Duke University Press, 1949.

ARTICLES

Silver, Rollo G. "Seven Letters," *American Literature*, VII, 46-81 (March, 1935).

————. "Thirty-one Letters of Walt Whitman," *American Literature*, VIII, 417-38 (January, 1937).

MANUSCRIPTS

Letter to Ellen O'Connor, November 15, 1863. Berg Collection, New York Public Library.

Letter to Ellen O'Connor, May 15, 1874. Berg Collection, New York Public Library.

III BIOGRAPHY AND CRITICISM

BOOKS

Allen, Gay Wilson. "Walt Whitman," *American Prosody*. New York: American Book Company, 1935. Pp. 217-42.

————. *Walt Whitman Handbook*. Chicago: Packard and Company, 1946.

Arvin, Newton. *Whitman*. New York: The Macmillan Company, 1938.

Bailey, John. *Walt Whitman*. London and New York: The Macmillan Company, 1926.

Barrus, Clara. *Whitman and Burroughs, Comrades*. Boston and New York: Houghton Mifflin Company, 1931.

Bazalgette, Leon. *Walt Whitman, the Man and His Work*. Translated by Ellen Fitzgerald. Garden City, New York: Doubleday, 1920.

Binns, Henry Bryan. *A Life of Walt Whitman*. New York: E. P. Dutton and Company, 1905.

Bucke, Dr. Richard Maurice. *Walt Whitman*. Philadelphia: David McKay, 1883.

Burroughs, John. *Notes on Walt Whitman as Poet and Person*. New York: American News Company, 1867.

————. *Whitman, A Study*. Boston: Houghton Mifflin and Company, 1896.

Canby, Henry Seidel. *Walt Whitman an American*. New York: Literary Classics. Distributed by Houghton Mifflin and Company, 1943.

Carpenter, Edward. *Days with Walt Whitman: with Some Notes on his Life and Works*. London: George Allen; New York: The Macmillan Company, 1906.

Carpenter, George Rice. *Walt Whitman*. English Men of Letters, New York: The Macmillan Company, 1909.

Catel, Jean. *Rythme et Langage dans la 1re Edition des "Leaves of Grass" (1855)*. Paris: Les Editions Rieder, 1930.

————. *Walt Whitman: La Naissance du Poète*. Paris: Les Editions Rieder, 1929.

Daggett, Gwynne Harris. *Whitman's Poetic Theory*. Unpublished Thesis, University of North Carolina, Chapel Hill, 1941.

De Selincourt, Basil. *Walt Whitman: A Critical Study*. New York: Mitchell Kennerly, 1914.

Donaldson, Thomas. *Walt Whitman, the Man.* New York: Francis P. Harper, 1896.

Fausset, Hugh I'Anson. *Walt Whitman: Poet of Democracy.* New Haven: Yale University Press, 1942.

Furness, Clifton Joseph. *Walt Whitman's Workshop.* Cambridge: Harvard University Press, 1928.

Garland, Hamlin. "Walt Whitman, Old and Poor," *Roadside Meetings.* New York: The Macmillan Company, 1930. Pp. 127-43.

Holloway, Emory. *Whitman, An Interpretation in Narrative.* New York and London: Alfred A. Knopf, 1926.

Huneker, James Gibbons. "Visit to Walt Whitman," *Essays,* Selected with an Introduction by H. L. Mencken. New York: Scribner's, 1929. Pp. 416-24.

Johnston, John. *Diary Notes of a Visit to Walt Whitman and Some of His Friends in 1890.* Manchester: Labour Press, Ltd., 1898.

Kennedy, William Sloane. *The Fight of a Book for the World.* Massachusetts: The Stonecroft Press, 1926.

————. *Reminiscences of Walt Whitman,* with extracts from his letters and remarks on his writings. London: Alexander Gardner, 1896.

Landauer, Bella. *Leaves of Music by Walt Whitman.* New York: Privately Printed, 1937.

Matthiessen, F. O. *American Renaissance.* New York: Oxford University Press, 1941.

Morris, Harrison S. *Walt Whitman: A Brief Biography with Reminiscences.* Cambridge: Harvard University Press, 1929.

O'Connor, William D. *The Good Gray Poet.* See Bucke, *Walt Whitman.*

Perry, Bliss. *Walt Whitman, His Life and Work.* New York: Houghton Mifflin and Company, 1906.

Shephard, Esther. *Walt Whitman's Prose.* New York: Harcourt, Brace and Company, 1938.

Smith, Logan P. "Walt Whitman," *Unforgotten Years.* Boston: Little, Brown and Company, 1939. Pp. 79-108.

Symonds, John Addington. *Walt Whitman, A Study.* New York: E. P. Dutton, 1893.

Thomson, James. *Walt Whitman, the Man and the Poet,* London: Bertram Dobell, 1910.

Traubel, Horace. *With Walt Whitman in Camden.* Vol. I, Boston: Small, Maynard and Company, 1906. Vol. II, New York: D. Appleton and Company, 1908. Vol. III, New York: Mitchell Kennerly, 1914.

Winwar, Frances. *American Giant: Walt Whitman and His Times.* New York: Harper and Brothers, 1941.

ARTICLES

Allen, Gay Wilson. "Biblical Analogies for Walt Whitman's Prosody," *Revue Anglo-Americaine,* X, 490-507 (August, 1933).

Bradley, Sculley. "The Fundamental Metrical Principle in Whitman's Poetry," *American Literature,* X, 437-59 (January, 1939).

————. "The Problem of a Variorum Edition of Whitman's *Leaves of*

Grass," *English Institute Annual, 1941.* New York: Columbia University Press, 1942. Pp. 129-57.

Campbell, Killis. "The Evolution of Whitman as Artist," *American Literature,* VI, 254-63 (November, 1934).

Cooke, Alice L. "Notes on Whitman's Musical Background," *New England Quarterly,* XIX, 224-35 (June, 1946).

Cowley, Malcolm. "Walt Whitman, The Miracle," *New Republic,* CXIV, 385-88 (March 18, 1946).

————. "Walt Whitman, The Secret," *New Republic,* CXIV, 481-84 (April 8, 1946).

Coy, Rebecca. "A Study of Whitman's Diction," *University of Texas Studies in English,* XVI, 115-24 (July, 1936).

Crocker, L. "Walt Whitman's Interest in Public Speaking," *Quarterly Journal of Speech,* XXVI, 657-67 (December, 1940).

————. "The Rhetorical Influence of Henry Ward Beecher," *Quarterly Journal of Speech,* XVIII, 82-87 (February, 1932).

Erskine, John. "A Note on Whitman's Prosody," *Studies in Philology,* XX, 336-44 (July, 1923).

Frend, Grace Gilchrist. "Walt Whitman as I Remember Him," *Bookman,* London, LXXII, 203 (July, 1927).

Furness, Clifton Joseph. "Review of Frances Winwar: American Giant," *American Literature,* XIII, 423-32 (January, 1942).

————. "Walt Whitman and Music," *News Bulletin,* Boston Chapter, Special Libraries Association, IV, No. 2, p. 2 (November, 1937).

Gohdes, Clarence. "Whitman and Emerson," *Sewanee Review,* XXXVII, 79-93 (January, 1929).

Goodale, Douglas. "Some of Walt Whitman's Borrowings," *American Literature,* X, 202-13 (May, 1938).

Holloway, Emory. "Some New Whitman Letters," *American Mercury,* XVI, 183-88 (February, 1929).

————. "Review of *Walt Whitman: Poet of Democracy* by Hugh I'Anson Fausset," *American Literature,* XIV, 319 (November, 1942).

————. "More Light on Whitman," *American Mercury,* I, 186 (February, 1924).

————. "Walt Whitman in New Orleans," *Yale Review,* V, 166-83 (October, 1915).

Hungerford, Edward. "Walt Whitman and His Chart of the Bumps," *American Literature,* II, 350-84 (January, 1931).

Pound, Louise. "Walt Whitman and Bird Poetry," *English Journal,* XIX, 31-36 (January, 1930).

————. "Walt Whitman and the French Language," *American Speech,* I, 421-30 (May, 1926).

————. "Walt Whitman and Italian Music," *American Mercury,* VI, 58-63 (September, 1925).

Ross, E. C. "Whitman's Verse," *Modern Language Notes,* XLV, 363-64 (June, 1930).

Spregelman, Julia. "Walt Whitman and Music," *South Atlantic Quarterly,* XLI, 167-76 (April, 1942).

Starke, Aubrey H. "Lanier's Appreciation of Whitman," *American Scholar*, II, 398-408 (October, 1933).

Stovall, Floyd. "Main Drifts in Whitman's Poetry," *American Literature*, IV, 3-21 (March, 1932).

Strauch, Carl F. "Structure of Walt Whitman's Song of Myself," *English Journal*, XXVII, 597-607 (September, 1938).

Swayne, Mattie. "Whitman's Catalogue Rhetoric," *University of Texas Studies in English*, No. 412, 162-78 (July, 1941).

Thayer, W. R. "Personal Recollections of Walt Whitman," *Scribner's*, LXV, 674-87 (June, 1919).

Trowbridge, John Townsend. "Reminiscences of Walt Whitman," *Atlantic Monthly*, LXXXIX, 163-75 (February, 1902).

Ware, Lois. "Poetic Conventions in *Leaves of Grass*," *Studies in Philology*, XXVI, 47-57 (January, 1929).

White, Cortland Y. "A Whitman Ornithology," *Cassinia*, XXXV, 12-22 (1945).

Wiley, Autrey Nell. "Reiterative Devices in *Leaves of Grass*," *American Literature*, I, 161-70 (May, 1929).

MANUSCRIPT

Manuscript Notebook of Herbert Gilchrist, 1876-77. Walt Whitman Collection, Library of The University of Pennsylvania.

IV MUSIC

Abbott, Lawrence. *Approach to Music*. New York: Farrar and Rinehart, 1940.

Brink, Carol. *Harps in the Wind*. New York: Macmillan, 1947.

Brockway, Wallace and Weinstock, Herbert. *The Opera, A History of Its Creation and Performance: 1600-1941*. New York: Simon and Schuster, 1941.

Edwards, H. S. *Rossini and His School*. New York: Scribner and Welford, 1881.

Ferris, George T. *Great Italian and French Composers*. New York: D. Appleton and Company, 1891.

Grove's Dictionary of Music and Musicians, ed. H. C. Colles. Third Edition, New York: Macmillan, 1927, 5 vols.

Hamilton, Clarence W. *Music Appreciation, Based on Methods of Literary Criticism*. Boston: Oliver Ditson, 1920.

International Cyclopedia of Music and Musicians, ed. Oscar Thompson. New York: Dodd, Mead and Company, 1939.

Jordan, Philip D. *Singin' Yankees*. Minneapolis: University of Minnesota Press, 1946.

Krehbiel, Henry E. *A Book of Operas, Their Histories, Their Plots, and Their Music*. Garden City, New York: Garden City Publishing Company, Inc., 1916.

————. *Chapters of Opera, The Lyric Drama in New York to 1909*. New York: Henry Holt, 1909.

Lahee, Henry Charles. *Annals of Music in America*. Boston: Marshall Jones, 1922.

Lahee, Henry Charles. *Grand Opera in America*. Boston: L. C. Page, 1902.

Maretzek, Max. *Crotchets and Quavers, or Revelations of an Opera Manager in America*. New York: Samuel French, 1855.

Mathews, W. S. B. (ed.) *A Hundred Years of Music in America*. Chicago: G. L. Howe, 1889.

Odell, George C. D. *Annals of the New York Stage*. New York: Columbia University Press, 1927-1938. 10 vols.

Ritter, Frederic Louis. *Music in America*. New York: Charles Scribner's Sons, 1883.

Sonneck, O. G. T. *Early Opera in America*. New York: Schirmer, 1915.

Streatfield, R. A. *The Opera*. Philadelphia: Lippincott, 1907.

Toye, Francis. *Rossini: A Study in Tragi-Comedy*. New York: Alfred A. Knopf, 1934.

————. *Giuseppe Verdi: His Life and Works*. London: William Heinemann, Ltd., 1931.

Newman, Ernest. *Stories of the Great Operas and Their Composers*. New York: Garden City Publishing Co., 1930. 3 vols.

ARTICLES

"The Story of New Orleans Rise as a Music Center," *Musical America*, XIX, 3 (March 14, 1914).

White, Richard Grant. "Opera in New York," *The Century, Illustrated Monthly Magazine*, New Series I, 686-703 (November, 1881); 864-82 (April, 1882); II, 31-43 (May, 1882); 193-210 (October, 1882).

NEWSPAPERS

New Orleans *Daily Delta* (February, 1848).

OPERA SCORES

Bellini, Vincenzo. *Norma, Tragedia Lirica*. Paris: Maurice Schlesinger, Undated.

Donizetti, Gaetano. *La Favorita*, Opera in four acts with Italian words and an English adaptation by Charles Lamb Kenney. Edited by Arthur Sullivan and J. Pittman. London and New York: Boosey and Company, Undated.

Verdi, Giuseppe. *Ernani*. A tragic opera in four acts, Edited and the pianoforte accompaniment revised by Berthold Tours. London: Novello, Ewer and Company, Undated.

V MISCELLANEOUS

A History and Criticism of American Public Address. W. N. Brigance, ed. New York: McGraw-Hill, 1943. 2 vols.

Rush, James. *Philosophy of the Human Voice*. Philadelphia: Grigg and Elliot, 1833.

Sears, Lorenzo. *The History of Oratory*. Chicago: Griggs, 1896.

Greene, T. M. *The Arts and the Art of Criticism*. Princeton University Press, 1940.

Lanier, Sidney. *The Science of English Verse*, Vol. II, Centennial Edition,

244 WALT WHITMAN AND OPERA

Paull Franklin Baum, ed. Baltimore: Johns Hopkins Press, 1945. First published, 1888.

Lowell, Amy. "Some Musical Analogies in Modern Poetry," *Musical Quarterly*, VI, 127-57 (January, 1920).

Omond, T. S. *A Study of Metre*. London: Alexander Moring, Ltd., 1920.

Sand, George. *Consuelo*. Translated from the latest Paris edition of Charpentier with all the new revisions and corrections of the author by Fayette Robinson, Esq. Philadelphia: T. B. Peterson and Brothers, 1851.

Index

245